Stephen G. Hall, Ullrich Heilemann, and Peter Pauly (Eds.)

Macroeconometric Models and
European Monetary Union

RWI : Schriften

Heft 73

Stephen G. Hall, Ullrich Heilemann,
and Peter Pauly (Eds.)

Macroeconometric Models and European Monetary Union

Duncker & Humblot · Berlin

Bibliografische Information Der Deutschen Bibliothek

Die Deutsche Bibliothek verzeichnet diese Publikation in
der Deutschen Nationalbibliografie; detaillierte bibliografische
Daten sind im Internet über <http://dnb.ddb.de> abrufbar.

Fotoprint: Berliner Buchdruckerei Union GmbH, Berlin
Printed in Germany

ISSN 0720-7212
ISBN 3-428-11398-5

Gedruckt auf alterungsbeständigem (säurefreiem) Papier
entsprechend ISO 9706 ⊖

Internet: http://www.duncker-humblot.de

Preface

This volume contains the contributions of a conference dealing with the consequences of the European Monetary Union for the macroeconometric modelling of the Euro area, which took place in Essen on November 17 and 18, 2000. The objective of the conference was to give an overview of the status and development of the econometric modelling in the Euro area based on a concentrated exchange of information and discussion among a comparatively small group of scientists. At the end of the conference the participants were convinced that the discussions including a great variety of theoretical, methodical and factual aspects from the producers' as well as the consumers' perspective will not fail to have a certain impact on the future development of macroeconometric modelling.

Once more it became clear, however, that an ideal way to a solution of the problems is still not in sight. The future development will be characterized by a plurality of approaches and models. Thus trends continue which have had a more or less strong, durable or temporary influence on the model landscape since the emergence of the monetarist revolution, the „rational expectations" or the "real business cycle"-models; their influence was clearly perceptible during the conference. We hope that the results and reported experiences will soon be included in the experts' discussions. We are still at the beginning of the theoretical and empirical exploration of the macroeconomic development of the Euro area, it is not always clearly perceptible what is transitory and what is permanent, and this openness should facilitate the reception of the experiences and results which have been presented.

The idea for this event was developed in the course of the *Project* LINK, our special thanks go to Professor Dr. Stephen Hall, London Business School, Professor Dr. Ullrich Heilemann, RWI, and Professor Dr. Peter Pauly, University of Toronto. One of the highlights of the conference was the participation of the nobel prize winner Professor Dr. Lawrence Klein – pioneer and Nestor of macroeconometric modelling – who, as his contribution shows, is following up the creation of the European Monetary Union with critical interest. The meeting was organized by Mrs. Hiltrud Nehls, graduated economist, she was supported by Mrs. Claudia Lohkamp. The editorial work was done by the very experienced Mr. Joachim Schmidt, who was assisted by Mrs. Anette Hermanowski. The organization of individual meetings was taken over by the editors of this volume and by Professor Dr. Bert Hickman, Stanford University, Professor Dr. Jean-Louis Brillet, INSEE, Paris, and Professor Dr. Manfred Deistler, Technical University Vienna. The institute would like to thank all of them as well as the speakers and those who participated in the discussions.

Last not least we have to mention the "Gesellschaft der Freunde und Förderer des RWI"; without their generous financial support this event would not have been possible.

Essen, October 2003
Rheinisch-Westfälisches Institut
für Wirtschaftsforschung

Christoph M. Schmidt

Contents

Stephen G. Hall, Ullrich Heilemann, and Peter Pauly

Introduction

On January 1, 1999, the most ambitious plan of European integration began – the European Monetary Union (EMU). Austria, Belgium, France, Finland, Germany, Greece (since 2001), Ireland, Italy, Luxemburg, the Netherlands, Portugal and Spain transferred their monetary sovereignty to the European Central Bank (ECB). Two years later, the national currencies of the 12 member states were replaced by a common currency, the Euro. The institutional change was preceded by a selection procedure based on the fulfilment of a number of macroeconomic criteria of monetary and fiscal stability and future commitments (Growth and stability pact). This process has been widely covered in the literature and neither this nor the debate regarding the final outcome of EMU must be repeated here. Surprisingly, much less attention has been devoted to another question: what will be the consequences of EMU for our analytical tools to forecast and simulate macroeconomic developments and policies. True, the European Commission and the European Monetary Institute (EMI), the predecessor of the ECB, had started to formulate and express their data needs already in the mid 1990s and much has been done to satisfy them. With the start of the publication of the Harmonized Index of Consumer Prices (HICP) and the construction of area wide data bases the main information gaps have been closed. However, the consequences of EMU for our analytical tools and models remains unclear.

The question has several dimensions. One is simply the instrumental aspect: whether existing models will satisfy future requirements, will monetary policy (still) be adequately modelled? Will their policy tools have to be modified? What about the changed external value of national currencies? A *second* dimension is formed by the question of how the changed institutional setting – one interest rate/monetary policy for all, fixed exchange rates, binding fiscal policy rules – and the now larger "currency area" will affect the reactions of the private sector and national economic policy. This question is harder to answer because there are no prior experiences. The difficulties are increased by the fact that the EMU started at a time when Europe and the world economy were in particular difficult times, and when structural and cyclical changes were hard to isolate from each other. A *third* question is rather technical again: In which way will the ECB modelling react on all these challenges?

From November 17 to 18, 2000 a group of modellers gathered in Essen, FRG, organized by *Project* LINK and the RWI to discuss these and associated problems. After an opening address by Nobel laureate *Lawrence Klein*, the organization of the discussions followed the topics listed above.

Klein opened the conference with a contribution examining some first standard experiences of *economic* integration, specifically NAFTA. He looked at it from the perspective of the US and Canada as well as from Mexico. As to be expected from international trade theory, there were considerable gains in employment for all three countries. But somewhat unexpected, the two northern participants experienced much stronger productivity gains than Mexico. While increasing returns to scale "can be detected in macroeconometric models that are open to exploitation of economies of scale, this is not so obvious in computable general equilibrium models (CGE), where there is often preoccupation with constant returns to scale and fixed coefficients of production." (p. 12). From this perspective it would be tempting to have a look back on the many studies evaluating the economics and welfare gains from NAFTA. For the future of the NAFTA concept Klein's verdict was favourable. This was not so for the EMU, where he argued that the Maastricht criteria could also have been met by a Canada/US- type strategy, that is high growth with employment, labour market improvements, budget surpluses, and low inflation and all at the same time.

The first part of the conference was occupied with "new models for Europe". *Michael Beeby*, *Stephen Hall* and *Brian Henry* present a supply-side approach to model the Euro-11 economy. Their 16 equations model of the Euro-11 area has a number of innovative features. Its supply-side is built up from an estimated production function, the labour market is based on wage bargaining theories where state-space modelling techniques are used to generate estimates of the return from not working, and agents are assumed to update their expectations each period i.e., they learn. The model is used for two purposes. First, to obtain estimates of the NAIRU in Euroland and second, to understand how the Euroland economy responds to different types of shocks. So far, results seem to suggest a rather high stability of economic reaction patterns. It will be interesting to see whether this holds also for the past 50 years as the authors plan to do. But even more important will be to see whether the EMU will change this.

Mika Kortelainen and *David Mayes* present results from EDGE, a dynamic general equilibrium model of the Euro area, a model with some nominal rigidities that has been calibrated on Euro area data. The model includes consumption/saving decisions using a Blanchard stochastic lifetimes approach; valuation of private financial wealth according to the present value of capital income; overlapping Calvo wage contracts in the labour market and a neoclassicial supply side with Cobb-Douglas technology. Key parameters to be calibrated to set the equilibrium path (equity premium, share of capital in the economy) are the real rate of growth and the rate of depreciation. The calibration is based on data from new Euro area statistics and on experience from the US. The model is deliberately designed to have a simple and transparent structure and properties. Even though the model has been developed for both forecasting and policy simulation purposes, the paper concentrates on its simulation properties with regard to the field of Euro monetary policy. The simulation results have several important lessons: the importance of credibility of ECB's actions, the importance of transparency of ECB's policy goals and actions and that the faster the private sector can learn the smaller his loss.

The paper by *David Rae* and *David Turner* describes the OECD's new small global forecasting model for the three main OECD economic regions: the United States, the Euro area, and Japan. The key variables – output, inflation, the trade balance, and import prices – are driven by monetary and fiscal policy, exchange rates, and world demand. The projections from the model are used as a starting point to help animate the early stages of the OECD's forecasting round. The model is essentially of the Keynes/Klein-type with a particular focus on the impact of global linkages and the transmission of influences between regions. The authors think of their work as preliminary and find that it should be expanded in several areas: first, monetary policy could be dealt with in greater depth; second, expectations as a transmission mechanism of policy both within and between regions should be further disaggregated; third, closer scrutiny of differences in dynamics across regions may be warranted and, finally, the "rest of the world" – 80 percent of Euro area trade-block should be disaggregated.

The ECB staff has started a number of activities to model the macroeconomics of the Euro area. In their paper on structural modelling of the Euro area, *Gabriel Fagan*, *Jerome Henry* and *Ricardo Mestre* provide an overview of these models. The paper recalls the context in which this task took place, namely the EMI assessment regarding a suitable econometric infrastructure for the ECB, implying the use of a suite of models comprising estimated structural macro models for the Euro area as a whole, as well as for the various member countries. The authors reveal some details on the structure of the area wide model employed for the Euro area such as single equation properties for key Euro area relations and illustrative full model simulation results. All in all, the authors find the ECB's investment in modelling worthwhile. In particular, the Euro area and the countries comprising it are now much better known, a first set of stylised facts has been derived and a benchmark is now available against which to evaluate judgements. But, not all too surprising, although the 1st generation of Euro area models have not yet been completed, plans for the next generation are already being made.

The ECB's activities are, because of its short history, of course an exception. In general modelling activities for the Euro area will not start from zero but will rely to a large degree on previous "country modelling experience". They were the topic of part II of the conference. *Jean Luis Brillet* and *Maria Dos Santos* gave an account of the *Macsim* system, a simplified multi-country system, relying on small single country macro econometric models, linked through trade flows. The set of countries chosen are European, with a sketchy Rest of the World. Even though the model's main goal is teaching macroeconomics, it can be used for economic policy analysis, particularly on issues such as EMU. Simulations can use different rules for the exchange rate and interest rates, in addition to the participation to EMU. To examine the consequences of Spain and Portugal joining EMU, a number of modifications of the model were necessary, mostly with particular consideration of the specific features of the member countries, which should lead to particular properties (for instance, Portugal is smaller, and has strong economic ties with Spain, more than the reverse). New and old estimation results and model reactions on demand and supply shocks were compared. All in all they confirm more or less previous findings of this and other models. New seems to be the emphasis which is given to the size of new member countries and also to the regional orientation of trade links which are often missing in policy discussions.

Ullrich Heilemann, György Barabas and *Hiltrud Nehls* try to answer the basic question of this part from an *autre monde* perspective. They ask whether in West Germany's macroeconomic behaviour effects of European Integration can be detected. After a short listing of major fields and effects of European integration, they simulate the trade effects of the customs union (1968), the EC enlargement (1973), the introduction of the EMS (1979) and the announcement of the single market (1987) and look for their consequence on major macroeconomic parameters. They use a modified version of the RWI-business cycle model, a quarterly medium sized macroeconometric model which has been in use for forecasting and simulation since the mid 1970. Given theoretical expectations, the results are somewhat disillusioning – trade creating effects are hardly discernible. One reason for this might be, the fact that all these effects mainly show up on the sector level. Net effects are small and stretch over longer periods, that start much before the laws come into force. For EMU this means that we will have to wait for some time until we will be able to identify their effects. To model builders and users these results may be comforting because they tell them that a slow and gradual adjustment of their models to the EMU regime may be well in order.

Policy in the new environment is the subject of two papers. *Ray Barrell*, *Karen Dury* and *Ian Hurst* examine the decision making within the ECB. They do this by evaluating simple monetary policy rules in an encompassing framework. They develop different types of rules that the ECB may consider to implement to assess their effectiveness in stabilising EMU member economies. Stochastic simulations on the National Institutes Global Econometric Model (NiGEM) are used to evaluate different types of rules and different parameterisations of the rules on the country level and for the aggregated Euro area. They find that more or less for both levels, the combined nominal GDP and inflation targeting rule, with a coefficient of 1.0 on inflation, is the best rule for maximising output and minimising inflation. Pure inflation targeting with a coefficient of 1.0 appears to be the least effective at stabilising the Euro area aggregates. It is also shown that the covariance structure of Euro area inflation can matter in terms of determining the best policy rule. As to the results and their implications for policy making at the ECB, the authors find that there is no immediate conflict within the decision making bodies of the ECB.

In the last paper *Christian Schumacher* and *Christian Dreger* look for evidence from panel cointegration tests on broad money demand (MH3) in Europe. For a group of fourteen European countries the null of no cointegration cannot be rejected. Only in a core sample consisting of Germany, France, Austria, the Netherlands and Belgium cointegration is found. Other studies using Euro area wide aggregated money demand functions show that aggregated time series money demand equations perform statistically better than their counterparts for single countries. The results found here indicate that this could be partly due to an averaging effect that overcompensates the missing cointegration feature in some of the countries. Although the panel methods have the advantage of higher efficiency than usual time series cointegration tests, they are not as much developed. Some drawbacks of the panel cointegration tests are possibly neglected cross section dependence and non availability of methods to control for structural breaks. It can be questioned whether the advantage of higher efficiency due to the inclusion of the cross section dimension overcompensates these drawbacks.

The discussion of this conference has made it clear that to date only a small part of the challenges the EMU poses for macroeconometric modelling has been resolved. Most progress has been made by simply building aggregate models covering the entire Euro area. The empirical quality of these models is difficult to compare to that of national country models – which by no means will vanish – but at least the new models seem to work. This indicates that there is the necessary amount of homogeneity of EMU member's economic behaviour and that is encouraging for model builder – and for ECB policy. It was not at all so clear that this is the case if we recall the many debates on "optimal currency area" that came up when in the mid 1990s the debate on EMU

started. No problem seems to be the proper modelling of the institutional setting, while the question of a proper catch of future reactions of the Euro area is
much harder to answer. It will be interesting to see whether past experiences
of a gradual absorption of the various steps of European integration will hold
here, too. Until then, the many results presented at the conference have improved our understanding of EMU's present and future problems and certainly also narrowed the debate.

Lawrence R. Klein

US and NAFTA – Some First Experiences and Modelling

It is quite appropriate, at this meeting focusing on Macroeconometric Models and European Monetary Union, to look at similar issues from the perspective of the effects of NAFTA on the US and the other two members, Canada and Mexico.

NAFTA is unusual in that it combines effects on both developed countries and a developing country. Although Mexico is a recent member of OECD, it has many of the characteristics of a developing country. The NAFTA organization is regional, as is the European Union, and it affects both trade in goods and services and in capital flows. It is not, however, involved with monetary union as is the European Union.

First, let us look at NAFTA issues from the point of view of Canada. Here I draw upon an interesting analysis by a one-time colleague from econometric model building research, Donald J. Daly, of York University, Canada (Daly 1998, 2000). There was great fear that Canada would lose jobs to Mexico, as would the United States, after the implementation of NAFTA. While it is true that Mexican employment gained considerable advantage from NAFTA, since Mexican wages are far smaller than those in Canada and the US (possibly only one-tenth the hourly rates in the more advanced economies), there have been both losers and gainers from sector to sector, and the gainers more than compensated for the job losses. Not only were there gainers, but there was an *overwhelming* gain for Canada and the US, in the sense that overall unemployment rates dropped significantly in the post-NAFTA period. This is something to think about when reasoning on behalf of EU countries. Had they tried to reach Maastricht targets by high growth, as did Canada and the United States, they might be having, on an all round basis, the same kinds of labor market improvements, domestic budget surpluses, and low inflation, all at the same time. There is no *unique* route to the kinds of target values set by Maastricht criteria.

Very low wage costs in Mexico were not sufficient to tip the balance against the weight of superior infrastructure (transport, communication, power, sanitation, water, education and other infrastructural facilities). These and other features made for much stronger *productivity* gains in Canada and the US. The gains from trade, which have been very real, as a result of lowering barriers through NAFTA enabled the advanced countries to achieve lower average and marginal costs with greater output levels; this is achieved through realizing *increasing returns to scale*, which have played a considerable role in the process of technical changes in Canada and the US.

The roots of economic efficiency go beyond NAFTA in an historical sense. Very good gains of this type were realized earlier by two predecessor agreements, namely the Canadian-US auto agreements (1965) and the Canadian-US Free Trade Agreement (FTA) which was crafted just before the introduction of NAFTA in 1994.

These predecessor agreements permitted high degrees of specialization. Automobile manufacturing benefited by outsourcing parts and supplies for final assembly, use of modern inventory practices, and using all the infrastructured advantages, especially for shipping to and fro across the Canadian-US border.

The concept of increasing returns to scale helped to identify gains for microchip production, software activities in a "business-to-business" mode. These kinds of gains can be detected in macroeconometric models that are open to exploitation of economies of scale, but not so obvious in computable general equilibrium models (CGE), where there is often preoccupation with constant returns to scale and fixed coefficients of production.

The Free Trade Agreement opened possibilities on a broader scale, beyond autos, and trade in manufactured products expanded as barriers were reduced, thus enabling scale economies to be more pervasive.

The analysis of economic relations between either Canada or the US with Mexico showed improvement after NAFTA was introduced, but these gains were temporarily halted by Mexico's financial crisis of December 1994. It was not only financial, but also very political. Now, the political situation has changed a great deal, and it is to be hoped that Mexico can set out on a fresh and productive path from 2000 onwards, under a new kind of leadership. It should be noted that some large foreign direct investment activities (FDI) continued expansion in spite of the crisis.

Economists broadly agree that free trade is a good thing, both from the viewpoint of welfare economics and for macroeconomic growth. At a regional level, as is the case with NAFTA, the conventional judgment is that a local agreement that does not *divert* trade but, instead *creates* trade, is economically desirable and I would surely argue that NAFTA creates trade. There are, however, winners *and* losers, but the prevailing economic environment in Canada,

US, and Mexico, after NAFTA began in 1994, was expansionary and helped all three countries. There were, nevertheless opponents and detractors who argued that Mexico's crisis in December 1994, was because of NAFTA. Prevailing opinion and analysis, however, concluded that political turbulence in the Mexican presidential campaign of 1994 in which the favored candidate was assassinated, political unrest in Chiapas, and a cover-up (lack of transparency) on the part of Mexican officials was responsible for the ultimate depletion of international financial reserves.

A stage was set for rapid recovery as a result of credit supplied by the IMF and the US government, continuing inflows of private capital (mainly through FDI), and very good performance in the border industries (*Maquiladoras*). All these activities contributed to a rapid recovery in which the loans of the United States were quickly repaid, with full interest.

There was a sharp recession in 1995, but it should be pointed out that the previous financial crisis of 1982-83 (the World Debt Crisis) put Mexico into a two-year recession before expansion could be resumed. Alfredo Coutiño and I authored a study in early 1995 that argued in favor of a prediction for a recovery after a one-year recession because Mexican domestic reforms, with support from NAFTA trade, would lift the economy out of crisis much faster and better than in the period of a decade earlier (Klein, Coutiño 2000).

Mexican trade, 1993-99, has expanded so much that Mexico's ranking has grown from 17th in world export volume to 13th, surpassing many countries that are well known for trade performance. In this period, Mexico's exports tripled, and imports more than doubled. Also FDI has expanded rapidly right after NAFTA, to reach values now in excess of $10 billion.

Bond ratings have improved, and Mexico is building earnings from a stronger energy sector by taking advantage more wisely than before, of the favorable prices for crude oil.

Future prospects

The two major advanced countries of NAFTA, Canada and the US have been leaders in world economic expansion for nearly a decade. Output has been growing vigorously, with low inflation, and technically advanced activity in information, biological, and other innovative sectors. The US has a problem of trade and current account deficits, but much of this is due to the leadership role of the US in a troubled world economy.

Mexico is in a different situation. After a period of political change it has an entirely different kind of government starting in 2001. President Fox has raised new hopes by taking an expansionist line. He aims for *sustained* GDP growth of 7%. He has yet to prove himself, but it is refreshing. Also he has found unusual cooperation from outgoing President Zedillo. Customarily, econometric models of Mexico have a "dummy variable" to designate economic discord at the end of each 6-year reign, but at the present time, it is expected that there will be a smooth transition from President Zedillo to President Fox. This is a good sign.

Fox is expected to pursue an active international policy, building on the gains of the past few years that have stemmed from the NAFTA accord. In 2000, Mexico will have expanded GDP by more than 5.5%, well on the way to the 7% target. The US economy is deliberately slowing, in order to work off some excesses such as incipient inflation of wage rates and a highly distorted stock market. It should, however, be able to avoid recession in 2001 and Canada should also remain prosperous, but feel the effects of a slowdown in the US.

Mexico has come to a position of low inflation (one at single-digit levels) and maintains an improving foreign exchange position. Unemployment remains steady.

At the time of signing the NAFTA agreement, President Clinton declared that he would try to expand NAFTA, to include strong economies in South America. Chile has been a favored choice. During his second term, he did not succeed in bringing Chile into NAFTA, but the new US government does show some interest in enlarging NAFTA membership in this same direction. At this time, the verdict is favorable in support of the NAFTA concept, and we can look forward to seeing the gradual expansion of a strong institution.

References

Daly, D.J. (1998), Canadian Research on the Production Effects of Free Trade: A Summary and Implications for Mexico. *North American Journal of Economics and Finance* 9: 147–167.

Daly, D.J. (2000), *Will North American Manufacturing Jobs Move to Mexico with NAFTA?* Paper presented at ASSA Meetings, Boston, January 9, 2000. Schulich School of Business, York University, North York, Ontario.

Klein, L.R. and A. Coutiño (1996), The Mexican Financial Crisis of December 1994 and Lessons to Be Learned. *Open Economies Review* 7 (Supplement 1): 501–510.

Klein, L.R. and A. Coutiño (2000), A Mexican Adjustment Scenario. Ensayos Sobre Aspectos Macroeconomicos de Mexico. Instituto de Investigation Economica y Social Lucas Alaman, A.C.

Michael Beeby, Stephen G. Hall, and S.G. Brian Henry[1]

Modelling the Euro-11 Economy: A Supply-Side Approach

1. Introduction

In this paper a medium sized econometric model of the Euro-11 (or Eurozone/ Euroland) economy is constructed. The motivation for this is to obtain a model that can be used to conduct policy simulations and obtain forecasts for those eleven countries that will be the inaugural members of European Monetary Union. Underlying the construction of the model has been the attempt to incorporate into macro-modelling recent developments that have occurred elsewhere in macroeconomics. Three features of the model are worth noting. First, given the greater emphasis placed on the supply-side, we provide a consistent treatment by estimating a production function for the Eurozone and including its implied marginal products as cointegrating vectors (CVs) in the dynamic earnings, employment and investment equations. Second, wage bargaining theories of the type associated with Layard/ Nickell/Jackman (1991) are included in the labour market equations. Unobserved components models are then used to obtain estimates of the return from not working (unemployment benefits etc.). Third, to overcome the apparently counterfactual dynamic responses resulting from the assumption of rational expectations, agents are assumed to learn, i.e. to update their expectations each period (each of these techniques are discussed in more detail below). Overall, the addition of these features should result in a model that is not only more theoretically consistent, but also in a model that has improved dynamic properties relative to econometric models that assume rational expectations.

At the heart of the model is an estimated Cobb-Douglas constant-returns-to-scale production function. From this production function the marginal products for labour and capital are derived and equated to their marginal costs (the real wage and the real rental rate of capital respectively) as required by the standard neo-classical theory of the firm. These equations are then used as the long-run equilibrium relationships (CVs) in the dynamic earnings, employ-

---
[1] We gratefully acknowledge funding from ESRC ROPA Award No. R/022/25/0187.

ment and investment equations. Given the size of econometric models, researchers typically proceed by estimating each equation individually and not as a system. One drawback from this approach is that usually only a single CV enters into each equation. This is an arbitrary restriction and not one that can be justified through either economic or econometric theory. Our approach is instead to take a more general modelling strategy. Although each equation is estimated individually we allow all CVs from the production side to enter into all the dynamic equations at the initial "general" stage. Testing down procedures then eliminate those CVs found to be insignificant. Thus more than one equilibrium relationship may enter into a single dynamic equation if their presence is not rejected by the data. This idea is based on the approach taken by Vector Error Correction models (VECMs). Although we do not estimate the equations as a system we do exploit the reduced rank characteristic of such systems. In brief, for a set of non-stationary variables let m cointegrating vectors exist, then the model may be written as,

$$\Delta Y_t = \Theta(L)\Delta Y_{t-1} + \alpha\beta' X_{t-1} + \varepsilon_t$$

where $\alpha\beta' X_t$ is the set of CVs with $X = (Y, Z)$, and where the variables are partitioned into endogenous (Y) and weakly exogenous variables (Z). CVs do not enter the dynamic equations for the weakly exogenous variables. The above equation is then the conditional model that has an accompanying marginal model, which is not stated here. The adjustment matrix α is of dimension $n \times m$ but it is not typically diagonal, each dynamic equation may include more than one CV.

The determinants of labour supply (and hence aggregate supply) within the model are set out in terms of a conventional structural econometric model enabling us to describe the main arguments in the standard union-firm model of Layard et al. In their model unions set the level of wages prevailing in the economy and in return unions agree to allow managers the right to set employment. To determine the level of wages demanded, unions need to know the value (or return) from not working. This is affected in part by the level of unemployment benefits. Data on the return from not working in the Euro-11 appears (as yet) unavailable and even if it was available, its interpretation might not be clear given the disparate levels of benefit offered by national governments. To overcome this an unobserved components model (i.e. Kalman Filter) is used to obtain some estimates of the return from not working. The advantage of this is twofold. First, estimates of the non-accelerating inflation rate of unemployment (NAIRU) can be obtained, an exercise that is conducted below. Second, the effects of policies that target changes in labour supply measures can be simulated and assessed. Our approach thus brings together structural (i.e. the union-firm model) and time-series models of the NAIRU.

The third innovative feature of this paper is the assumption that individuals update their expectations each period (i.e. they learn), rather than simply assuming that agents have rational expectations. Introducing learning into econometric models has potentially large rewards. Unlike in small analytical models, the introduction of RE has changed the short-run policy responses of the larger models in ways that are not totally plausible. For instance, if the government announces that interest rates will increase by one per cent, exchange rates in large-scale models will typically jump by approximately fifty per cent – a highly implausible result (Fisher et al. 1990). However RE does have big theoretical advantages since it assumes that agents use their information set optimally, and it is the dominant assumption in modern macroeconomics. Learning can potentially maintain the long-run advantages of RE (since learning has been shown to converge asymptotically to the RE solution under rather general conditions), while overcoming its poor short-run policy responses in large-scale models. Expectations can enter these models in many areas, but it is in the exchange rate sector where they have been shown to have the largest effect. Typically expectations have been introduced via a forward-looking open arbitrage exchange rate equation. The easiest way to introduce a shock is through an exogenous price, usually the world price of oil. In this paper learning also enters via the exchange rate equation, though the model will be subjected to more than just a single shock.

The outline of the paper is as follows. Section 2 describes the data, the methods used to construct a single aggregate from the eleven individual series, and plots the behavior of the main series over the past fifteen to twenty years. The model is presented in Section 3 with the estimation results shown in Section 4. Section 5 contains estimates of the NAIRU for Euroland and Section 6 describes the results from some simulation exercises. Section 7 concludes.

2. The data

Methodological issues
Aggregating data across countries is of course problematic. Movements in exchange rates rule out simply adding up series across countries. Methods that use estimates of exchange rates that are instead based on purchasing power parity (PPP) are also unsatisfactory since PPP estimates are themselves not uncontroversial and may be sample dependent. This means that before any aggregation method can be chosen the following decisions need to be made. First is the aggregation across levels or growth rates? Second, are the weights on each country's series assumed to be fixed (e.g. as with Paasche and Laspeyres indices) or time varying? There are four available choices. The approach here is to use data that is aggregated across growth rates and where the weights are time varying. Beyer et al. (2000) have subsequently shown that this approach is superior to other methods. Their reasons are discussed below.

The weights attached to each individual country's series are assumed to vary
over time. This approach was chosen since one major drawback with using
fixed weights is that they fail to capture any large changes to relative prices
that may occur. With data from the Euro-11 there have clearly been periods
where large devaluations and exchange rate movements have occurred. However, applying varying weights to series in levels results in distortions to the
data following exchange rate movements, distortions that can be shown to not
occur if the aggregated data is in growth rates. For these reasons the chosen
method of aggregation was to use the series in growth rates with the applied
weights allowed to vary over time.

For an aggregate real series Y, and its two country components Y_1 and Y_2, the
aggregation method used and the derivation of the weights is as follows.

$$\Delta y_t = \log Y_t - \log Y_{t-1} \approx \frac{\Delta Y_t}{Y_{t-1}} \equiv \frac{\Delta Y_{1t} + \Delta Y_{2t}}{Y_{t-1}} = \Delta y_{1t}\omega_{1t-1} + \Delta y_{2t}\omega_{2t-1}$$

where Δ is the first difference operator, y is the log of Y, and the weights ω_i, for
i = 1 to 2 are

$$\omega_{1t} = \frac{E_{1t}Y_{1t}}{E_{1t}Y_{1t} + E_{2t}Y_{2t}} = \frac{Y_{1t}}{Y_{1t} + E_{2t}Y_{2t}/E_{1t}}$$

where E is the exchange rate used to convert the values into a common currency (a similar formula exists for ω_2). Exchange rate movements then alter
the magnitude of the weights attached to a country's series and can be expected to vary over time. However the magnitudes of any individual series are
computed from growth rates and are not affected by changes to exchange
rates.

Euro-11 data
Figure 1 plots the Euro-11 data for some key Euroland series. The upper part
plots the annual change in output (GDP), consumption (C) and business investment (I). The series display a strong degree of procyclicality with consumption in particular tracking changes to GDP. Throughout the 1980s the
Euro-11 economy exhibited steady growth without any of the booms/reces-
sions that were observed in the individual countries. Aggregating across the
eleven economies has had the effect of evening out these deviations from
trend, implying that country specific cycles may have become less synchro-
nised. During the 1990s however the smoothness of the series becomes less
prevalent with the beginning of this decade marked by a strong boom in GDP
and consumption. A sharp downturn in the economy then begins, bottoming
out in 1993, before a sustained period of steady growth is again maintained.
One last fact to note is the high volatility of the investment series. Fluctuations
in investment are much more severe than for any of the other series documented, a fact that has been well documented within individual countries.

Figure 1

Key economic aggregates for the Euro-11 economy

1981-1 to 1999-4; in %

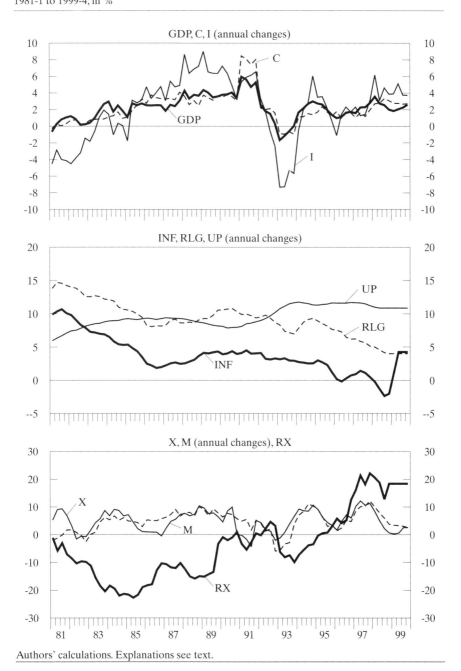

Authors' calculations. Explanations see text.

Figure 1 middle part plots the inflation (INF) rate, the unemployment (UP) rate, and nominal long interest rates (RLG). Over this almost twenty year period unemployment has continued to increase. A brief period of respite occurred towards the end of the 1980s but over the mid to late 1990s unemployment has shown no tendency to fall. This is particularly worrying given that this period has been one of steady growth and explains why the term "jobless growth" is an appropriate description of Euroland's performance. One success has been in the conduct of monetary policy however. Inflation has declined steadily over this period and appears to be well under control. Inflation's decline also explains the downward path of nominal long rates over this period.

Open economy series are plotted in Figure 1, lower part. Both exports (X) and imports (M) are characterised by a series of short cycles, with their growth rates rarely falling below zero. During the late 1990s both series showed strong growth with annual growth rates averaging about five per cent a year. The nominal effective exchange rate (measured as foreign currencies per Euros and re-based for purposes of clarity so that 1995 = 0) has appreciated since the mid 1980s in contrast to the early 1980s when the dollar was dominant (the US averages about thirty per cent of Euro-11 trade). Recent falls in the Euro are yet to show through given that the data ends in 1999 quarter one.

3. The model

From Layard et al. the standard labour market model comprises of a model of the wage bargain between unions and managers, and technology and product demand assumptions. In the model economy there are many firms (indexed by i) that are all unionised. Unions are assumed to maximise with respect to nominal wages a function that is the weighted average of the difference between the nominal wage paid by firm i (W_i) and the expected real income of a worker who loses his job (A), which can be thought of as the level of unemployment benefits, a transition function (S) that governs the ease with which an unemployed person can find employment (and vice versa) and π_i^e, the ith firm's expected profits that are themselves determined by the amount of wages paid,

$$\max \Omega = \left(W_i - A \right)^\beta S \left(W_i \right)^\beta \pi_i^e \left(W_i \right) \qquad (1)$$

Product demand is assumed to be a constant elasticity demand function,

$$Y_i = P_i^{-\eta} Y_{di} \qquad (2)$$

where P_i is the real price of firm i's output, Y_{di} is a demand shift variable and η is the price elasticity. Without any loss of generality, the production function for each firm is assumed to be Cobb-Douglas,

$$Y_i = N_i^\alpha K_i^{1-\alpha} \qquad (3)$$

Since all firms are by assumption identical, we can delete the index i since $W_i = W$, $K_i = K$, $N_i = N$ and $P_i = 1$. By maximising the Nash product in (1), and by assuming profit maximisation using (2) and (3), a key equation relating the amount of labour supplied to the aggregate wage can be obtained,

$$W = f(K/N, \kappa, \beta, A, U, \alpha) \tag{4}$$

Nominal wages are a function of the firm's capital – labour ratio, a measure of competitiveness $(k = 1 - 1/\eta)$, the strength of union power (β), a variable (A) that captures everything that determines the return from not working except unemployment, unemployment (U) itself and the degree of labour intensity (α). This relationship can be thought of as a labour supply condition since these factors determine how willing workers are to supply their labour each period. The firm's first order profit maximising conditions for labour and capital are,

$$\frac{W}{P} = \alpha k \left(\frac{K}{N} \right)^{1-\alpha} \tag{5}$$

$$\frac{R}{P} = (1-\alpha)k \left(\frac{K}{N} \right)^{\alpha}. \tag{6}$$

Equations (4) – (6) are three long-run relationships that can be estimated and included as cointegrating vectors in the dynamic equations, where we allow for the possibility that these long-run relationships may enter more than one regression. Note that Layard et al. interchangeably use (5) as an employment or a price equation, in their model it has both interpretations.

The empirical implementation of the wage bargaining model can be problematic even in countries where there are no data problems: what variables are to be used that can capture exactly the value of the alternative to work (A)? For the Euro-11 data it is even more difficult. As far as we are aware no data exists on aggregate values for such series as unemployment benefits, and even if they did their interpretation could be difficult given the large differences that prevail across countries. However, the advantages from incorporating some measure of A are big. Simulation exercises that analyse the response of the economy to changes in labour supply measures could be conducted and superior measures of the NAIRU obtained. Therefore, the approach taken here was to use an unobserved components (UC) model to obtain an estimate of this variable. UC models are being increasingly used for estimating models of the NAIRU over the business cycle (see Richardson et al. 2000, Laubach 1999, Orlandi, Pichelmann 2000 for NAIRU models; Artis, Zhang 1999 for an application to business cycles). For our purposes such pure time-series models have considerable drawbacks. Although they treat the NAIRU as time varying, they do not enable us to attribute these variations to changes in labour supply variables for example. Little guidance can then be offered on the policy implications of the persistently high levels of unemployment in Europe, or indeed its sources. For this a structural model is needed.

Laubach (1999) is an example of the pure time-series approach. He estimates a univariate model of the form

$$\Delta\pi = \gamma(L)\left(u_{t-1} - u_{t-1}^n\right) \tag{7}$$

where for simplicity lags are ignored, and where   is the deviation of inflation from its expected rate, and u^n the (unobserved) NAIRU (note that Laubach's Phillips Curve specification actually uses other lagged supply-side variables such as the nominal exchange rate and commodity prices so it is not entirely devoid of structure). Laubach estimates the NAIRU as a UC model assuming that the NAIRU follows a random walk with drift,

$$u_t^n = u_{t-1}^n + \mu_{\tau-1} + v_t$$

$$\mu_t = \mu_{t-1} + \varsigma_t.$$

This assumption is in contrast to that made in Gordon (1997), for example, who assumed that the US NAIRU was a random walk without drift. Laubach's model would appear to be an improvement on this, but even so he finds that the NAIRU estimates he gets are subject to great imprecision (even with the addition of a second equation for the unemployment gap which forces it to be mean reverting).

Our method combines both structural and time-series techniques so goes some way to overcoming the problems noted in the other studies. In turn, we adopt a (partial) time series approach because of a major problem in trying to estimate a long run wage equation of the standard form as represented by equation (7) above for the Euro-11. In the case of the Euro-11 there is a lack of data for variables affecting the transition probability and alternative wage. That is, apart from unemployment, other variables that affect the wage out of work (A) and the relative strength of unions (β) are unobtainable.

Our approach to resolving this problem is to use an unobserved components model for that part of the wage model which represents the "union" part of the Nash bargain given by equation (1). Implicitly the "firm" part of the equation (i.e. the $\pi(.)$ term) is taken to be the marginal productivity condition – as it is in most applications. What remains after this, measurable, component is partialled out is then treated as due to the union side of the bargain (and which we loosely refer to as labour supply factors).

More formally we can write the UC model as the dynamic nominal wage equation,

$$\Delta \ln W_t - \Delta \ln W_{t-1} = \alpha_0 + \alpha_1 \left(\ln W_{t-1} - \ln P_{t-1} - \ln F'_{Nt-1} \right);$$
$$+ \alpha_2 \left(\ln W_{t-1} - \ln P_{t-1} + \alpha_3 U_{t-1} - \alpha_4 A_{t-1} \right) + dynamics + \varepsilon_{0t} \tag{8}$$

$$\varepsilon_{0t} \sim N(0, W_t)$$

where α_1, α_2 are negative, α_3 is positive and F'_N is the marginal product of employment. This is an equation that includes both the dynamics and labour demand terms (such as the standard neo-classical marginal product of labour/real wage equality). We can then condition on these terms to estimate the unobserved union/laboursupply term (A). To put this model into a form that can be estimated, we need some assumptions about the process driving A, and to use these in setting up the model in a Kalman Filter form. We assume that the A process is,

$$A_t = A_{t-1} + ST_t + \varepsilon_{it}; \quad \varepsilon_{1t} \sim N(0, Q_{1t}) \tag{9}$$

$$ST_t = ST_{t-1} + \varepsilon_{2t}; \quad \varepsilon_{2t} \sim N(0, Q_{2t}). \tag{10}$$

Equations (8) – (10) are then estimated by the Kalman Filter where (8) is the measurement equation, and (9) and (10) the state equations. In these latter equations a slightly more general approach has been taken that allows the state variable to be a random walk with drift (the drift term being given by ST). A is thus assumed to follow a random walk with a stochastic trend (ST). The motivation for the inclusion of a stochastic trend in the union/labour supply process is to capture the perceived upward trend in the value of the alternatives to work, matching the upward trend in nominal wages over time.

Although estimation is by single equation methods we allow for the possibility that each dynamic equation may contain more than one long-run cointegrating relationship. The set of dynamic equations for nominal wages, prices, employment and capital take the following general form,

$$\theta_{11}(L)\Delta W_t = \theta_{12}(L)\Delta P_{t-1} + \alpha_{11}\left(F'_{Nt-1} - W_{t-1}/P_{t-1} \right) + \tag{11}$$

$$\alpha_{12}\left(W_{t-1}/P_{t-1} + \alpha_1 U_{t-1} - A_{t-1} \right)$$

$$\theta_{21}(L)\Delta P_t = \theta_{22}(L)\Delta W_{t-1} + \alpha_{21}\left(F'_{Nt-1} - W_{t-1}/P_{t-1} \right) \tag{12}$$

$$\theta_{31}(L)\Delta N_t = \theta_{32}(L)\Delta\left(W_{t-1}/P_{t-1} \right) + \alpha_{31}\left(F'_{Nt-1} - W_{t-1}/P_{t-1} \right) + \tag{13}$$

$$\alpha_{32}\left(Y_{t-1} - f\left(N_{t-1}, K_{t-1} \right) \right)$$

$$\theta_{41}(L)\Delta K_t = \theta_{42}(L)\Delta r_{t-1} + \alpha_{41}\left(F'_{Kt-1} - r_{t-1} \right). \tag{14}$$

The final term in (11) is the empirical implementation of the long-run wage equation (5) where U is unemployment and A is the return from not working, estimated by the UC model. The other equation to note is the employment equation (13), where both the marginal product condition (6) and a term capturing the difference between actual GDP and the level of GDP determined by supply factors (i.e. the production function) enter. The inclusion of both terms can be thought of as capturing the fact that some firms are not output constrained and hence employ workers according to the neo-classical demand function. At the same time there are other firms that are output constrained and this final term $\alpha_{32}(\ )$ captures this by assuming that they meet their output target by varying their labour input, given their capital stock.

Clearly other items are required to complete and close the model but since the rest of the model is straightforward it can be summarised briefly. The long run levels part of consumption allows for the familiar theoretical considerations. Consumption is assumed to be a function of income, net wealth (NW), and the long-term real interest rate (RLG-INF), all expressed in real terms. Homogeneity is also imposed on the level of real income so that explosive behaviour for consumption as the economy expands is ruled out,

$$C_t = f\left(NW_t, Y_t RLG_t, INF_t\right) \tag{15}$$

The aggregate price level (the producer price index is used here) is assumed to be a weighted average of unit wage costs (total employment multiplied by earnings divided by output) and import prices (PM).

$$P_t = f\left(N_t, W_t, Y_t, PM_t\right) \tag{16}$$

Import prices have been included to capture price changes for those goods imported by producers. Data problems for the Euro-11 mean however that the import price measure incorporates the prices of goods traded between the Euro-11 countries, as well as the prices of goods from outside this area. To overcome this a separate equation for import prices was estimated explicitly allowing for the possibility that the import price measure may incorporate domestic prices.

$$PM_t = f\left(P_t, WP_t\right), \tag{17}$$

Over the long-run import prices are assumed to be a function of a competitiveness measure (here world prices, WP) and domestic prices. Incorporating domestic prices should directly correct for the presence of intra-traded goods in the import price measure.

Open economy effects are captured by the import (M) and export (X) regressions. Both equations contain a price and a quantity variable. The chosen price variable, or measure of competitiveness, is relative wage costs (WCR). Variations in quantities are captured by total final expenditure ($TFE = GDP + M$) in the imports equation, and by a world trade (WT) measure in the exports equation.

$$M_t = f(TFE, WCR_t),$$ (18)

$$X_t = f(WT_t, WCR_t),$$ (19)

We also have a technical relation for the consumer price (P_c) linking it to the producer price (P) in (5),

$$\Delta P_{ct} = \Delta P_t$$ (20)

In aggregate a resource constraint binds,

$$GDP_t = C_t + I_t + GC_t + X_t - M_t$$ (21)

where I is business investment and government consumption (GC) is assumed to be exogenous. Equation (14) describes the evolution of the capital stock with investment changing over time in the usual manner,

$$I_t = K_t - (1-\delta)K_{t-1}.$$ (22)

Finally, we can note the policy rules used. The monetary rule adjusts the nominal interest rate such that deviations of inflation from its target rate are minimised (using the conventional proportional, integral, differential (PID) formula). Fiscal rules (again using a PID form) adjust tax rates such that the government's budget constraint is met, where for the moment government spending is assumed exogenous.

4. Estimation results

Results from estimating each of the equations are given in the appendix. The production function was calibrated such that the share of capital in output was 0.36, the value typically chosen in the real business cycle literature (e.g. Kydland, Prescott 1982). Constant returns to scale was also assumed. From these equations it is straightforward to obtain estimates of the marginal products of capital and labour.

In the long-run consumption function wealth effects are reasonably strong. A one per cent increase in the ratio of real net wealth to real personal disposable income leads to a rise in consumption of 0.13 per cent. Long-term real interest rates also enter the CV for consumption though its effects are not particularly large. The hypothesis of homogeneity in consumption and income could not be rejected. Underlying the estimation process was the decision to obtain results that are parsimonious and that have good dynamic properties. The dynamic consumption equation typifies this. Dynamics enter solely from the change in real personal disposable income (lagged one quarter). Lagged terms in consumption, income, inflation and real interest rates were also included at the initial first stage but their t-statistics were either very low or entered with the incorrect sign. The estimated dynamic investment equation contains lagged dynamic terms in both GDP and investment. Its CV is the difference between the real interest rate (used to proxy capital's marginal cost) and the marginal product of capital. If the interest rate is above capital's marginal product, investment falls so that the capital stock can return to its long-run level.

The dynamic employment equation contains two long-run relationships. One is the difference between actual output and the level of output that can currently be produced by supply- constrained firms. This term enters with a coefficient of 0.13. The second CV is the difference between the real wage (labour's marginal cost) and the marginal product of labour. If labour's marginal product is above its marginal cost then the level of employment increases since firms seek to employ more workers. The coefficient on this term is 0.02. Dynamics enter via two lagged changes in employment. The earnings equation also contains two long-run terms. One being the difference between actual output and a measure of output by the supply constrained firms. The second term is from the wage bargaining model. Unions choose the wage dependent upon the level of unemployment (a proxy for the probability that workers may lose their job if the chosen wage is too high) and the return from not working (A). The series for A was obtained by a Kalman Filter estimation process with A assumed to be an unobserved variable. Also included in the Kalman Filter was the level of unemployment and the real wage. The residuals from this regression then enter the dynamic wage equation. Interpretation of the coefficients isn't straightforward. For instance, the coefficient on the lagged unemployment term is –0.02, which seems small but simulation exercises suggest that this has a strong effect on the simulation properties of the model.

Aggregate prices in the long run are a weighted average of unit wage costs and import prices, with UWC having the largest weight (0.82). The dynamic price equation then contains this CV (with a coefficient of 0.2) plus a lagged dynamic price term and the change in earnings lagged one quarter. In turn, import prices are a weighted average of the log of prices plus the log of world prices, with both having approximately equal weight.

The final set of estimated equations concern the open economy effects from the trade equations. In the long run exports equation, exports move one-for-one with world trade, and the coefficient of relative wage costs is 0.38. This CV enters the dynamic exports equation with a coefficient of 0.19. The other term is a lagged dynamics term. The CV for imports has total final expenditure as the quantity variable, again imposed with a unit coefficient, and relative wage costs which are more important for imports since its coefficient is now 0.64. In the dynamic imports equation the error-correction mechanism enters with a coefficient of –0.18, implying a return to equilibrium reasonably quickly each quarter. Also included are three lagged dependent variables with coefficients of 0.13, 0.25 and 0.18 respectively. This completes a description of the econometric results.

5. Estimating the NAIRU in the Euro-11

In this section the model is used to obtain two estimates of the NAIRU. The first estimate is perhaps more appropriately termed the NAWRU, since it is earnings inflation that is being targeted and not price inflation. The estimate is obtained by asking what the unemployment rate should be to set the current period's wage inflation rate equal to the previous period's rate. The mechanics of this exercise simply involve inverting the earnings equation. A plot of the resulting estimate is shown in Figure 2. From these figures it appears that the short-run NAWRU closely tracks the actual unemployment rate. The biggest discernable difference between the two series is over the period 1991 – 1995 when the estimated NAWRU is consistently lower than the actual unemployment rate. This occurs at a time when the inflation rate was steadily falling.

Figure 2 lower part plots a long-run version of the NAIRU. This series was obtained by asking what level of unemployment would be necessary for the price level to be equal to the long-run level of prices implied by the cointegrating vector in the price equation. Based on these figures and in contrast to the short-run NAWRU estimates, the NAIRU has proved remarkably invariant given the changes that have occurred in the Eurozone over this period. From 1993 the NAIRU begins to gradually rise as the actual unemployment rate increases into double digits. The net effect is that the NAIRU is now half of one per cent higher in the 1990s than it was in the 1980s. It may seem surprising that our estimates for the NAIRU are relatively invariant over time. However these results are not unusual. Laubach used a Kalman Filter to estimate NAIRU's for the G7 and also found his estimates to be approximately constant for each of the countries[2].

6. Simulation exercises

In this section the response of the model to two types of shocks is presented. First, the model is subjected to a temporary shock to government consumption. Second, the return to not working is shocked temporarily.

---

[2] It may be that our specification of the dynamic wage equation (8) is responsible for the constancy of the NAIRU. The return from not working (A) is modelled as a Kalman Filter process and it may be that any movements in the NAIRU are being captured by this variable.

Figure 2
The short-run NAIRU for the Euro-11
1985-1 to 1999-4; in %

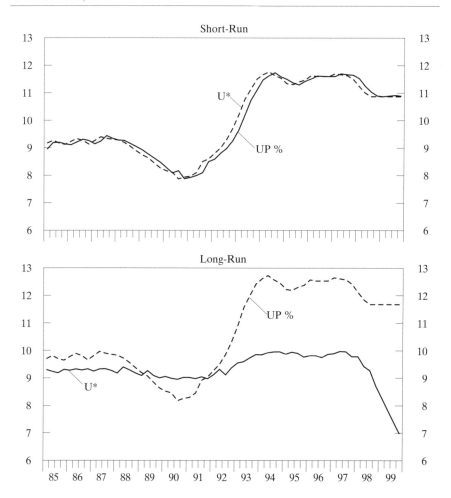

Authors' calculations. Explanations see text.

A temporary shock to government consumption

For this shock government consumption is increased by 5 % over the period
1987Q1 to 1990Q1 (results are presented in Figures 3 and 4). Figure 3 plots the
responses of GDP, consumption and investment. Since government consumption is a component of GDP from the resource constraint, GDP is higher for
the duration of the increase in GC. Consumption, which is a function of real
disposable income, rises gradually following GDP's increase. Surprisingly
there is little effect upon investment. By the end of the sample period invest-

Figure 3

Temporary shock to government consumption

1988-1 to 1999-4; in %

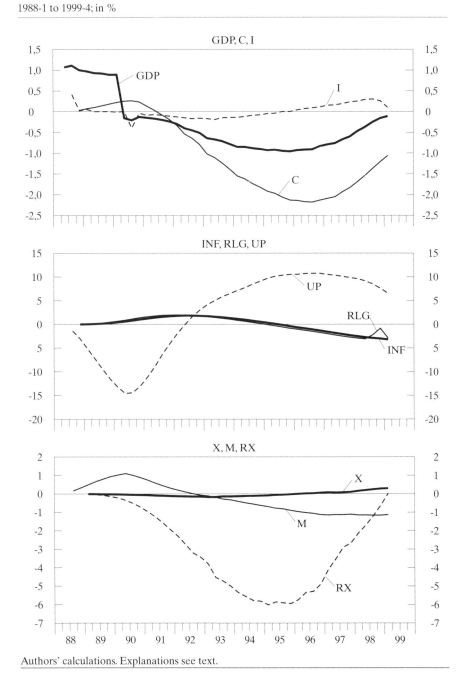

Authors' calculations. Explanations see text.

Figure 4
Learning parameters following a government shock
1988-1 to 1998-4; in %

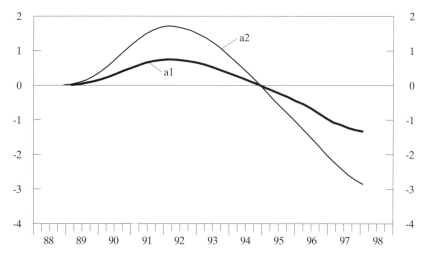

Authors' calculations. Explanations see text.

ment begins to rise as interest rates fall (see Figure 3 middle) following the decreases in output. Inflation too is unchanged following the shock but unemployment falls during the period of the increased expenditure before beginning a sustained period of recovery. Positively correlated with the decline in
GDP is the depreciation of the nominal effective exchange rate (RX), plotted
in Figure 3 lower part. Occurring with the depreciation is a decline in imports,
though the change in exports is much smaller.

Expectations enter into the model via an open arbitrage equation requiring
the difference in the levels of real interest rates between two countries to be
equal to the expected change in the real exchange rate. Under rational expectations the expected exchange rate next period would be equal to the actual
exchange rate, subject to any shock. Under learning it is instead assumed that
agents use a rule to predict the expected exchange rate. This expected exchange rate rule can be a function of any of the other variables, though for the
purposes of modelling a parsimonious specification is usually chosen. Each
period, as new information becomes available, agents update the rule as they
learn which variables are relevant for forecasting the exchange rate and which
variables are not. Marcet/Sargent (1989) have shown that so long as the learning rule contains some information that is correlated with the true process
driving exchange rates then the exchange rate under learning will converge to
the exchange rate equilibrium derived under rational expectations.

Figure 5

Temporary shock to the labour supply

1987-1 to 1990-1; in %

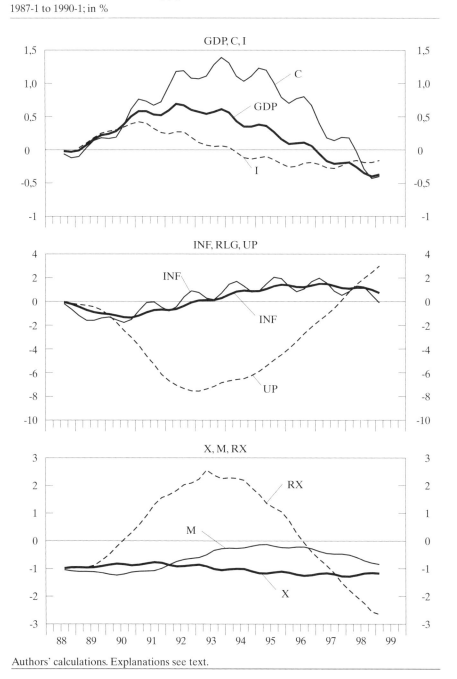

Authors' calculations. Explanations see text.

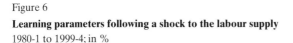

Figure 6

Learning parameters following a shock to the labour supply

1980-1 to 1999-4; in %

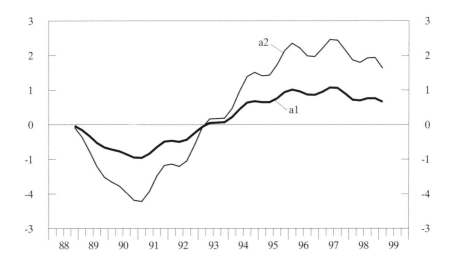

Authors' calculations. Explanations see text.

In our model the expected real effective exchange rate (between Euroland and the rest of the world) is assumed to be a linear function of lagged nominal effective exchange rates. Figure 4 plots how the learning parameters evolve over time, with a_1 being the constant and a_2 the coefficient on lagged exchange rates. One would expect these parameters to converge over time as the exchange rate converges asymptotically onto the rational expectations solution although here, ten years after the shock, there is still some way to go before this has occurred.

A temporary shock to the return from not working

As above, the shock to the return from not working (which can be interpreted as a decrease in unemployment benefits) is temporary and also lasts for the period 1987Q1 to 1990Q1. Given the bargaining framework, any decrease in unemployment benefits results in a fall in the wage paid by firms, and demanded by unions, since there is a lower return available elsewhere in the economy. Figure 5 indicates that GDP, consumption and investment are all higher than prior to the decrease in benefits. The amount of labour supplied increases in this economy as the wage falls resulting in higher GDP, consumption and investment. Inflation (a function of unit wage costs) rises along with the real long rate. Unemployment falls as the amount of labour supplied in the economy is raised. Nominal exchange rates appreciate for the five years following the shock with imports rising as their price has fallen (following a short lag).

Exports are again unresponsive to these exchange rate movements. The learning parameters a_1 and a_2 show a higher degree of convergence following this shock and appear well on their way to converging (Figure 6).

7. Conclusion

This paper has estimated a medium-sized model of the Euro-11 area. Three features of the model are worth noting. First, a specific supply-side built up from a Cobb- Douglas production model was constructed and estimated. Second, a general form for each equation was specified so that more than one long-run relationship could enter into each dynamic regression. Third, the model was simulated under the assumption that agents learn. The model was then used for two purposes. First, to estimate the level of the NAIRU in the Euro-11 area. Two measures were constructed: one short run and one long run measure. The short-run measure was found to closely track actual unemployment over the sample period. In contrast the long-run measure of the NAIRU was relatively stable at 9 per cent, though there was some evidence to suggest that it may be beginning to fall. Second, the model was used to study how the Euro-11 economy responds to different types of shocks. Temporary shocks to government expenditure and unemployment benefits were each found to act as stimulants to GDP and other key series for the first five years at least before the effect of higher real interest rates began to feed in. In future work, we intend to extend the model's database by approximately fifty years so that questions concerning the stability of the model can be addressed and experiments conducted where the duration of the shock (policy change) is much longer.

Appendix: Estimation Results

Production

$$y_t = 0.36 k_t + (1 - 0.36) n_t + dummies \qquad (A1)$$

where lower case letters denote logs. From (i) the marginal products of capital (MPK) and labour (MPL) are next derived which in turn are set equal to the real rental rate of capital and real wage respectively.

Consumption

$$ECMC_t = c_t - y_t + 0.08 - 0.14(nw_t - y_t) + 0.002(RLG_t - INF_t) + dummies + \varepsilon_t \ (A2)$$

$$\Delta c_t = 0.004 + 0.24 \Delta rpdi_{t-1} - 0.12 ECMC_t + dummies + \varepsilon_t \qquad (A3)$$
$$(5.15) \phantom{\Delta rpdi_{t-1} -} (2.84)$$

$$R^2 = 0.86; \sigma = 0.003; \chi(4) sc = 2.84; \chi(2)_N = 1.51; \chi(1)_H = 0.48.$$

Investment

$$ECMK_t = RLG_t - INF_t - MPK_t + 0.26 \qquad \text{(A4)}$$

$$\Delta i_t = 0.006 + 0.37\left(\Delta y_{t-1} - \Delta y_{t-2}\right) + 0.22\Delta i_{t-1} - 0.03 ECMK_{t-1} + dummies + \varepsilon_t \quad \text{(A5)}$$
$$(2.47)(1.45) \qquad\qquad (1.70) \qquad (2.33)$$

$$R^2 = 0.42; \sigma = 0.014; \chi(4)sc = 3.59; \chi(2)_N = 0.26; \chi(1)_H = 2.03.$$

Employment

$$ECMW_t = w_t - p_t + 5.06 - mpl_t \qquad \text{(A6)}$$

$$ECMY_t = y_t - 0.36k_t - (1 - 0.36)\, n_t - dummies \qquad \text{(A7)}$$

i.e. the difference between actual output and supply constrained output.

$$\Delta n_t = 0.0005 + 0.19\Delta n_{t-1} + 0.45\Delta n_{t-2} + 0.133 ecmy_{t-1} - \qquad \text{(A8)}$$
$$(1.62) \quad (1.99) \qquad (4.85) \qquad (2.10)$$

$$0.002 ecmw_{t-1} + dummies + \varepsilon_t$$
$$(1.26)$$

$$R^2 = 0.48; \sigma = 0.003; \chi(4)sc = 7.53; \chi(2)_N = 1.86; \chi(1)_H = 0.51.$$

Earnings

$$\Delta er_t = -0.74 + 1.266 A_t - 0.38 ecmw_{t-1} - 0.56\left(er_{t-1} - p_{t-1}\right) - \qquad \text{(A9)}$$
$$(11.5) \qquad (6.52) \qquad\quad (9.29)$$

$$0.02 UP_{t-1} + dummies + \varepsilon_t$$
$$(12.27)$$

$$R^2 = 0.94; \sigma = 0.011; \chi(4)sc = 7.49; \chi(1)_H = 0.80.$$

Prices

$$ECMP_t = p_t - 0.06 - 0.82\left(n_t + er_t - y_t\right) - (1 - 0.82)*pm_t \qquad \text{(A10)}$$

$$\Delta p_t - \Delta p_{t-1} = 0.003 - 0.2 ecm_{t-1} + \varepsilon_t \qquad \text{(A11)}$$
$$(2.06)$$

$$R^2 = 0.79; \sigma = 0.003; \chi(4)sc = 2.49; \chi(2)_N = 0.20; \chi(1)_H = 0.68.$$

$$\Delta pm_t = -0.67 + 0.49 p_t + 0.51 wp_t + dummies + \varepsilon_t \qquad \text{(A12)}$$
$$(85.2)(9.13) \quad (9.13)$$

$$R^2 = 0.92; \sigma = 0.04; \chi(4)sc = 4.90; \chi(2)_N = 0.98; \chi(1)_H = 0.04.$$

Exports

$$ECMX_t = x_t - wt_t - 3.16 + 0.39wcr_t + dummies \qquad (A13)$$

$$\Delta x_t = 0.01 + 0.2444\Delta x_{t-1} - 0.199ecmx_{t-1} + dummies + \varepsilon_t \qquad (A14)$$
$$(5.30)\quad(2.78)\qquad(2.55)$$

$$R^2 = 0.43; \sigma = 0.01; \chi(4)sc = 5.80; \chi(2)_N = 1.20; \chi(1)_H = 0.49.$$

Imports

$$ECMM_t = m_t - tfe_t + 4.96 - 0.64wcr_t + dummies \qquad (A15)$$

where *tfe* is total final expenditure (GDP + M)

$$\Delta m_t = 0.005 + 0.14\Delta m_{t-1} + 0.26\Delta m_{t-2} + 0.18\Delta m_{t-3} - \qquad (xvi)$$
$$(2.35)\ (1.22)\qquad(2.49)\qquad(1.72)$$

$$0.18ecmm_{t-1} + dummies + \varepsilon_t$$
$$(1.00)$$

$$R^2 = 0.36; \sigma = 0.01; \chi(4)sc = 2.99; \chi(2)_N = 2.25; \chi(1)_H = 1.20.$$

Note:
ó : standard error of the regression;
$\chi(4)_{sc}$: LM test for serial correlation with a Chi-squared distribution with 4 d.o.f.;
$\chi(2)_N$: LM test for normality with a Chi-squared distribution and 2 d.o.f.;
$\chi(1)_H$: LM test for heteroscedasticity with a Chi-squared distribution and 1 d.o.f.

References

Artis, M. and Y. Zhang (1997). International Business Cycles and the ERM: Is there a European Business Cycle? *International Journal of Finance and Economics* (2): 1–16.

Beyer, A., J. Doornik and D.F. Hendry (2000), *Constructing Historical Euro-Zone Data*. Nuffield College, Oxford, unpublished Mimeo.

Fisher, P.G., S.K. Tanner, D.S. Turner, K.F. Wallis and J.D. Whitley (1990), Econometric Evaluation of the Exchange Rate in Models of the UK Economy. *Economic Journal* 100: 1230–1244.

Gordon, R. (1997), The Time Varying NAIRU and its Implications for Economic Policy. *Journal of Economic Perspectives* 11 (1): 11–32.

Kydland, F. and E.C. Prescott (1982), Time to Build and Aggregate Fluctuations. *Econometrica* 50: 1345-70.

Laubach, T. (1999), *Measuring the NAIRU: Evidence from Seven Economies*. Federal Reserve Bank of Kansas City, unpublished Mimeo.

Layard, R., S. Nickell and R. Jackman (1991), *Unemployment – Macroeconomic Performance and the Labour Market*. Oxford: Oxford University Press.

Marcet, A. and T.J. Sargent (1989), Convergence of Least Squares Learning Mechanisms in Self-Referential Linear Stochastic Models. *Journal of Economic Theory* 48: 337–368.

McMorrow, K. and W. Roeger (2000), Time-Varying NAIRU/NAWRU Estimates for the EU's Member States. EC Working Papers Series 145. European Commission, Brussels.

Orlandi, F. and K. Pichelmann (2000), Disentangling Trend and Cycle in the EUR-11 Unemployment Series: An Unobserved Component Modelling Approach. EC Working Papers Series 140. European Commission, Brussels.

Richardson, P., L. Boone, C. Giorno, M. Meacci, D. Rae and D. Turner (2000), The Concept, Policy Use and Measurement of Structural Unemployment: Estimating a Time-Varying NAIRU Across 21 OECD Countries. OECD Working Paper 250. OECD, Paris.

Mika Kortelainen and David G. Mayes

Using EDGE – A Dynamic General Equilibrium Model of the Euro Area

As a member of the Eurosystem the Bank of Finland has to be able to make its own judgements about the prospects for price stability in the euro area and about the implications this has for setting policy in the Eurosystem. In order to provide consistent and coherent advice from a clear point of view it is sensible to base this process on a relatively simple and analytically understandable macroeconomic model. As the Bank of Finland has been developing its view of the Finnish economy over a long period of time and incorporating that in a series of econometric models, the latest of which is BOF5 (Willman et al. 1998), this would seem a sensible starting point for a euro area model. At least there is some experience in how models of this sort work and some confidence in their use. A key issue for the Bank is transparency. Transparency is normally thought of as making the Bank's thinking transparent with respect to the outside world but in the current context it also needs to be trans- parent within the Eurosystem. The other National Central Banks and the ECB need to be able understand readily how the Bank of Finland views the workings of the euro economy and therefore be able to understand the ex ante advice as well as the ex post analysis of the effects of different shocks, assumptions and policy reactions.

Although the euro area is sixty times as large as Finland in economic terms and rather more closed and complex, there is no reason why the same sort of macroeconomic framework should not apply but with different parameters. However, BOF5 is quite a large model, with nearly 400 equations 60 of which are estimated. Even if it were possible, replicating this at the euro level would be a major and long-term exercise. Policy has had to be made with the tools available from the outset of the Eurosystem (effectively late 1998 although the euro did not come into being until 4th January 1999). It therefore seemed sensible to start with a smaller model which incorporated the main theoretical features. EDGE has therefore been designed to have the minimum structure consistent with incorporating the main relationships in the economy relating to the operation of monetary policy. It has 40 equations 13 of which are behavioural. The remainder are definitions, identities and policy rules. The model is deliberately designed to have a similar structure of variables to the ECB's Area-Wide Model (AWM) for comparability and use in the policy process (Fagan et al. 2001).

However, modelling the euro area presents two further fundamental problems. The euro area is a new construct. Although its constituent member states existed before, they were not operating together in the same way even in the period immediately beforehand. Estimating a model using data related to the past is therefore not necessarily a very good guide to what behaviour will be in the future. After all the whole point of Economic and Monetary Union is to change the behaviour of the euro economy, making it more flexible, more dynamic and hence able to grow faster in real terms on the one hand and more stable both in nominal (price) terms and in terms of real fluctuations round the faster growth path on the other. The model therefore has to be able to cope with structural change and have a structure that allows us to explore the implications of changes in behaviour. Secondly, even if we could set up such a model for estimation the data did not exist. We have therefore created our own database from published sources (Table 4, Appendix) but many of the series are very short[1]. Therefore, despite the advantages of estimation there is no alternative initially to calibrating the model on the basis of international evidence of parameter values, consistent with the characteristics of the new information held in the euro database. As time passes no doubt it will become possible to move nearer an estimated model.

In Section 1, which follows, we outline the structure and thinking behind EDGE and list its equations. A fuller version is published in Kortelainen (2001). The key requirements for the model are that it is forward-looking and incorporates model consistent expectations, that there be a private sector that can respond to foreign and domestic demand and supply shocks, that there be a foreign sector and fiscal and monetary authorities that can set policy in a describable manner. The model needs to converge towards a coherent steady state with plausible adjustment paths. Section 2 therefore describes how we derived the parameter values and the adjustment paths in the light of existing evidence and indications about how the euro area may work.

The main part of the paper is, however, Sections 3 and 4, where we examine how the model works in practice. In Section 3 we show how the model responds to a range of common shocks including changes in fiscal and monetary policy, domestic and foreign demand and supply shocks. Given recent and widely discussed prospects we include exchange rate and stock market shocks.

---

[1] An earlier version of this model used a database developed by Fagan et al. 2001. The new database and the calibration is described in detail in Kortelainen 2002.

Section 4 on the other hand explores how the monetary authority – the Euro-system – interacts with the rest of the economy. We explore three straight-forward cases.

In the first case we explore the importance of "credibility" and show the difference in impact on the economy of a policy change if the bank is credible and the difference in impact if the Eurosystem acts as if it were credible when it is not. In the second two cases we consider problems of a structural change in the economy, firstly in the NAIRU and secondly in real rate of interest. Both of these are treated as aspects of either a "new economy" or simply the impact of closer integration stemming from EMU. We show the differences in impact if the central bank and the private sector perceive the change from when they do not and explore how different learning mechanisms affect the outcome. In particular we explore the consequences if the private sector misperceives the central bank's reaction function. Thus we solve the model with the central bank basing its decisions on one reaction function and the private sector basing its decisions on a different central bank reaction function.

1. An outline of the EDGE model

The economy modelled in EDGE is divided into five sectors: households, firms, the government, the monetary authority and the rest of the world. The model itself (Appendix) has some 40 equations, 13 of which are behavioural, 5 define public policy, with the remaining 22 being identities. While the model is set out in dynamic form, it converges to a steady state in which stock equilibrium is defined and the real rate of growth is set (Appendix).

We follow the representative agent approach for both households and firms. Households are assumed to maximise the discounted value of lifetime consumption, using the Blanchard (1985) stochastic lifetime approach in a similar manner to that implemented in Sefton/in't Veld (1999). Behaviour is thus forward-looking with households basing their current actions on their expected wealth, derived from both financial assets and income (human wealth). Firms face a Cobb-Douglas technology (although Ripatti/Vilmunen (2001) show how this can be extended to a CES framework). The representative firm maximises the discounted value of expected real dividends (profits). This generates an adjustment process for capital and labour demand derived from inverting the production function and a demand for inventories. Wages are negotiated along the lines of overlapping Calvo (1983) contracts. Thus in determining capital, labour and wages the behaviour is forward-looking. Adjustment process are deliberately simple but unlike many similar models there is no attempt to add in subsequent adjustment processes to put more grit in the wheels of change. In the case of real wages the bargain depends on marginal product of labour and the departure of unemployment from the "NAIRU".

Prices tend to short-run marginal labour cost in the long run, adjusting accord-ing to a quadratic loss function.

The modelling of the foreign sector is based on trade equations rather than on the net acquisition of foreign assets. This approach is not yet satisfactory as the available statistics include trade within the euro area as well as outside it. Prices of both exports and exports depend upon foreign and domestic prices and the CPI (and investment deflator) depend on domestic and import prices. Completing the model, we assume that government adjusts the direct tax rate to achieve the steady-state debt to nominal GDP ratio, given decisions over public investment, consumption and indirect taxes. The path is controlled by the net lending to GDP condition as in the Maastricht Treaty. Similarly, given an inflation target the monetary authority sets interest rates following a Taylor rule (using the "unemployment gap" described in the case of wage setting rather than an output gap in addition to the deviation of inflation from the target). The exchange rate is then determined by uncovered interest rate pari-ty, given the exogenously determined foreign rate of interest.

2. Calibration

It is not possible to use simple estimation to derive the parameters of a euro area model as there is no past history of the area. It is therefore necessary to approach the problem in a more complex and indirect manner. We can try to infer the likely behaviour of the euro area by (a) considering how its compo-nents functioned in the past (b) observing how behaviour has been changing in recent years as the member states have sought to converge (c) projecting such changes into the future (d) comparing the projected behaviour with that in similar areas – principally the United States (e) comparing the process of structural change with that observed in other instances. In conducting these steps we can use a combination of our own new estimates and the cumulation of modelling experience of others.

This strategy represents a process of calibration, using the evidence available to derive plausible values for the model parameters. However, this is only a starting point as such a process works best for individual parameters and char-acteristics of the steady state. It does not work so well for deriving the proper-ties of the model as a whole. Two things are required for the complete model. One is that it fits quite well to the characteristics of the data we can create for the euro area, particularly in the most recent periods. The second is that the simulation properties of the model seem plausible – again in the light of previ-ous experience with the member states and experience with models of other large "countries".

The bulk of this paper is concerned with the model's simulation properties, which we turn to in the next section. Here we deal with the earlier steps in the calibration process, using the database described in the previous section.

The key parameters to be established for the *steady state* (Table 1) are

g : the real rate of growth

δ : the rate of depreciation

to set the equilibrium path

χ : the equity premium

β : the share of capital in the economy

and a series of other parameters to set the steady-state ratios for inventories, government transfers, debt, real consumption, real investment and other income to GDP. Weights need to be determined for the components of the price indexes and the trade equations need to be calibrated as a whole in a manner consistent with stable exchange rate determination. Values have to be assigned to the NAIRU and to the two key parameters in the consumption function – the subjective discount factor and the probability of death. Lastly the adjustment speeds of labour demand, wages and the GDP deflator need to be set.

The results of these choices are set out in the Appendix. Where series were stable we used estimated or average values from the data period available for the euro area. Where they were unstable we used values prevailing at the end of the period, particularly for the projection of the model into the future. Thus, for example, g was calibrated as 0.5 % per quarter to omit the slower growth associated with convergence to the Maastricht criteria but without a return to the higher rates occurring before the 1990s or any strong new economy effect. Such prospects are best left to simulations. In the same way the NAIRU was estimated as an HP filter through the data period with its most recent value projected forward. Again it may very well be appropriate to argue that structural reforms will enable this value to fall in the future and hence this can be entered into the simulations as we explore in the next section.

The calibration of the equity premium is largely based on the US experience (Siegel 1992). Calibrating the consumption equation proved a little difficult as the parameter values that fit the data well imply a sensible marginal propensity to consume but rather implausibly high values for the subjective discount factor and probability of death. Rather than solve this by the traditional method of adding somewhat arbitrary lags to the consumption equation we decided to remain data consistent as an initial step.

While we can fix the government sector according to practice prevailing in the data period as described, the monetary authority's reaction function is probably the most important choice from our point of view. Again what is necessary is a simple starting point from which simulations of different functions can be run as we will demonstrate in the next section. We therefore posit a Taylor rule based on the foreign real rate of interest and equal weights on the inflation and unemployment gaps. No smoothing is assumed, although the specification of the equation allows this. Taking all these calibrations together and filling the model across the data period generates a reasonable fit, as indicated by Table 2.

The second step is to calibrate the dynamic model. This involves the computation of leads and lags for the principal equations (Table 3). Kortelainen (2002) shows the results from some stochastic simulations to determine how well the calibrated model seems to track the properties of the data.

3. Simulations to set the characteristics of the model

EDGE is coded and solved in TROLL, using the Laffarque-Boucekkine-Juillard algorithm to solve the model forward. In setting up the simulations we first need to run the steady state model far enough forward to generate suitable terminal conditions for the dynamic model. We have used 800 periods (200 years). Then in solving the dynamic model over the same time horizon we insert a correcting factor for all the nominal and price variables in the terminal period to equate the differences between the dynamic and steady state models. Thus while the real variables converge to their steady state values there is no such requirement for the nominal variables.

We did not experience problems of convergence and EDGE appears to be dynamically stable over the long run. This therefore should give a suitable base from which to compute policy simulations.

In order to set the properties of the model we ran a series of standard shocks to the policy variables: taxes, government spending and the inflation target; to drivers of the model: rate of growth of the labour force, world demand, equity premium etc. However, some shocks can only be temporary, such as those to the exchange rate and interest rates, if the steady state is to be regained. To illustrate this we show examples of the following shocks in this section:

1. A shock from government policy in the form of a permanent increase in public consumption equivalent to 1 % of GDP.

2. A domestic shock in the form of a permanent increase in the equity premium by 1 %.

3. A foreign shock in the form of a permanent increase in world demand by 1 %.

It is important to have some yardstick against which to judge the resultant paths. Hunt (2000) was particularly helpful in providing a comparison with the responses of the IMF's MULTIMOD. (There is always a danger of circularity here in that if models are calibrated[2] against each other they may embody modellers' prejudices rather than observed behaviour.)

3.1 A shock from government policy

The key feature of the model that this simulation, increasing public consumption permanently by the equivalent of 1 % of GDP, illustrates is that a shift of resources towards the government reduces overall GDP, as productivity in the public sector tends to be below that in the private sector (the picture is shown in Figure 1). This of course is mainly because of the higher levels and growth rates of productivity that are possible in manufacturing industry compared with more service based activities. In the short run there is an increase in activity as it takes time for the increase in taxation required to finance the increased public expenditure to reduce private sector spending. The counterweight to this is that unemployment falls as a result of the sectoral shift towards more labour intensive activities. Because spending runs ahead of tax revenue in the short run public debt increases, inflation also rises and along with that nominal interest rates rise as the central bank tries to maintain price stability. The interest rate increase is sufficiently large for it to be a real as well as a nominal increase. This in turn leads the real and nominal exchange rates to increase as well. Because of the size of the initial shock to government debt it takes a long time for nominal magnitudes to return to equilibrium and a noticeable proportion of the adjustment process is still to come after the 15 years shown in the Figure.

3.2 A permanent increase in the equity premium

An increase in the equity premium is in effect a downward shock to wealth as a result of an increase in risk in the corporate sector. The immediate effect is a cutback in consumption as the private sector tries to adjust (Figure 2). This slows the economy, inflation falls, the real exchange rate falls and unemployment rises. The jump in these variables is largely the result of the impact of expectations of the future problems being discounted back into current asset prices. Monetary policy can ease under these circumstances and real wages fall. What is interesting in this example is that monetary policy cannot solve the adjustment problem. Because the shock is to wealth, a stock variable, the adjustment is not nearly complete even within the 15 year period shown. If nominal interest rates were to be cut even further in the hope of having a rath-

---

[2] The simulations shown stem from an earlier version of the model but the changes do not affect the qualitative results and in most cases have little visible impact on the graphs shown.

Figure 1

**A shock from government policy in the form of a permanent increase
in public consumption equivalent to 1% of GDP**

Difference from baseline

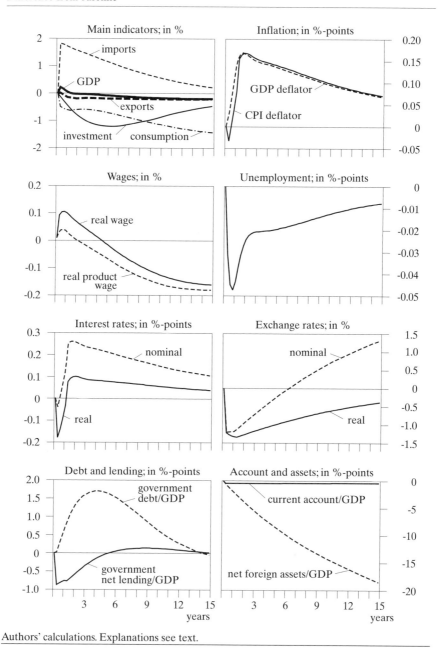

Authors' calculations. Explanations see text.

Figure 2

A domestic shock in the form of a permanent increase in equity premium by 1%-point
Difference from baseline

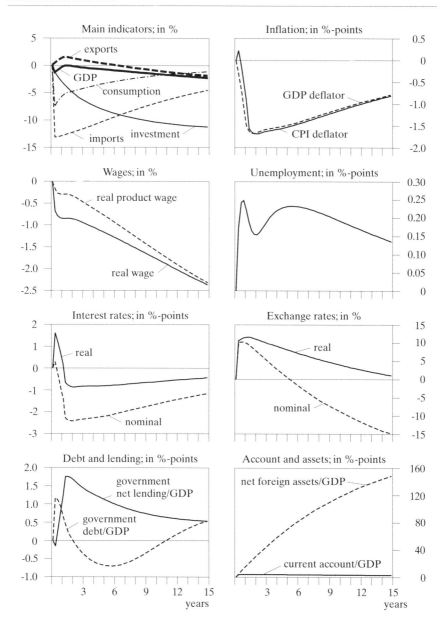

Authors' calculations. Explanations see text.

Figure 3

A foreign shock in the form of a permanent increase in world demand by 1%

Difference from baseline

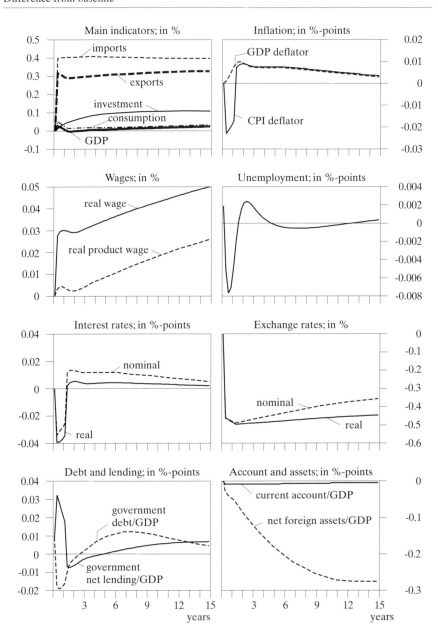

Authors' calculations. Explanations see text.

er smaller cut in inflation then the real adjustment process for wealth would merely be dragged out rather longer, making the loss on the unemployment side of the Taylor rule greater. The result would therefore look rather different if the central bank were purely targeting inflation.

3.3 A permanent increase in world demand

What is interesting from the simulation of a foreign demand shock is that it has very little impact on the economy (Figure 3), with the exception of the trade variables themselves. Because the shock is seen to be permanent it has an immediate effect on behaviour through expectations, even though the realisation, period by period will come through much more steadily. The immediate effect of this increase in demand comes through partly on trade volumes and partly through an appreciation in the real and nominal exchange rate. As a result imports increase more than exports as in effect the terms of trade move in favour of the euro area.

4. Monetary policy simulations

Thus far the shocks we have imposed show the central bank responding following a simple Taylor rule. Clearly the areas of greatest interest to us are to explore what happens when the central bank is itself the initiator of shocks and how the way the bank operates can affect the operation of the economy. One of the obvious changes, which we do not explore here, is that rule itself could be changed. We could alter the weights in the rule or indeed replace the Taylor rule by an inflation forecast targeting rule (Amano et al. 1999). An inflation targeting rule is more difficult to implement as we have to be able to solve the model for the inflation forecast before then implementing the rule. Since the rule itself is part of the forecast this is a tedious process. However, in this paper we focus on three aspects of the operation of the Taylor rule itself. The first is simply to assess what happens when monetary policy settings change in the form of

4. A temporary shock in the form of a two year increase in interest rates by 1 %[3].

In this case the shock is not anticipated but it is not a "surprise" in the sense that central bank is deviating from its anticipated rule for a short-run advantage. It is merely responding to information that it has, in the expected manner. There is thus an asymmetry in the first period when the change is implemented.

---

[3] This simulation is labelled 4 as it follows on from the three in the previous section.

However this "straightforward" form of shock has only limited interest for the policy maker. We, therefore go on to show what happens if the central bank tries to implement a change in policy in the form of a change in the inflation target. We are concerned in this instance to show the importance of "credibility". If a central bank is "credible" in this sense then the private sector will expect the policy change to succeed and inflation expectations will shift by the full extent of the change in target. Our simulation in this case is thus:

5. An exploration of the importance of *credibility* in the form of a monetary policy shock of a 1 % increase in the inflation target

a   when the central bank is credible

b   when the central bank is not believed and the central bank and private sectors act simultaneously

c   when the central bank is not believed and the central bank acts first.

The importance of simulation 5c is that in this case the private sector has the opportunity of observing the central bank's action. We can perhaps relate this simulation to the discussion of transparency. If the private sector can be better informed about what the central bank is doing then the costs of policy will be lower.

Even so the case explored here is rather extreme. It seems unlikely on the one hand that a large policy change would be fully credible immediately. At least some of the private sector would doubt that it would be sustained. Hence to some extent credibility would be earned by experience (see Vilmunen 1998 and Mattila 1998 for a discussion of these "peso" problems). On the other hand it also seems unlikely that the central bank would not eventually gain a substantial measure of credibility if it persevered with its policy. In some respects this is akin to the process of learning (Tetlow et al. 1999). If events do not turn out as anticipated then one would expect that both the central bank and the private sector we realise that their view of the world may be incorrect and slowly adjust their behaviour towards the new circumstances.

Our next step therefore is to take the case of an external shock and show the difference in impact when central bank recognises the shock from when it does not. The particular shock is as follows:

6. An examination of the impact of the central bank's failure to recognise a structural shift in the economy in the form of a 1 % fall in the NAIRU.

Two simulations have to be run in this instance, the first showing what happens when the central bank does recognise the structural shift and the second when it does not. This issue is one of the most important in monetary policy as structural shifts are always difficult to detect (unless due to regulatory change, in which case the debate is over the size of the response) and confusion by the central bank of a shift in a relationship with a shock to the relationship[4] can have major consequences, particularly since it may mislead the private sector.

We take one such example of learning but rather than just exploring how the private sector might learn whether the monetary authority has actually changed its behaviour we take the case of a change in the supply-side of the economy and consider the effect on the behaviour of the model of different learning processes:

7. An exploration of learning in the form of a 1 % reduction in the real rate of interest

a   when both central bank and private sector perceive it immediately

b   when the central bank fails to realise it

c   when the central bank and the private sector learn of the change linearly over 5 years

4.1 A temporary interest rate shock

The three shocks we have shown thus far (in the previous Section) can be permanent, although in the case of the government spending shock it is because of a matching increase in financing. It is rational for the private sector to act as if these shocks were permanent in the light of no other evidence as future shocks could be of either sign, unless of course public expenditure is reaching the bounds of plausibility as a share of GDP. A change in interest rates on the other hand is inherently a short run temporary phenomenon unless there has been a change to expected growth rates, productivity or the inflation target. As is clear from Figure 4, a 2 year (nominal) interest rate rise has no long-term impact on the economy. In almost all cases variables have returned to the steady state after 3 years, i.e. within one year of the ending of the shock. However, as there is a one-off fall in inflation, this will result in a permanent appreciation in the nominal exchange rate (temporary appreciation in the real exchange rate). Net foreign assets will also make a one-off permanent adjustment. The rise in unemployment (fall in GDP) is substantial – over 2 % of GDP – in the short run but rapidly disappears. As before the impacts of the shock are spread among quantities and prices, with the real wage falling temporarily as well as unemployment rising. Thus stickiness in the system is clearly limited.

Even in the case of a temporary interest rate shock it is necessary to find the cause somewhere in order to conduct a logically coherent simulation. Otherwise it will merely appear as a monetary policy surprise that will generate expectations of changes in the target of monetary policy. In this case we assume it

---

[4] i.e. confusing a shift in a curve with a shift along it.

Figure 4

A temporary shock in the form of a two years increase in interest rates by 1%

Difference from baseline

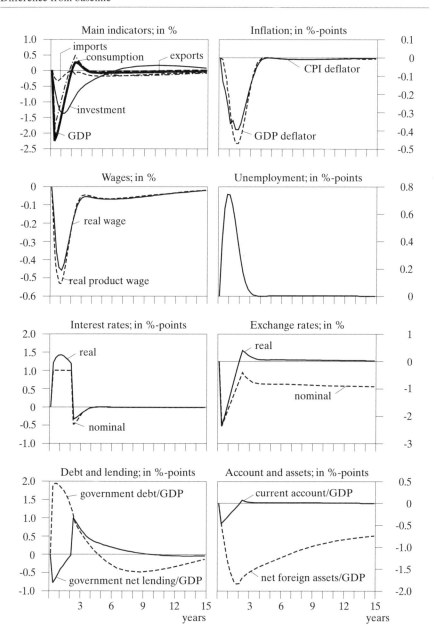

Authors' calculations. Explanations see text.

is a shock to foreign interest rates that requires a response of domestic monetary policy through the Taylor rule.

4.2 The importance of *credibility* in monetary policy

Thus far the only policy shock we have considered is a fiscal policy shock. The change in interest rates in the previous simulation was not a monetary policy shock but an external shock to which monetary policy responded in a predictable manner. In this set of simulations we explore how much the credibility of the central bank affects the impact on the economy.

In Figure 5a we consider the case where the central bank is credible. The shock takes the form of an announced increase in the inflation target by 1 %. Nominal interest rates have to increase permanently by 1 % as well. The nominal exchange rate will now depreciate steadily by 1 % a year compared to the base level. The interest burden on government is also increased permanently, although the response of taxes ensures that this cost is fully financed in the long run. Perhaps the most interesting result is that there is a one-off gain in real terms from this move. There is a jump in GDP, mainly through exports and consumption in the short run before returning towards the steady state in the second year. This is the real counterpart of the increase in inflation.

In Figures 5b and 5c we consider the consequences if the central bank is not believed. Since increases in inflation targets are only too believable we have considered the case of a reduction in the inflation target (by 1 %). Here although the inflation rate falls the central bank is unable to get it to fall by 1 %, it only falls by 0.15 %. Whereas in the case of a credible policy change the real interest rate falls back to the steady-state value very quickly, when the central bank is not credible, it deviates permanently by almost half a percentage point. Thus instead of there being an upward blip in the real interest rate and single step down in activity, the effect is permanently adverse to the tune of 0.1 % of GDP. The permanently higher real interest rate draws in foreign funds, accumulating foreign assets with a small trade surplus (imports fall more than exports) and the real exchange rate depreciates.

In the simulation shown in Figure 5b the model is solved simultaneously so the central bank sets policy in the light of its lack of credibility. An alternative way of looking at this, shown in Figure 5c is to assume that the central bank sets policy on the assumption that it will be believed and then the private sector responds. In this case the costs are lower in the case of the domestic economy and inflation returns to the steady-state value steadily over the period. Although real and nominal interest rates are still somewhat higher than in the credible case the margin is now considerably smaller. The effect on the foreign sector is however greater as the exchange rate depreciated by more and the trade gap is wider, also increasing net foreign assets.

Figure 5a

An exploration of the importance of credibility in the form of a monetary policy shock of a 1%-point increase in inflation target when the central bank is credible

Difference from baseline

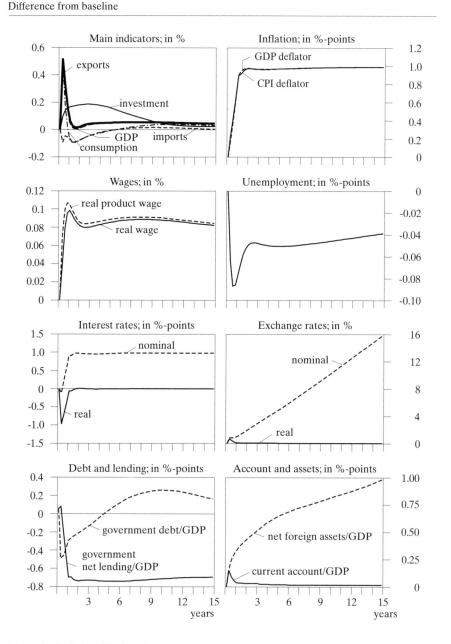

Authors' calculations. Explanations see text.

Figure 5b

**An exploration of the importance of credibility in the form of a monetary policy shock
of a 1%-point decrease in inflation target when central bank is not believed
and central bank and private sector act simultaneously**

Difference from baseline

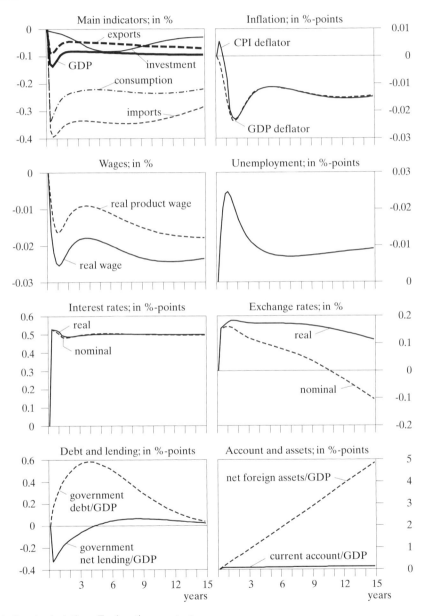

Authors' calculations. Explanations see text.

Figure 5c

An exploration of the importance of credibility in the form of a monetary policy shock of a 1%-point decrease in inflation target when central bank is not believed and the central bank acts first

Difference from baseline

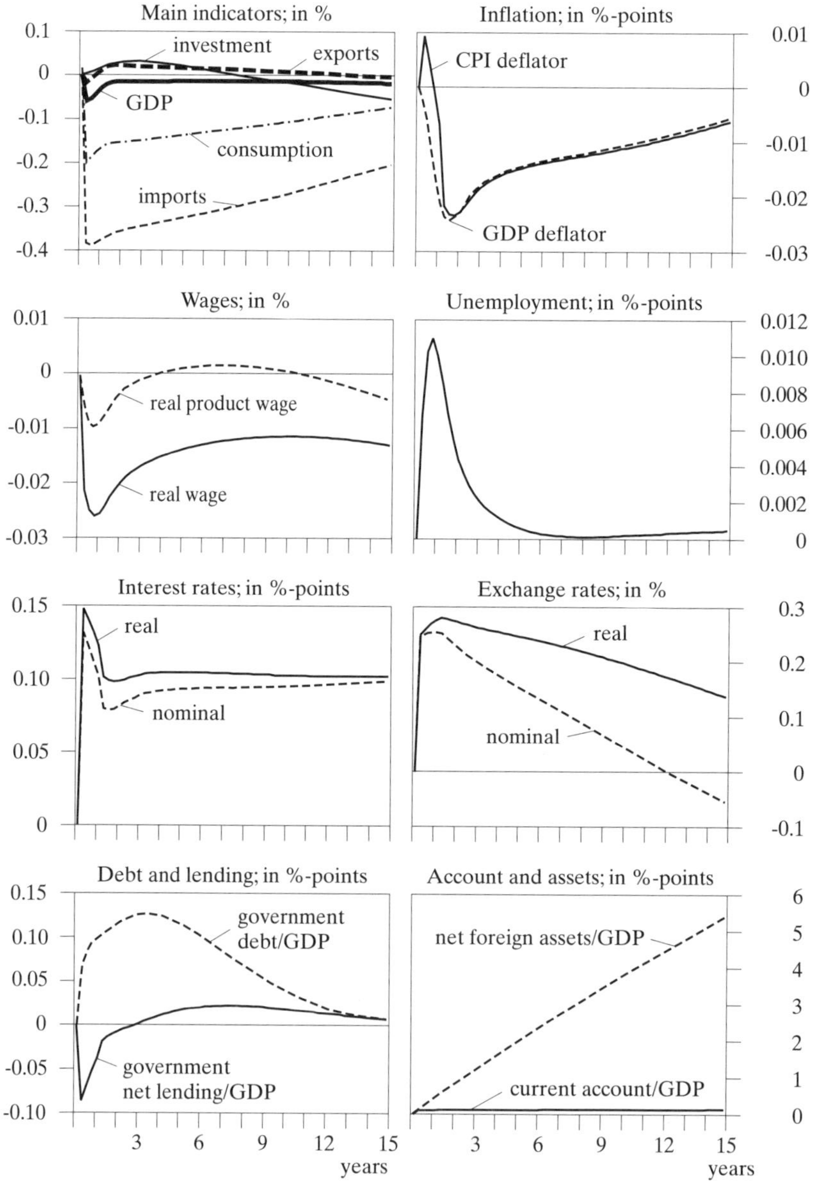

Authors' calculations. Explanations see text.

4.3 Learning

It is rather unrealistic to assume that the central bank could carry on period after period in the assumption that it was credible, when the evidence revealed it was not. In the same way the private sector could be expected to adjust its behaviour as the central bank repeated its response. It would be more realistic to assume that the parties learn form each other.

The central bank's reaction function is of the form

$$R = r* + \pi + 0.5 \cdot (\pi - \overline{\pi}) - 0.5 \cdot (1 - \beta) \cdot (U - \overline{U})$$

where $r*$ is the equilibrium real rate of interest and $\overline{U}$ the NAIRU. Currently the NAIRU is exogenous in the model. We can therefore readily explore the idea that an element of the "new economy" emerges in the euro area and as a result the NAIRU falls. One of the key problems for monetary policy (see Wieland 1998) for example, is that the monetary authority may not observe this change. If we take the case of the fall in the rate of productivity growth in the 1970s (Orphanides 2000) this failure of perception can be quite long standing. If the central bank were to spot the change immediately this would have a favourable effect on the real economy right from the outset (Figure 6a). All the components of GDP would rise and unemployment would fall rapidly by the amount of the change in the NAIRU. Monetary policy would initially ease because of the downward shock on inflationary pressures, although it would have to rise slightly as the economy approaches new capacity constraints. As the benefit is purely domestic, imports will rise more than exports, the exchange rate depreciate and the net foreign assets will be lower compared to GDP. If the central bank does not notice the change in the NAIRU then the gains are slightly more muted. (Figure 6b) shows the differences if the gain is not recognised. The GDP gain is smaller, the unemployment gain smaller – indeed unemployment never falls by the extent of the fall in the NAIRU and monetary policy is run permanently tighter to the extent of nearly 30 basis points. If we compare Figures 6a and 6b we can see that this is a striking difference in stance. Instead of a brief initial cut in interest rates and then only a 5 basis point rise, policy is tighter because the central bank interprets the increase in economic activity as a threat to future inflation. The inflation does actually materialise although not to the anticipated extent.

To implement learning we return to the case where the shock is a permanent fall in $r*$ as this represents the simplest change to the Taylor rule. In the first case (Figure 7a) we therefore explore what would happen if the central bank failed to adjust immediately and learnt steadily over a period of 5 years, by imposing a linear adjustment on $r*$ in the Taylor rule. (We experimented with a number of other exogenous learning processes but the results were qualitatively similar.) As the bank learns, so real (and nominal) interest rates fall and

Figure 6a

A permanent fall in NAIRU by 1%-point central bank does see the fall in NAIRU

Difference from baseline

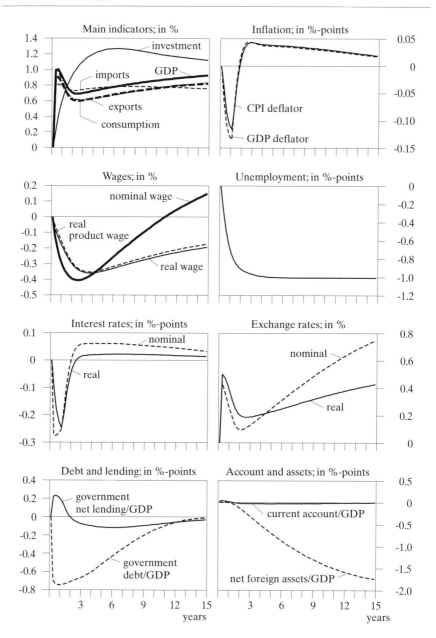

Authors' calculations. Explanations see text.

Figure 6b

A permanent fall in NAIRU by 1%-point Myopics vs. sharp-eyed central bank

Difference from baseline

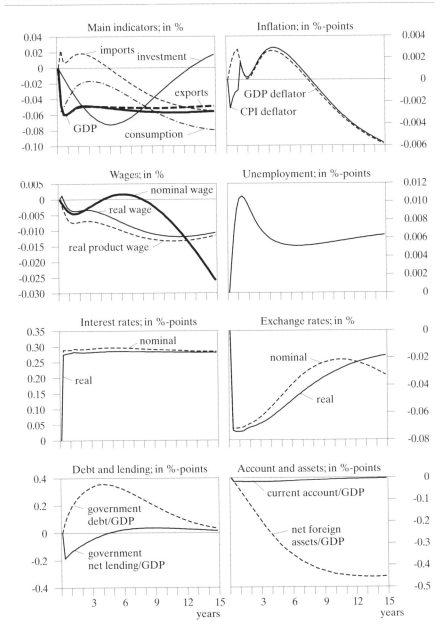

Authors' calculations. Explanations see text.

Figure 7a

**An exploration of learning in the form of a 1%-point reduction
in the real rate of interest when the central bank fails to realise it**

Difference from baseline

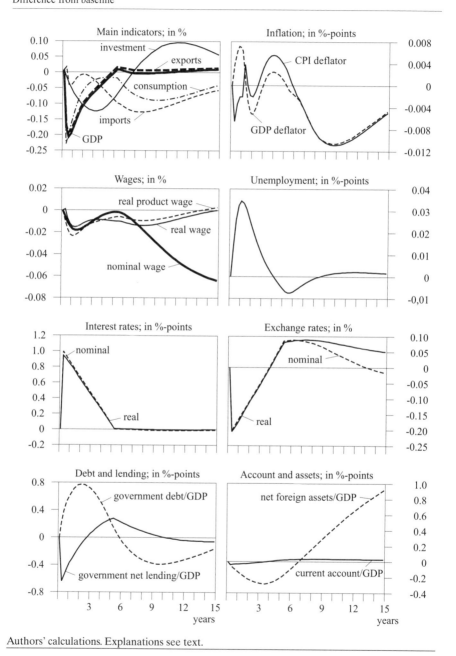

Authors' calculations. Explanations see text.

Figure 7b

An exploration of learning in the form of a 1%-point reduction in the real rate of interest when the central bank and the private sector learn of the change linearly over 5 years

Difference from baseline

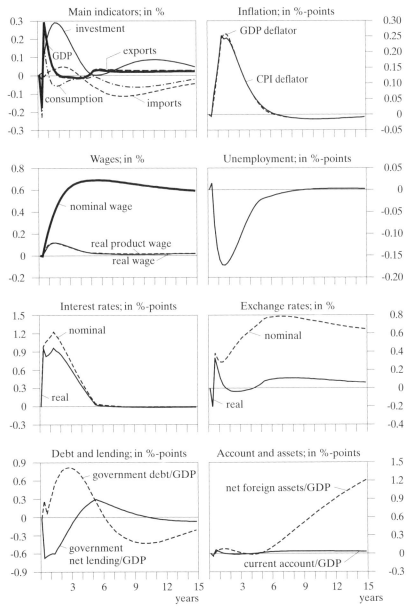

Authors' calculations. Explanations see text.

the real economy falls back to the baseline path. The short-run oscillations are quite complex; financial, product and labour markets adjust at different rates, leading to an uneven path for inflation. Unemployment, government debt and net lending, net foreign assets and the current account all show reversals in their time paths.

If we assume that the same exogenous process of linear learning also applies to the private sector then the results are both more substantial and different in character (Figure 7b). The initial effect is now positive as the private sector expands activity, assuming that the policy reaction implies a change in the inflation target (upward). The impact on inflation is much more substantial. Unemployment falls by 0.24 percentage points instead of rising by 0.35 points. Real wages converge to the steady-state from above and not below. Thus there are actually real gains to the economy from the slower learning, although inflation performance is worse. This is, however, a result of the particular simulation and other forms of slower learning would generate different results. The key feature is that if the central bank is slower at learning than the private sector then there are real costs, in part because the private sector confuses the slow learning with a policy change. If the central bank were very transparent then its thinking could be clear to the private sector and this error would not be made. An exploration of transparency in that sort of detail is however beyond the current analysis.

5. Implications

The EDGE model that we have developed illustrates five important lessons for euro area monetary policy.

- The first is the importance of credibility. If the private sector does not believe that the central bank will succeed in its actions then this forecast tends to be self-fulfilling as expectations of inflation do not change. In so far as the bank can achieve its policy aims this will be at much greater cost in terms of output and unemployment. The other side of this relationship is also worth recalling, as it implies that a credible central bank that responds as expected will have to do relatively little to achieve its policy objectives, as inflation expectations are not jolted by shocks.

- Secondly, it shows the importance of transparency. If the private sector cannot readily detect when the central bank has reacted to new information it will tend to assume that it is the goals of policy that have changed. This also will add to the costs of monetary policy.

- Thirdly the model suggests that the faster the private sector can learn the smaller the loss.

- Fourthly, if the central bank fails to recognise a structural shift it can negate the benefits of that shift by applying an unchanged policy rule. The problem is worsened if the private sector notices the shift but the central bank does not.

– Taking these together, if the central bank thinks that a structural shift may be taking place and wants to adjust policy in the light of that probability, it needs to make its actions explicit rather than trying to hedge its assessment in secrecy. This last circumstance is probably the most important for the euro area as a new system. Neither the Eurosystem nor any of the other participants in the economy have really good evidence on how it works. They form judgements based on past behaviour and their knowledge of the requirements of the future and update them in the light of experience. Mistakes in that process are inevitable but the way the process of learning is undertaken affects its cost.

The simulations illustrate the importance of three key features of the model itself. In the first place it illustrates the importance of forward-looking behaviour with respect to wealth and the valuation of assets. Shocks affecting those values have substantial effects in the short run but adjustment processes can be very long lived, exceeding the 15 years illustrated in the Figures. Secondly behaviour differs markedly if a shock is perceived to be transitory rather than permanent and the impact is much more limited. This also has a clear implication for monetary policy. Monetary policy actions that are not expected to endure will be relatively ineffective. Thirdly it illustrates the key importance of building the reaction of both fiscal and monetary policy into the model. Private sector actions depend crucially on what they think the monetary and fiscal authorities will do in the future. The effectiveness of current policy depends on private sector expectations of future policy. Non-convergent rules will not be credible.

The policy rules illustrated in the paper are just that, illustrations. They do not imply that authorities have to follow rigid rules but they illustrate the interaction between the behaviour patterns that the authorities have and the behaviour patterns the private sector thinks they have. In the circumstances we illustrate it is not normally beneficial for the authorities to disguise their intentions because the private sector is well aware of the incentives and the longer term consequences of nonsustainable actions. Particularly in the case of monetary policy, there are substantial payoffs to designing some sort of "precommitment technology" that allows the private sector to believe that the monetary authority will actually carry out the actions necessary to maintain its objective of price stability in the future.

This is a young model, which will develop as we gain experience in using it. The calibration process is a continuing one as new evidence about parameter values and plausible properties appears. With the euro area only being in place for only two years the learning curve is likely to be steep for some time to come.

Appendix

1. List of equations

Labour demand:

$$L_t = 0.483 \cdot E_t L_{t+1} + 0.492 \cdot L_{t-1} + 0.025 \cdot \left(\frac{Y_t}{TK_t^{0.41}} \right)^{1.69} \tag{A1}$$

Capital stock:

$$\Delta \log K_t = -0.324 \cdot E_t \Delta \log K_{t+2} + 0.986 \cdot E_t \Delta \log K_{t+1} + \tag{A2}$$

$$0.3378 \cdot \Delta \log K_{t-1} + 0.0005 \cdot \left(\frac{PF_t}{PI_t} \left(\frac{0.41 \cdot Y_t}{K_t} \right) - \frac{(r_t + \chi + 0.01)}{1 + r_t + \chi} \frac{PI_t}{PC_t} \right)$$

Nominal wages:

$$WN_t = 0.49 \cdot E_t WN_{t+1} + 0.5 \cdot WN_{t-1} + 0.01 \cdot \left[0.59 \cdot Y_t / N_t \cdot PF_t \cdot \left(1 - 3 \cdot (U_t - \overline{U}_t) \right) \right] \tag{A3}$$

GDP deflator:

$$P_t = 0.495 \cdot P_{t-1} + 0.485 \cdot E_t P_{t+1} + 0.02 \cdot \left(\frac{WN_t}{(1 - \tau_t^{indirect})} \cdot \frac{L_t}{0.59 \cdot Y_t} \right) \tag{A4}$$

Consumption:

$$C_t = 0.6 \cdot \frac{1}{1 + r_t + \chi} \cdot E_t C_{t+1} + 0.015 \cdot \left((1 + \varsigma_t) \cdot \frac{A_{t-1}}{PC_t} + \frac{YDN_t}{PC_t} \right) \tag{A5}$$

Windfall gain:

$$\varsigma_t = \frac{A_t}{A_{t-1}} - 1 - \frac{YDN_t - C_t \cdot PC_t}{A_{t-1}} - \pi_{t-1} \tag{A6}$$

Wealth:

$$A_t = \frac{1}{1 + R_t / 400 + \chi} E_t \left(A_{t+1} + GDN_{t+1} + NFA_{t+1} \right) + \tag{A7}$$

$$\left(PF_t \cdot Y_t - WN_t \cdot L_t - 0.01 \cdot PI_t \cdot K_{t-1} - 0.33 \cdot GOY_t \right) + GDN_t + NFA_t$$

Inventories:

$$KI_t = 0.88 \cdot T \cdot L_t^{0.59} K_t^{0.41} - 0.5 \cdot \left(Y_t - T \cdot L_t^{0.59} K_t^{0.41} \right) + \tag{A8}$$

$$0.494 \cdot E_t \left(Y_{t+1} - T \cdot L_{t+1}^{0.59} K_{t+1}^{0.41} \right)$$

Exports:

$$\log X_t = 0.48 \cdot \log Y_t^* + 0.72 \cdot \log DD_t - 0.41 \cdot \log\left(\frac{PX_t}{P_t^* \cdot e_t}\right) + 0.63 \quad \text{(A9)}$$

Imports:

$$\log M_t = 1.2 \cdot \log DD_t - 0.9 \cdot \log\left(\frac{PM_t}{P_t}\right) - 3.9 \quad \text{(A10)}$$

Export prices:

$$\log PX_t = 0.32 \cdot \log P_t + 0.68 \cdot \log\left(P_t^* \cdot e_t\right) - 0.05 \quad \text{(A11)}$$

Import prices:

$$\log PM_t = 0.48 \cdot \log PX_t + 0.38 \cdot \log\left(P_t^* \cdot e_t\right) + 0.14 \cdot \log\left(PC_t^* \cdot e_t\right) - 0.65 \text{ (A12)}$$

Consumer price deflator:

$$\log PC_t = 0.90 \cdot \log P_t + 0.10 \cdot \log PM_t + 0.01 \quad \text{(A13)}$$

Investment deflator:

$$\log PI_t = 0.85 \cdot \log PF_t + 0.15 \cdot \log PM_t + 0.10 \quad \text{(A14)}$$

Identities

Private nominal disposable income:

$$YDN_t = YFN_t - TAX_t + INN_t + TRF_t - GOY_t + NFN_t - 0.01 \cdot PI_t \cdot K_{t-1} \quad \text{(A15)}$$

Real GDP:

$$Y_t = C_t + CG_t + I_t + X_t - M_t + \Delta KI_t \quad \text{(A16)}$$

Capital accumulation equation:

$$I_t = K_t - 0.99 \cdot K_{t-1} \quad \text{(A17)}$$

Indirect taxes:

$$TIN_t = \tau_t^{indirect} \cdot YEN_t \quad \text{(A18)}$$

Direct taxes:

$$TAX_t = \tau_t^{direct} \cdot YEN_t \quad \text{(A19)}$$

Public disposable income:

$$GYN_t = TAX_t + TIN_t + GOY_t - TRF_t - INN_t \quad \text{(A20)}$$

Interest outlays of government:

$$INN_t = R_t / 400 \cdot GDN_{t-1} \qquad \text{(A21)}$$

Net foreign assets:

$$NFA_t = NFA_{t-1} \cdot \left(e_t / e_{t-1} \right) + CA_t \qquad \text{(A22)}$$

Net factor income from abroad:

$$NFN_t = R_t^* / 400 \cdot NFA_{t-1} \qquad \text{(A23)}$$

Current account:

$$CA_t = X_t \cdot PX_t - M_t \cdot PM_t + NFN_t \qquad \text{(A24)}$$

Public debt:

$$GDN_t = GDN_{t-1} - GLN_t \qquad \text{(A25)}$$

Public net lending:

$$GLN_t = -GCN_t - GIN_t + GYN_t \qquad \text{(A26)}$$

Domestic demand:

$$DD_t = C_t + CG_t + I_t + \Delta KI_t \qquad \text{(A27)}$$

Nominal GDP as factor cost:

$$YFN_t = Y_t \cdot PF_t \qquad \text{(A28)}$$

Nominal GDP:

$$YEN_t = Y_t \cdot P_t \qquad \text{(A29)}$$

GDP deflator at factor price:

$$PF_t = P_t \cdot \left(1 - \tau_t^{indirect} \right) \qquad \text{(A30)}$$

Expected inflation rate, quarterly:

$$\pi_t = \log PC_{t+1} - \log PC_t \qquad \text{(A31)}$$

Expected real interest rate:

$$r_t = R_t / 400 - \pi_t \qquad \text{(A32)}$$

Effective exchange rate (UIRP):

$$\log e_t = \log e_{t+1} + \left(R_t^* - R_t \right) / 400 \qquad \text{(A33)}$$

Unemployment rate:

$$U_t = \left(N_t - L_t \right) / N_t \qquad \text{(A34)}$$

Public nominal consumption:
$$GCN_t = CG_t \cdot P_t \qquad (A35)$$

Public nominal investment:
$$GIN_t = IG_t \cdot PI_t \qquad (A36)$$

Public other income:
$$GOY_t = 0.20 \cdot YEN_t \qquad (A37)$$

Public real consumption:
$$CG_t = \gamma \cdot Y_t \qquad (A38)$$

Policy parameters

Transfers:
$$TRF_t / YEN_t = 0.25 \cdot U_t + 0.20 \qquad (A39)$$

Direct tax rate:
$$\Delta\tau_t^{direct} = 0.05 \cdot \left(GDN_t / YEN_t - \psi \right) - 0.1 \cdot \left(GLN_t / YEN_t + \psi \cdot \left(\pi_{t-1} + g \right) \right) \qquad (A40)$$

Inflation rate target:
$$\bar{\pi}_t = 0.0027 \qquad (A41)$$

Taylor rule:
$$R_t = (1-\Omega) \cdot R_{t-1} \quad \Omega \cdot \begin{bmatrix} 400 \cdot r^* + 100 \cdot \log\left(PC_t / PC_{t-4} \right) \\ +50 \cdot \left[\log\left(PC_t / PC_{t-4} \right) - 4 \cdot \bar{\pi}_t \right] \\ -50 \cdot 0.59 \cdot \left(U_t - \bar{U}_t \right) \end{bmatrix} \qquad (A42)$$

2. The steady state model

Output:
$$Y = TK^{0.41} L^{0.59} \qquad (B1)$$

Capital stock:
$$K = (PF / PI) \cdot 0.41 \cdot Y / \left(r + \chi + 0.01 \right) \qquad (B2)$$

Wages:
$$WN = 0.59 \cdot PF \cdot Y / L \qquad (B3)$$

Consumption:

$$C = \left(\frac{1+r+\chi - 0.6 \cdot (1+g)}{1+r+\chi} \right)^{-1} \cdot 0.015 \cdot (A+YDN)/PC \qquad (B4)$$

Private wealth:

$$A = (r+\chi-g)^{-1} \cdot (PF \cdot 0.41 \cdot Y - 0.01 \cdot PI \cdot K - 0.33 \cdot GOY) + GDN + NFA \qquad (B5)$$

Change in inventories:

$$\Delta KI = 0.88 \cdot g \cdot Y \qquad (B6)$$

Exports:

$$\log X = 0.48 \cdot \log Y^* + 0.72 \cdot \log(C+CG+I+\Delta KI) - \qquad (B7)$$
$$0.41 \cdot \log(PX/(P^* \cdot e)) + 0.63$$

Imports:

$$\log M = 1.2 \cdot \log(C+CG+I+\Delta KI) - 0.64 \cdot \log(PM/P) - 3.9 \qquad (B8)$$

Export prices:

$$\log PX = 0.32 \cdot \log P + 0.68 \cdot \log(P^* \cdot e) - 0.05 \qquad (B9)$$

Import prices:

$$\log PM = 0.48 \cdot \log PX + 0.38 \cdot \log(P^* \cdot e) + 0.14 \cdot \log(PC^* \cdot e) - 0.65 \qquad (B10)$$

Consumer price deflator:

$$\log PC = 0.90 \cdot \log P + 0.10 \cdot \log PM + 0.01 \qquad (B11)$$

Investment deflator:

$$\log PI = 0.85 \cdot \log PF + 0.15 \cdot \log PM + 0.10 \qquad (B12)$$

Identities

Employment:

$$L = N \cdot (1-U) \qquad (B13)$$

Technical progress:

$$\log T = \log T_{-1} + g \cdot 0.59 \qquad (B14)$$

Public interest outlays:

$$INN = R/400 \cdot GDN \qquad (B15)$$

Net factor income from abroad:
$$NFN = R^* / 400 \cdot NFA \qquad \text{(B16)}$$

Government other income:
$$GOY = 0.20 \cdot YEN \qquad \text{(B17)}$$

Government budget constraint:
$$TAX = GLN - TIN - GOY + GCN + GIN + TRF + INN \qquad \text{(B18)}$$

Private nominal disposable income:
$$YDN = YFN - TAX + TRF + INN - GOY + NFN - 0.01 \cdot PI \cdot K \qquad \text{(B19)}$$

GDP identity:
$$Y = C + CG + I + X - M + \Delta KI \qquad \text{(B20)}$$

Current account:
$$CA = X \cdot PX - M \cdot PM + NFN \qquad \text{(B21)}$$

Nominal GDP at factor cost:
$$YFN = Y \cdot PF \qquad \text{(B22)}$$

Nominal GDP:
$$YEN = Y \cdot P \qquad \text{(B23)}$$

Government nominal consumption:
$$GCN = CG \cdot P \qquad \text{(B24)}$$

Government nominal investment:
$$GIN = IG \cdot PI \qquad \text{(B25)}$$

GDP deflator at factor price:
$$PF = P \cdot \left(1 - \tau^{indirect}\right) \qquad \text{(B26)}$$

Domestic real interest rate:
$$r = R / 400 - \pi \qquad \text{(B27)}$$

Inflation rate:
$$\log PC = \log PC_{-1} + \pi \qquad \text{(B28)}$$

Policy variables

Indirect taxes:
$$TIN = \tau^{indirect} \cdot YEN \qquad \text{(B29)}$$

Transfers:

$$TRF / YEN = \omega_1 \cdot U + \omega_2 \tag{B30}$$

Government real consumption:

$$CG = \gamma \cdot Y \tag{B31}$$

Government real investments:

$$IG = \xi \cdot Y \tag{B32}$$

Steady-state conditions

Unemployment rate:

$$U = \overline{U} \tag{B33}$$

Investment:

$$I = (0.01 + g) \cdot K \tag{B34}$$

Government net lending:

$$GLN = -GDN \cdot (g + \pi) \tag{B35}$$

Government debt:

$$GDN = \psi \cdot YEN \tag{B36}$$

Net foreign assets:

$$NFA = CA / (g + \pi) \tag{B37}$$

Domestic nominal interest rate:

$$R = 100 \cdot \log(PC / PC_{-4}) + 400 \cdot r^* \tag{B38}$$

Inflation rate:

$$\pi = \overline{\pi} \tag{B39}$$

List of names of variables

Symbol	Explanation	Symbol	Explanation
A	Asset wealth	$P*$	Foreign prices
C	Consumption	PM	Import prices
CA	Current account	PI	Gross investment deflator
CG	Public consumption, real	PX	Export prices
DD	Domestic demand	π	Inflation rate
e	Effective exchange rate	$\bar{\pi}$	Inflation target
g	Real growth rate in steady-state	r	Real interest rate, domestic
GCN	Public consumption, nominal	$r*$	Real interest rate, foreign
GDN	Public debt, nominal	R	Nominal interest rate, domestic
GIN	Public investment, nominal	$R*$	Nominal interest rate, foreign
GLN	Public net lending	T	Technical progress
GOY	Public other income, nominal	TAX	Direct taxes by households
GYN	Public disposable income, nominal	τ^{direct}	Direct tax rate
I	Investment, real	$\tau^{indirect}$	Indirect tax rate
IG	Public investment, real	TIN	Indirect taxes
INN	Public interest outlays, nominal	TRF	Public transfers
K	Capital stock	U	Unemployment rate
KI	Change in inventories	$\bar{U}$	NAIRU
KI	Inventories	W	Real wages
N	Labour force	WN	Nominal wages per employee
L	Labour demand	χ	Equity premium
M	Imports	X	Exports
NFA	Net foreign assets	Y	Real GD P
NFN	Net factor income from abroad	$Y*$	World GDP, real
P	GDP deflator	YDN	Private disposable income, nominal
PC	Conumer price deflator	YEN	Nominal GDP
$PC*$	World commodity prices	YFN	Nominal GDP at factor cost
PF	GDP deflator at factor price	ζ	Windfall gain

List of parameters

β	The factor share of capital in production
ψ	Steady-state government debt to nominal GDP ratio
ω_1, ω_2	Steady-state transfers equation parameters
ξ	Steady-state government real investments to GDP ratio
γ	Steady-state government real consumption to GDP ratio

Table 1

Calibration of the steady-state model

Parameter	Value	Description
β	0.415726	The income share of capital
δ	0.01	The depreciation rate
χ	0.009	Equity premium
	0.6	The coefficient of the lead in consumption equation
	0.015	The coefficient of the fundament in consumption equation
g	0.005	Real growth in steady-state
v	0.33	The share of profits that is paid to the public sector
k	0.883242	The ratio of the stock of inventories to real GDP
	1.2	The elasticity of exports with respect to foreign demand
	–0.409181	The elasticity of exports with respect to relative prices
	0.63	Constant in exports equation
	1.2	The elasticity of imports with respect to domestic demand
	–0.9	The elasticity of imports with respect to relative prices
	–3.9	Constant in imports equation
	0.32	The elasticity of export prices with respect to domestic prices
	–0.05	Constant in export price equation
	0.48	The elasticity of import prices with respect to export prices
	0.38	The elasticity of import prices with respect to foreign prices
	–0.65	Constant in import price equation
	0.9	The elasticity of consumer prices with respect to GDP deflator
	0.01	Constant in consumer price equation
	0.85	The elasticity of inv. prices w.r.t. the GDP deflator at factor cost
	0.10	Constant in investment price equation
	0.25	The coefficient of unemployment rate in transfers to GDP
	0.2	Constant in investment price equation
γ	0.2	The ratio of government real consumption to GDP
ξ	0.028	The ratio of public real investement to GDP
ψ	0.7	The ratio of nominal public debt to GDP
b_4	0.2	The ratio of other public income to GDP

Table 2

Ex post simulation accuracy of the steady-state model

		MD	MAD	RMSE	MAPE
Real GDP	Y	–2.09	2.09	2.31	2.11
Private consumption	C	2.09	2.60	3.05	2.58
Fixed investment	I	–2.91	3.17	3.48	3.15
Exports	X	0.58	2.06	2.44	2.07
Imports	M	7.00	7.01	7.78	7.09
GDP deflator	P	0.56	0.57	0.69	0.57
Consumer price deflator	PC	0.70	0.70	0.82	0.70
Investment price deflator	PI	–0,01	0.35	0.39	0.35
Export price deflator	PX	2.41	2.54	2.80	2.55
Import price deflator	PM	2.62	2.62	2.81	2.62
Real wages	WR	–1.64	1.64	2.21	1.65
Labour demand	L	0.03	0.30	0.35	0.30
Nominal exchange rate	e	–2.04	3.34	4.72	3.26
Annual inflation rate	INFY	1.05	1.05	1.06	
Unemployment rate	U	–0.03	0.27	0.31	
Nominal interest rate	R	0.67	0.70	0.90	
Budget deficit to GDP	GLN/YEN	–0.32	0.34	0.52	
Public debt to GDP	GDN/YEN	–14.27	14.27	14.89	
Current account to GDP	CAN/YEN	–1.12	1.12	1.39	
Net foreign assets/GDP	NFA/YEN	–32.71	41.13	62.44	

Authors' calculations. – MD: mean deviation; MAD: mean absolute deviation; RMSE: root mean square error; MAPE: mean average percentage error. – For lower panel MD, MAD and RMSE are not divided by the aggregaze level of variable.

Table 3

Calibration of the dynamic model

Value	Description
0.483	The coefficient of the lead in labour demand equation
0.492	The coefficient of the lag in labour demand equation
0.025	The coefficient of the fundament in labour demand equation
–0.324	The coefficient of the second lead in investment equation
0.986	The coefficient of the lead in investment equation
0.3378	The coefficient of the lag in investment equation
0.0005	The coefficient of the fundament in investment equation
0.49	The coefficient of the lead in wage equation
0.5	The coefficient of the lag in wage equation
0.01	The coefficient of the fundament in wage equation
0.485	The coefficient of the lead in price equation
0.495	The coefficient of the lag in price equation
0.02	The coefficient of the fundament in price equation
–0,5	The coefficient of the deviation of production in inventories equation
0.494	The coefficient of the lead of the deviation in inventories equation

Authors' calculations.

Data Sources

Model code	TROLL code	Explanation	Source
A	AST	Asset wealth	See Appendix
C	PCR	Real consumption	ECB Monthly Bulletin Table 5.1 c12
CA	CAN	Current account	ECB Monthly Bulletin Table 8.1 c1
CG	GCR	Real public consumption	ECB Monthly Bulletin Table 5.1 c13
DD	FDD	Real domestic demand	ECB Monthly Bulletin Table 5.1 c11
e	EEN	Nominal effective exhange rate	ECB Monthly Bulletin Table 10 c1
g	g	Real growth in steady-state	Calibrated
GCN	GCN	Nominal public consumption	ECB Monthly Bulletin Table 5.1 c4
GDN	GDN	Nominal public debt	ECB Monthly Bulletin Table 7.2 c1
GIN	GIN	Nominal public investment	ECB Monthly Bulletin Table 7.1 c11
GLN	GLN	Public net lending	GYN - GIN - GCN
GOY	GOY	Nominal public other income	ECB Monthly Bulletin Table 7.1 c8 + 7.1 c11 + 7.1 c12
GYN	GYN	Nominal public dispos. income	TAX + TIN + GOY - TRF - INN
I	ITR	Real investment	ECB Monthly Bulletin Table 5.1 c14
IG	GIR	Real public investment	GIN / PI
INN	INN	Nominal public inter. outlays	ECB Monthly Bulletin Table 7.1 2 c5
K	KSR	Fixed capital stock	$(1 - \delta) \cdot K(-1) + I$
ΔKI	DLSR	Change in inventories	ECB Monthly Bulletin Table 5.1 c15
KI	LSR	Inventories	KI(-1)+ΔKI
N	LFN	Labour force	ECB Monthly Bulletin Table 5.4 c7 / 5.4 c8
L	LNN	Labour demand	N - Table 5.4 c7
M	MTR	Imports	ECB Monthly Bulletin Table 5.1 c18
NFA	NFA	Net foreign assets	ECB Monthly Bulletin Table 8.7 c1
NFN	NFN	Net factor income from abroad	ECB Monthly Bulletin Table 8.1 c4 + 8.1 c5
P	YED	GDP deflator	ECB Monthly Bulletin Table 5.1 c1 / 5.1 c10
PC	PCD	Consumer price deflator	ECB Monthly Bulletin Table 5.1 c3 / 5.1 c12
PC*	COMPR	World commodity prices	HWWA-Institut für Wirtschaftsforschung, HWWA Raw materials price index, 1990 = 100, USD, rebased (1995 = 100)
PF	YFD	GDP deflator at factor price	$P \cdot \left(1 - \tau^{indirect}\right)$
P*	YWD	OECD GDP deflator	OECD Economic Outlook
PM	MTD	Import price deflator	ECB Monthly Bulletin Table 5.1 c9 / 5.1 c18
PI	ITD	Investment deflator	ECB Monthly Bulletin Table 5.1 c5 / 5.1 c14
PX	XTD	Export price deflator	ECB Monthly Bulletin Table 5.1 c8 / 5.1 c17
π	INFQ	Quarterly inflation rate	log (PC/PC(-1))
$\bar{\pi}$	INFT	Quarterly inflation target	Calibrated
R	STRQ	Domestic real interest rate	R / 400 - π
r*	STRQF	Foreign real interest rate	R* / 400 log (P*/P*(-1))
R	STN	Domestic nominal interest rate	ECB Monthly Bulletin Table 3.1 c3
R*	STNF	Foreign nominal interest rate	ECB Monthly Bulletin Table 3.1 c6
T	TFT	Technical progress	Solow residual
TAX	TAX	Direct taxes by households	ECB Monthly Bulletin Table 7.1 1 c3
τ^{direct}	TAR	Direct tax rate	TAX/YEN
$\tau^{indirect}$	TIR	Indirect tax rate	TIN/YEN
TIN	TIN	Indirect taxes	ECB Monthly Bulletin Table 7.1 1 c6
TRF	TRF	Public transfers	ECB Monthly Bulletin Table 7.1 2 c6
U	URX	Unemployment	ECB Monthly Bulletin Table 5.4 c8
$\bar{U}$	URT	NAIRU	Hodrick-Prescott (1600) filtered U
WN	WIN/L	Nominal wages per employee	Hodrick-Prescott (1600) filtered U
	WIN	Nominal wage sum	Eurostat new_cronos
χ	χ	Equity premium	Calibrated
X	XTR	Exports	ECB Monthly Bulletin Table 5.1 c17
Y	YER	Real GDP	ECB Monthly Bulletin Table 5.1 c10
Y*	YWR	Real OECD GDP	OECD Economic Outlook
YDN	YDN	Nominal private dispos. income	YFN–TAX+INN+TRF-GOY+NFN–$\delta \cdot PI \cdot K$
YEN	YEN	Nominal GDP	ECB Monthly Bulletin Table 5.1 c10 * P
YFN	YFN	Nominal GDP at factor cost	$Y \cdot PF$
ξ	ξ	Windfall gain	See Appendix

References

Amano, R., D. Coletti and T. Macklem (1999), Monetary Rules when Economic Behaviour Changes. In B. Hunt and A. Orr (eds.) (1999), 157–200.

Blanchard, O. (1985), Debt Deficits and Finite Horizons. *Journal of Political Economy* 93 (2): 223–247.

Calvo, G. (1983), Staggered Prices in a Utility-Maximizing Framework. *Journal of Monetary Economics* 12 (3): 383–398.

Fagan, G., J. Henry and R. Mestre (2001), An Area-Wide Model (AWM) for the Euro Area. ECB Working Paper 42. ECB, Frakfurt.

Hunt, B. (2000), Comments on "Actual and Perceived Monetary Policy Rules in a Dynamic General Equilibrium Model of the Euro Area", Bank of Canada Workshop on "Advances in Econometric Model Building", Ottawa, August 2000, printed in Kortelainen (2001).

Hunt, B. and A. Orr (eds.) (1999), *Monetary Policy Under Uncertainty*. Reserve Bank of New Zealand, Wellington.

Kortelainen, M. (2001), Actual and Perceived Monetary Policy Rules in a Dynamic General Equilibrium Model of the Euro Area. Bank of Finland Discussion Papers 3/2001. Bank of Finland, Helsinki.

Kortelainen, M. (2002), EDGE: a Model of the Euro Area with Applications to Monetary Policy. Bank of Finland, Helsinki, Mimeo, forthcoming.

Mattila, V.-M. (1998), Simulating the Effects of Imperfect Credibility: How Does the Peso Problem Affect the Real Economy. Bank of Finland Discussion Paper 24/98. Bank of Finland, Helsinki.

Orphanides, A. (2000), Activist Stabilization Policy and Inflation: The Taylor Rule in the 1970s. Finance and Economics Discussion Series 2000-13. Board of Governors of the Federal Reserve System, Washington, DC.

Ripatti, A. and J. Vilmunen (2001), Declining Labour Share – Evidence of a Change in Underlying Production Technology? Bank of Finland Discussion Papers 10/2001. Bank of Finland, Helsinki.

Sefton, J. and J. in't Veld (1999), Consumption and Wealth: An International Comparison. *Manchester School of Economic Studies* 67 (4): 525–544.

Siegel, J.J. (1992), The Real Rate of Interest from 1800–1900: A Study of the US and the UK. *Journal of Monetary Economics* 29 (2): 227–252.

Taylor, J.B. (1993), Discretion versus Policy Rules in Practice. *Carnegie-Rochester Conference Series on Public Policy* 39: 195–214.

Tetlow, R., P. von zur Muehlen and F. Finan (1999), Learning and the Complexity of Monetary Policy Rules. In B. Hunt and A. Orr (eds.) (1999), 113–153.

Vilmunen, J. (1998), Macroeconomic Effects of Looming Policy Shifts: Non-Falsified Expectations and Peso Problems. Bank of Finland Discussion Paper 13/98. Bank of Finland, Helsinki.

Wieland, V. (1998), Monetary Policy under Uncertainty about the Natural Unemployment Rate. Finance and Economics Discussion Series 1998-22. Board of Governors of the Federal Reserve System, Washington, DC.

Willman, A., M. Kortelainen, H.-L. Männistö and M. Tujula (1998), The BOF5 Macroeconomic Model of Finland. Structure and Equations. Bank of Finland Discussion Paper 10/98. Bank of Finland, Helsinki.

David Rae and David Turner[1]

A Small Global Forecasting Model

1. Introduction

This paper describes the OECD's new small global forecasting model. The main focus of the model is the production of globally-consistent short-term forecasts of the major aggregates for the three main OECD economic regions: the United States, the euro area, and Japan. The rest of the world is modelled as a fourth composite region, albeit in a crude way. The key variables – which include output, inflation, the trade balance, and import prices – are driven by monetary and fiscal policy, exchange rates, and world demand. The projections from the model are used as a starting point to help animate the early stages of the OECD's forecasting round.

A particular focus of the model is the impact of global linkages and the transmission of influences between regions. Consequently, the three regional models are linked directly *via* trade, interest rates, and exchange rates. There are two additional link- ages. First, output and inflation in the rest of the world depend on developments in the three main regions, and feed back on them through the trade equations. Second, commodity prices are endogenous and depend on world output and inflation. Both linkages provide important additional channels through which shocks are propagated across regions.

The model is essentially a demand-side model. Output is based on an IS-style relationship, although this has been split into domestic demand and net export components rather than being modelled as a single reduced form equation. Potential output is assumed to be exogenous, and the model can therefore be written in terms of an output gap. In other words, the model explains why growth may differ from the potential growth rate but does not attempt to ex-

[1] The paper reflects helpful comments from numerous colleagues, including Laurence Boone, Thomas Dalsgaard, Jorgen Elmeskov, Michael Feiner, Pete Richardson, and Ignazio Visco. Special thanks to Laurence Le Fouler and Isabelle Wanner for their excellent research assistance; and also to Rosemary Chahed and Jan-Cathryn Davies for document preparation. – The paper was also published as OECD Working Paper ECO/WKP(2001)12.

plain changes in potential growth. This approach seems to be a reasonable simplification given the model's primary roles of short term forecasting and analysis of global linkages. However, it does mean that it has a limited ability to analyse the impact of supply side factors that may be expected to change potential output.

Subject to the above constraints, the primary design criterion is that it be small in order to provide simple direct insights into specific forecast judgements on the basis of clear model properties. In addition, being small implies that few inputs or exogenous assumptions are required and makes it easier to decompose the influences behind the forecasts of each variable. In particular, the main equations have been solved out in terms of their explanatory variables so that the particular contributions to inflation or growth can be identified at any point in time.

A further design criterion has been to ensure that extra relationships can be added without major re-estimation or re-coding. For example, a standard forecasting application would have exogenous exchange rates and short-term and long-term interest rates, and (mostly) backward-looking inflation expectations. However, monetary policy reaction functions can be added (as demonstrated later in the paper), along with alternative assumptions regarding the formation of expectations. This allows a little more economic richness to be temporarily added to the model when it is used for policy analyses, especially for those situations in which financial markets and expectations play important roles in the transmission of shocks within and between regions.

Another feature is that it incorporates several concepts that provide a consistent point of contact between the model and the larger projection exercise. Demand and the composition of output are modelled relative to a specific (and exogenous) view about potential output,[2] inflation is modelled in a framework in which the output gap is important and real exchange rates and relative demand pressures play important roles. While very different in size and structure, the small model can be thought of as a simplified version of INTERLINK's demand side. One difference, however, is that this model is based on quarterly data whereas INTERLINK and the forecasting round use semi-annual data. In this respect, the model is able to take better account of short-term developments in key variables.

As with any model, there is a trade-off between the goodness-of-fit of individual equations and the model having properties that conform to priors about macroeconomics. The equations reported in this paper reflect a compromise between these choices. The estimation philosophy is that differences in equati-

---

[2] Potential output is estimated in a consistent way across countries, based on a production function approach; see Giorno et al. 1995 for details.

on specifications across regions appear only where there is a clear economic rationale. For example, the empirical importance of stock market wealth to the United States economy has led to the inclusion of such a variable in the United States domestic demand equation.[3] Otherwise, coefficient values are relatively freely estimated. However, a few coefficients have been restricted, particularly where they were poorly determined, in order to deliver properties closer to our priors or to be more consistent with results for other regions. Various homogeneity and global closure restrictions are also imposed to ensure that the model settles down to a sensible steady-state path. Goodness-of-fit is an important criterion for a forecasting model but particular weight has been given to accuracy in recent years, partly because the short-run dynamics of highly-reduced form equations may not remain stable over long spans of history.

2. Overview of the model

Each of the three OECD regions (the United States, the euro area, and Japan) consists of four main blocks:[4]

– *Output* is determined through an IS-style relationship, although domestic demand and net exports are modelled separately, partly for econometric reasons, and partly to emphasise the model's role of capturing international linkages. Potential output growth and fiscal policy are exogenous.

– *Inflation*. The main inflation variable is core CPI inflation, which is modelled using a Phillips curve. Inflation therefore depends on the output gap and various components of imported inflation. Headline CPI inflation depends on core inflation plus a wedge that is determined by commodity and oil price inflation.

– *Import Prices*. Manufacturing and service import prices are modelled, and depend on foreign and domestic consumer prices, the exchange rate, and commodity prices.

– *Financial Variables*. For forecasting purposes, short-term and long-term interest rates and nominal exchange rates are exogenous. For simulations, short-term interest rates can be determined by forward-looking monetary policy rules in which short-term interest rates depend on the output gap and the expected future core inflation rate (relative to an exogenous target rate). Bond rates will then depend on expected future short-term rates. Exchange rates can be endogenised using a (risk-adjusted) uncovered interest parity condition.

---

[3] Such effects are less easy to identify in other regions.

[4] Recent examples of this style of model include Duguay 1994; Bharucha, Kent 1998; Ball 1998; Hargreaves 1999; Beechey et al. 2000.

A separate block covers the rest of the world:

- *Commodity Prices* are modelled explicitly in order to capture an important mechanism through which global demand shocks can have inflationary consequences and be propagated between regions. Oil prices are exogenous.

- *Output and Inflation*. The output gap and inflation in the rest of the world are linked to output and inflation in the three main regions, and therefore provide other feedback channels for the main regions.

Key features and estimation results for each block are discussed in more detail below.

2.1 Inflation

The main inflation variable is core CPI inflation, defined as the CPI excluding food and energy. This was chosen because it is possibly the best single measure of the general inflationary pressures that monetary policy is concerned with. The exclusion of energy prices is also useful when monetary policy reaction functions are added the model, to ensure for example that policy does not react to (i.e., "lets through") the direct effects of an oil shock while reacting to second-round effects, such as the shock feeding through to inflation expectations. Core inflation is determined by a Phillips curve, where the explanatory variables are a pressure of demand term, in the form of the output gap, and supply shocks in the form of various components of import prices:

$$\pi = \pi^e + \alpha_0 ygap + lags\left(\omega\left(\pi^m - \pi\right)\right) + lags\left(\omega\Delta\pi^m\right) + lags\left(\nu\Delta\pi^{com}\right) + lags\left(\gamma\Delta\pi^{oil}\right), \quad (1)$$

where π is core CPI inflation, π^e is expected inflation, and *ygap* is the output gap.[5] The remaining terms capture import prices, where the inflation rate of import prices of manufactures and services (π^m) is separated out from commodity price inflation (π^{com}) and oil price inflation (π^{oil}). All import prices are measured in local currency terms, and the lags are designed to capture slow passthrough. Non-commodity, non-oil import prices are weighted by the degree of openness of the economy, ω, which is measured by the share of these imports in total value added. This measure of openness has risen over time in all the regions to reach its current level of 11 per cent for the United States, 12 per cent in the euro area, and 6 per cent for Japan. Commodity price inflation is weighted by the share of manufacturing in GDP (ν) while oil price inflation is weighted by an index of oil intensity in production (γ) which has halved since the early 1970s in all regions. All these weights are exogenous in model simulations.

---

[5] The *lags* function is shorthand for a general distributed lag, which may include current-dated values. Detailed data definitions and sources are given in an Annex.

Table 1

Core CPI inflation

Dependent Variable: $\Delta\pi = \Delta\,(100\,\Delta\log$ *core*-CPI)

	United States	Euro Area	Japan
Lagged dependent variables			
Lag 1	−0.551***	−0.473***	−0.636***
Lag 2	−0.366***	−0.168**	−0.251***
Lag 4	−0.145**		
Gaps			
Output Gap	0.045***	0.055***	
Output Gap$_{-1}$			0.075[a]***
ΔDomestic demand$_{-1}$			0.107**
Import prices[1]			
$\omega_{-1}(\pi^m - \pi)_{-1}$	0.501*	0.518***	0.302[b]
$\Delta\pi^m$	0.242		0.515***
$\Delta\pi^m_{-2}$			0.515***
Commodity Prices[2]			
Average, lags 1–8	0.411***		0.255**
Average, lags 1–4		0.117***	
Oil Prices[3]			
Full sample			0.149***
pre-1980	0.141***	0.040**	
post-1980	0.066	0.029	
Sacrifice Ratio	2.9	1.9	1.6 (6.3)[c]
Dummies		93q1	97q2
Estimation period	63:2 – 00:4	74:2 – 00:1	71:2 – 00:1
Standard error	0.23 %	0.16 %	0.46 %

Authors'c calculations. Data definitions are in an Annex. - One, two, and three stars denote significance at 10, 5, and 1 percent levels. – [1]Manufactures and services. – [2]Calculated as $v\Delta\pi^{com}_{-1}$ where v is the weight of manufacturing in OECD value added. – [3]Calculated as $\gamma\Delta\pi^{oil}_{-1}$, where γ is a measure of intensity of oil use in production. The lag structure is as follows: US: Average of lags 1–3; Euro Area: lag 1; Japan: lags 0 and 1. – [a]If gap is negative and inflation is less than 1 % p.a. then coefficient is one-quarter of the reported value. – [b]Three quarter lag. – [c]The sacrifice ratio in brackets is for the "flat" portion of the Phillips curve (i.e., low and falling inflation).

	Recent residuals (positive value means under-prediction)		
	1997		
Q1	0.12	0.00	−0.14
Q2	0.10	−0.06	0.00
Q3	−0.12	0.01	0.00
Q4	0.10	0.07	−0.22
	1998		
Q1	0.08	0.12	−0.37
Q2	0.19	0.23	−0.11
Q3	0.04	0.12	−0.17
Q4	−0.04	0.13	0.77
	1999		
Q1	−0.18	−0.18	0.30
Q2	0.05	0.14	−0.01
Q3	−0.13	0.02	−0.16
Q4	−0.11	0.00	0.29
	2000		
Q1	−0.19	−0.09	0.35

Authors' calculations.

Figure 1

Impacts on headline inflation (single equation properties)

Deviations from baseline (annual inflation rate, percentage points)

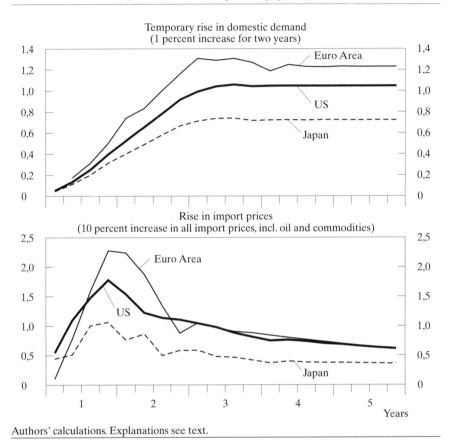

Temporary rise in domestic demand
(1 percent increase for two years)

Rise in import prices
(10 percent increase in all import prices, incl. oil and commodities)

Authors' calculations. Explanations see text.

For estimation purposes and in the standard version of the model, the coefficients on the lagged inflation terms are assumed to sum to unity, proxying the combined effects of nominal inertia and (backward-looking) inflation expectations. In that case the Phillips curve can be written in terms of the change in the inflation rate ($\Delta\pi$). Alternative specifications could include a weighted average of forward-looking and backward-looking expectations.

Each of the three regions also has a simple equation linking core CPI to headline CPI:

$$\pi^{head} = \pi + lags\left(\pi^{com}\right) + lags\left(\pi^{oil}\right). \qquad (2)$$

Here the headline CPI inflation rate (π^{head}) is built up from the core rate by adding the direct (or accounting) impact of oil and commodity prices. With

Table 2

Headline CPI inflation

Dependent Variable: $\pi^h = 100\ \Delta\log CPI$

	United States	Euro Area	Japan
Core Inflation	0.964***	0.976***	0.964***
Commodity Price Inflation			
Lag 0	0.010**		
Lag 1			0.019***
Lag 2	0.010***		
Lag 3		0.013***	
Oil Price Inflation			
Lag 0	0.016***	0.006**	0.006***
Lag 1		0.005**	
Lag 2			0.011***
Estimation period	63:2 - 00:1	80:1 - 00:1	70:4 - 00:1
Standard error	0.27 %	0.20 %	0.30 %

Authors' calculations. Data definitions are in an Annex. – One, two, and three stars denote significance at 10, 5, and 1 percent levels. – Coefficients restricted to sum to one.

this formulation it is possible to distinguish the direct (or accounting) effects of oil and commodity price shocks from the indirect or second-round effects, in which they may get built into the general inflation process.

The estimation results are shown in Tables 1 and 2, and the single equation dynamic properties are presented in Figure 1. Detailed data definitions are given in an Annex. The output gap is strongly significant for each region, although the gap appears in a non-linear form in the Japanese equation. Japan's equation has a goal-line effect, in which it is difficult to drive inflation lower when it is already very low.[6] Specifically, when inflation is below 1 per cent per annum, a negative output gap will only reduce inflation by 1 quarter of the amount that it would otherwise. This feature is important when trying to explain Japanese inflation over the past few years. A similar effect was tested for in the United States and euro equations but was not found to be empirically important, possibly because those two regions have not had Japan's experience of a prolonged period of low inflation. Although measured with some uncertainty, the sacrifice ratios are broadly consistent with those found in other Phillips curve work, including Richardson et al. (2000) and Turner/Seghezza (1999).

Manufacturing and services import prices are statistically significant for each region, and their impact on inflation is quite large. The $(\pi^m - \pi)$ term ensures that manufacturing and service import prices are eventually fully passed on to

---

[6] The analogy comes from American football, where the closer to the goal-line you are, the harder it is to gain extra yardage. The cut-off of 1 per cent per annum is fairly arbitrary but was chosen after experimenting with several values.

Figure 2

Impacts on inflation of a 50% rise in oil prices (single equation properties)

Deviations from baseline (annual inflation rate, percentage points)

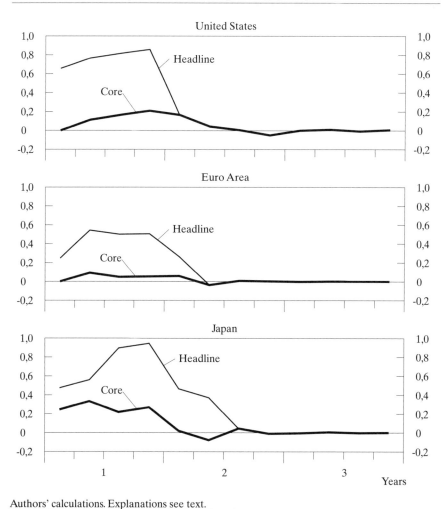

Authors' calculations. Explanations see text.

consumer prices,[7] but the adjustment is significantly slower in Japan than in the other two regions. That is partly because the import price coefficient is estimated to be lower, and partly because Japan's economy is more closed in the

---

[7] The model-wide implications of this term depend on the assumed exchange rate regime. Under fixed exchange rates, this term forces all countries to have the same steady state inflation rate (in order that real exchange rates are untrended). However, under floating rates each country can have its own inflation rate with the nominal exchange rate moving according to the inflation differentials between countries.

sense that imports represent a substantially smaller share of GDP. Commodity price inflation is also significant in a macroeconomic and econometric sense, with the long lag structure implying that only sustained changes in commodity prices feed through to the core inflation rate, while short-term blips tend to be discounted. There is some evidence that the impact of oil prices appears to have changed over time, at least for the United States and euro area. Even after accounting for the declining importance of oil in production, the estimated feed-through of oil prices to core inflation is less than half as strong in the post-1980 period as it was before 1980 (Hooker 1999). Finally, because only terms in $\Delta\pi$ are included, commodity and oil price inflation has the property that it "drops in and drops out" of consumer price inflation.

Figure 2 illustrates the different responses of headline and core inflation following a rise in oil prices. Note that the Figure shows the single equation properties, not a full model simulation. A rise in oil prices by 50 per cent has a large and relatively quick impact on headline inflation, which rises by between ½ and 1 per cent, although the impact drops out within 12–18 months (the lags are slightly longer in Japan). The core inflation rate rises by considerably less, by around 0.1 to 0.25 per cent.

2.2 GDP and the output gap

The output gap, *ygap*, is based on an IS-curve relationship, as a function of real interest rates (r), fiscal variables (g), the real exchange rate (rer), and other variables:

$$\Delta ygap = \mathrm{f}(r, g, rer, ...). \tag{3}$$

Given that GDP (y) and *ygap* are related by the identity $ygap = 100.(y/y^*-1)$ where y^* is potential output, equation (3) can be re-written as:

$$\Delta\log y = \Delta\log y^* + \mathrm{g}(r, g, rer, ...). \tag{4}$$

Consequently, an advantage of treating potential output as exogenous and writing the model in terms of the gap is that it avoids having to model or explain changes in potential output. In other words, the long term or trend changes in growth can be taken as given so that the model can focus on short term or cyclical variations in growth. That considerably simplifies the estimation and is likely to lead to equations that are econometrically more sound.[8]

---

[8] As evidenced by the burgeoning literature on the empirical determinants of trend growth, it is difficult to econometrically estimate robust equations that explain potential output. In more technical terms, the approach followed here assumes that potential is weakly exogenous with respect to the other explanatory variables (r, g, *etc*) – at least over business cycle frequencies – which seems a reasonable first approximation.

In keeping with the need to keep the model small, a single IS curve for each region was initially estimated. However, it quickly became clear that several important coefficients were poorly determined or had the wrong sign. Thus the output gap (*ygap*) was split into two components: domestic demand and net exports. Obviously output can be cut any number of ways but this disaggregation seemed most useful and relevant given the purpose of the model. Hence *ygap* is written:

$$ygap = 100.\big((dd+nx)\,/\,y* - 1\big) \equiv ddgap + nxgap \qquad (5)$$

where *dd* and *nx* are domestic demand and net exports respectively. These are discussed separately in the following two sections.

Domestic demand
The equation for the domestic demand gap, *ddgap*, takes the following form,

$$\Delta ddgap = -\delta(r-c) + lags\big(\Delta ddgap\big) + lags\big(\Delta irs\big) + lags\big(\Delta\Delta xmgap\big) + \qquad (6)$$

$$lags\big(\Delta\Delta gspend\big) + lags\big(\Delta\Delta grev\big)$$

where *r* is a measure of real long-term interest rates,[9] *c* is a constant, *irs* is the short-term interest rate, *gspend* is cyclically-adjusted government spending (as a proportion of potential output), and *grev* is cyclically adjusted government revenues (*grev* minus *gspend* equals the cyclically adjusted budget balance).

The first term captures the level of long-term real interest rates: high real interest rates will keep the growth rate of domestic demand permanently below the potential growth rate. Given that the other terms in the equation will eventually go to zero, the only way to ensure that domestic demand growth returns to its potential rate is for the real interest rate to return to its equilibrium level, *c*. Consequently, there is a policy-neutral real interest rate implicit in the model. This formulation also implies that there is no error-correction mechanism in this equation that ensures the gap "automatically" returns to zero. However, a non-zero gap has consequences for inflation and therefore for trade competitiveness, so the model as a whole has the property that gaps will eventually close. Of course, equilibrium can be restored more quickly by explicit monetary or fiscal policy action.

The other terms in the equation are relatively simple. Lagged dependent variables capture slow adjustment. Lags of net exports (relative to potential) capture the feed-through from foreign trade to domestic demand. For example, a depreciation of the exchange rate that leads to a rise in exports will lead to

---

[9] For the purposes of estimation, the inflation expectations component of real interest rates is proxied by a very smooth Hodrick Prescott filter through actual inflation. In model simulation, these expectations can be substituted out with model-consistent forward expectations of inflation.

greater income of producers and workers in the tradeables sector, which
should feed through to domestic demand with a lag. Changes in short-term interest rates capture monetary policy influences and allow a richer dynamic response to changes in policy than the simple equilibrium real interest rate term.
Finally, fiscal policy is captured through the separate influences of government
spending and revenue. Spending and revenue are treated separately because
the dynamic response to spending and tax shocks is likely to be considerably
different.[10] The dynamic functional form of the fiscal and net export variables
(specifically, that they have been double-differenced) ensures they will have
only temporary effects on output. For example, a permanent rise of government spending of 1 per cent of GDP will eventually be fully crowded out by a
1 per cent fall in private domestic spending. Such crowding-out effects are
somewhat mechanistic given the size and reduced form nature of the model,
proxying transmission mechanisms that are treated more explicitly in larger
models.

Several country-specific variables have been added to the domestic demand
equations in order to capture recent experience. For the United States, a measure of share-market wealth relative to disposable income has been an important recent determinant of domestic demand. The Japanese equation includes
the real price of land because the 1990s cannot be explained by monetary and
fiscal variables alone. The long stagnation is partly driven by balance sheet
problems in the financial sector, which in turn is partly the result of the collapse of asset prices since the late 1980s.

The estimation results are shown in Table 3 and the single-equation simulation
properties are shown in Figure 3.[11] Key results are:

– There is a strong feed-through from net exports to domestic demand in all
  regions, with a lag of 1-2 quarters.

– Changes in short-term interest rates are strongly significant and operate
  with a lag of around 2 quarters in the United States and euro area, and
  1 quarter in Japan. The coefficients on long-term real interest rates are
  relatively small[12] so this term will have only a small impact on short-term
  forecasts, but has an important stabilising role in the model when used for

[10] Making this distinction led to substantial improvements in the equations compared with earlier versions.

[11] In this and other equations, dynamics have initially been freely estimated but then often simplified by imposing the same coefficient on different lags. For example, the coefficients on lags 1-3
of $\Delta ddgap$ in the Japanese equation have been imposed to be equal because they were approximately equal when freely estimated.

[12] The Euro coefficient was imposed at –0.06 (a restriction accepted at the 10 per cent level) because the freely estimated coefficient was too small.

Table 3

Domestic demand

Dependent variable: $\Delta(\text{DD/potential}-1)\cdot 100$

	United States	Euro Area	Japan
Lagged dependents			
ΔDom Demand gap$_{-1}$		0.308***	0.249***
ΔDom Demand gap$_{-2}$		0.162*	0.249***
ΔDom Demand gap$_{-3}$			0.249***
Δ_4 Dom Demand gap$_{-1}$	0.130***		
Net exports			
$\Delta\Delta$Net Exports gap$_{-1}$	0.197		
$\Delta\Delta$Net Exports gap$_{-2}$	0.451**	0.383***	0.326**
$\Delta\Delta$Net Exports gap$_{-3}$	0.166		0.326**
$\Delta\Delta$Net Exports gap$_{-4}$			0.326**
$\Delta\Delta$Net Exports gap$_{-5}$			0.326**
Interest rates			
Real IRL[1]	−0.066	−0.06[a]	−0.064
ΔIRS$_{-1}$			−0.214***
ΔIRS$_{-2}$	−0.316	−0.100***	
ΔIRS$_{-3}$	−0.053	−0.100***	−0.214***
ΔIRS$_{-4}$	−0.179***	−0.100***	
Fiscal policy			
$\Delta\Delta$Spending	0.862***	1.573***	0.663***
$\Delta\Delta$Spending$_{-1}$	0.971***	0.544	1.632***
$\Delta\Delta$Spending$_{-2}$	0.678**	0.544	
$\Delta\Delta$Spending$_{-3}$	0.214	0.544	
$\Delta\Delta$Tax		0.545	
$\Delta\Delta$Tax$_{-1}$		−0.398	−1.091**
$\Delta\Delta$Tax$_{-2}$		0.402	
$\Delta\Delta$Tax$_{-3}$		0.150	−0.449**
$\Delta\Delta$Tax$_{-4}$	−0.210	−0.228	−0.622***
Other variables			
$\Delta\Delta$Sharemarket wealth$_{-1}$[2]	0.022***		
$\Delta\Delta$Land prices$_{-1}$[3]			0.488***
$\Delta\Delta$Land prices$_{-3}$			0.380***
Dummies	70q4, 78q2, 80q2	93q1	97q2
Estimation period	66:1 − 00:1	75:4 − 00:1	75:4 − 00:1
Stadard error	0.55	0.38	0.63

Authors' calculations. Data definitions are in an Annex. – One, two, and three stars denote significance at 10, 5, and 1 percent levels. – [1]Real interest rates minus equilibrium level. The equilibrium is estimated (it equals the constant term in the regression divided by the real IRL coefficient). Inflation expectations area mixture of forward and backward looking, as proxied by a smooth Hodrick-Prescott filter of actual inflation. – [2]Sharemarket wealth as a proportion of disposable income, including indirect holdings. An (econometrically estimated) 8-quarter lag structure is built into this variable. – [3]Urban land price index/CPI. – [a]Coefficient imposed.

Table 3 (continued)

Domestic demand

Dependent variable: $\Delta(DD/potential-1)\cdot100$

Recent residuals (positive value means under-prediction)		
1997		
Q1	0.2 (0.1)	0.0 (−0.2)	0.3 (0.4)
Q2	0.0 (0.0)	0.3 (0.5)	0.0 (0.0)
Q3	−0.2 (−0.3)	−0.1 (0.0)	−0.3 (−0.5)
Q4	−0.5 (−0.4)	0.4 (0.3)	−0.3 (−0.2)
1998		
Q1	0.1 (0.0)	0.2 (0.2)	−0.1 (−0.5)
Q2	−0.8 (−1.0)	0.0 (0.1)	−0.5 (−0.3)
Q3	−0.8 (−0.7)	−0.1 (0.0)	−1.0 (−1.3)
Q4	−0.9 (−0.6)	0.2 (−0.3)	−0.7 (−1.0)
1999		
Q1	1.5 (1.1)	−0.2 (−0.3)	1.2 (1.3)
Q2	1.3 (1.0)	−0.2 (−0.2)	1.3 (1.4)
Q3	−1.2 (−1.2)	−0.4 (0.0)	−0.9 (−0.6)
Q4	−0.1 (0.1)	−0.1 (−0.2)	−0.1 (−0.6)
2000		
Q1	1.1 (0.9)	−0.1 (−0.2)	0.9 (2.0)

Authors' calculations. Value in brackets is the residual for the total output gap.

simulations. Figure 3 shows that the total interest rate effect is weaker in the euro area than in the other two regions.

– The government spending multiplier is initially around 1 or higher implying that private spending is crowded in to begin with, but crowding out occurs relatively quickly; after two years, around two-thirds of the initial shock has been offset by a reduction in private spending.

– A 10 per cent rise in United States stock prices has a strong but temporary impact on domestic demand, with demand peaking around 1–1.5 per cent higher after 18 months. This is in line with a "3–5¢ rule" for consumption (whereby a $1 increase in wealth will lead to an eventual increase in consumption of between 3 and 5 cents), plus an extra effect for business investment.[13] The impact on domestic demand relative to potential output is temporary because the required portfolio adjustments will not be permanent.

---

[13] Sharemarket wealth is close to 200 per cent of disposable income, and consumption is around two-thirds of GDP. Hence, a 10 per cent rise in share prices corresponds in dollar terms to 20 per cent of GDP and 30 per cent of consumption. If 4¢ of each dollar is spent, consumption will rise by $4/100 \times 30 = 1.2$ per cent. Hence GDP will increase by approximately 0.8 per cent. The remaining effect comes from the extra investment generated by higher household demand (Meredith (1997) finds that the investment boost may be worth at least as much as the direct rise in consumption).

Figure 3

Impacts on domestic demand (single equation properties)

Deviations from baseline (percent)

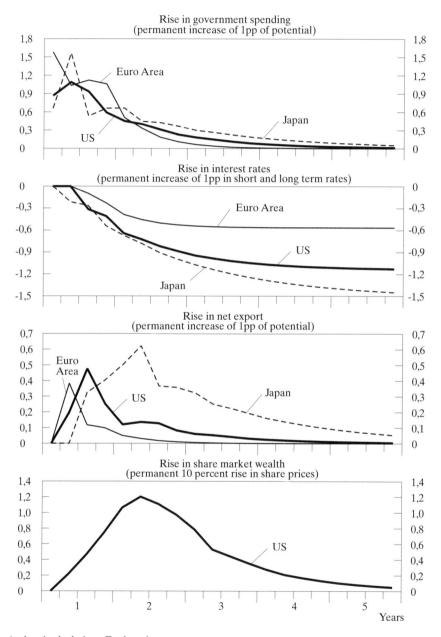

– Finally, two specification checks were performed. First, export growth (relative to potential) was added to each equation. This "trade multiplier" effect
  was added because it is possible that domestic demand will respond to an
  increase in the volume of trade even if *net* exports remain unchanged. However, this additional multiplier was insignificant in each region suggesting
  that the net export formulation is a useful simplification. Second, richer dynamic adjustment from potential output to actual output was tested by adding lags of potential growth. However, they were insignificant in each region.

Net exports
Net exports as a proportion of potential output are explained by the real effective exchange rate, the local domestic demand gap, and the trade-weighted

Figure 4

Impacts on net exports (single equation properties)
Deviations from baseline (percentage points of potential GDP)

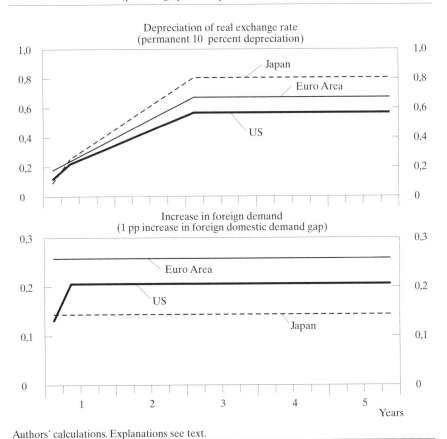

Authors' calculations. Explanations see text.

Table 4

Net exports

Dependent variable: Δ(net exports/potential) $\cdot$ 100

	United States	Euro Area	Japan
Δlog Real Exchange Rate			
Lag 0	–1.157**	–1.856***	–1.237***
Lag 1	–1.157**		–1.237***
Average, lags 2–8	–3.652***		–5.445***
Average, lags 1–8		–5.202***	
Relative Domestic Demand Gap[1]			
ΔRelative gap	0.130***	0.258***	0.135***
ΔRelative gap$_{-1}$	0.076***		
Dummies	78q1		
Estimation period	74:4 – 00:1	74:3 – 00:1	74:3 – 00:1
Standard error	0.19	0.18	0.30

Authors' calculations. – Data definitions are in an Annex. – One, two, and three stars denote significance at 10, 5, and 1 percent levels. – [1]Foreign minus domestic gap.

Recent residuals (positive value means under-prediction)			
	1997		
Q1	–0.2	–0.2	0.1
Q2	0.0	0.2	0.0
Q3	–0.1	0.1	–0.2
Q4	0.1	–0.1	0.1
	1998		
Q1	–0.1	0.0	–0.4
Q2	–0.2	0.1	0.1
Q3	0.1	0.0	–0.3
Q4	0.3	–0.5	–0.3
	1999		
Q1	–0.4	–0.1	0.1
Q2	–0.3	0.0	0.1
Q3	0.0	0.4	0.2
Q4	0.2	0.0	–0.5
	2000		
Q1	–0.2	0.0	1.1

Authors' calculations.

foreign domestic demand gap. Although differences in openness or import propensities may lead to the coefficients being different on local and foreign domestic demand gaps, in practice the restriction that the coefficients are equal but opposite in sign was accepted for each region. In that case, the equation can be rewritten in terms of the *relative* gap:

$$xmgap = lags\ (\ xmgap) + lags\ (\ rer) + lags\ (\ relgap) \qquad (7)$$

where *rer* is the log real effective exchange rate (based on relative CPIs) and *relgap* is the relative domestic demand gap (foreign minus domestic).

The estimation results are in Table 4 and Figure 4. The real exchange rate has a strong and significant impact on net exports in each region. The lag structure is quite long in each case, up to two years, implying that a sustained real exchange rate change is more important than an equal-sized short-term blip. The long-term elasticities are fairly similar across regions: a ten per cent depreciation of the real exchange rate will raise net exports as a share of GDP by 0.6 per cent in the United States, 0.7 per cent in the euro area, and 0.8 per cent in Japan. The size and timing of these responses is consistent with a short-run J-curve effect and with other evidence, including from interlink.

2.3 Import prices

Manufacturing and service import prices are assumed to be a weighted average of price-taking and price-making behaviour. For price takers, the import price is simply equal to foreign prices divided by the nominal exchange rate. For price makers, the import price is determined by the local price of competing goods, which is proxied by the domestic CPI. With this formulation, long run import prices can be written as a function of the real exchange rate, commodity prices, and domestic consumer prices. An error-correction equation is used to determine short run import prices. A time trend is also included to capture the long term decline in import prices relative to consumer prices.

Unfortunately there is no suitable time-series for euro area import prices that excludes intra-euro-area trade. This is particularly a problem when trying to estimate a real exchange rate elasticity because the trade-weighted real exchange rate excludes intra-euro currencies. Consequently, the coefficients of the euro equation have been imposed at values similar to the United States-Japan average but making adjustments in order to improve recent forecasting performance.[14]

Results are shown in Table 5. The relative weight on domestic prices versus foreign prices implies that Japan is significantly more of a price-taker than is the United States.[15] Speed of adjustment to long-run equilibrium is reasonably fast, and around half of the exchange rate impact comes through in the first quarter. Commodity prices have a significant impact on non-commodity

---

[14] Despite being imposed, the residuals from the long-run part of the equation are stationary implying that the long run represents a valid cointegrating relationship.

[15] The long-run equation can be rewritten so that relative import prices (PM/CPI) are a function of the real exchange rate. In that case, the real exchange rate elasticity is –0.45 for the United States and –0.74 for Japan.

Table 5

Import prices

Dependent variable: p = log (PM/CPI), PM is manufactures and services import prices

	Implicit Long Run
US	log PM = const + 0.547 log CPI + 0.453 log p^f/e - 0.008 trend[1]
Euro	log PM = const + 0.4 log CPI + 0.6 log p^f/e - 0.0057 trend
Japan	log PM = const + 0.260 log CPI + 0.740 log p^f/e - 0.00083 trend[2]

	Short Run		
	United States	Euro Area[3]	Japan
Equilibrium Correction			
p_{-1}	–0.163***	–0.2	–0.254***
rer_{-1} (= log p.e/p^t)	–0.074***	–0.12	–0.187***
Lagged dependents			
Lag 1	0.139**	0.1	
Lag 4			
ΔReal exchange rate			
Lag 0	–0.267***	–0.2	–0.483***
Lag 4			–0.158***
Commodity Prices			
Δlog (pcom/cpi)		0.07	0.131***
Δlog (pcom/cpi)$_{-2}$	0.052***		
Trend/100	–0.130***	–0.114***	–0.207***
Dummies	87q1		
Estimation period	77:1 – 00:1	(imposed)	80:1 – 00:1
Standard error	0.67 %	0.82 %[4]	1.50 %

Authors' calculations. Data definitions are in an Annex. – One, two, and three stars denote significance at 10, 5, and 1 percent levels. – [1]Trend applies after 1980 only. – [2]Trend applies before 1994 only. – [3]Coefficients imposed. See text for a discussion. – [4]Standard error and residuals (below) for euro based on implicit residuals from imposed equation, 1980 – 2000.

	Recent residuals (positive value means under-prediction), in %		
	1997		
Q1	0.0	–1.2	–1.9
Q2	–0.3	0.0	–0.2
Q3	–0.2	–0.6	1.8
Q4	0.2	–0.2	0.5
	1998		
Q1	0.2	0.3	3.6
Q2	0.2	–0.6	–0.1
Q3	0.6	0.5	0.1
Q4	–0.2	–0.1	–1.5
	1999		
Q1	0.4	–0.8	–1.0
Q2	0.2	–1.2	–0.7
Q3	0.3	–0.9	0.1
Q4	–0.2	0.4	–0.2
	2000		
Q1	0.9	–1.5	–2.1

Authors' calculations.

import prices, implying effects that work through the production chain, but the effect is only temporary. Oil prices were not significant.

2.4 Commodity prices

As mentioned earlier, commodity prices can be an important channel through which global demand shocks are magnified and propagated across regions. Commodity prices tend to be much more volatile than prices for final output, but have an asymmetry in their behaviour. Price rises tend to be large and quick, while price declines tend to be milder but to last longer. In addition, there is a strong commodity price cycle, and this cycle is highly correlated with the world demand cycle.

Commodity prices are determined by a complex interaction of supply and demand factors, but for the purposes of this model the key features can be simplified and modelled as follows. It is assumed that the inflation rate of non-oil commodity prices measured in US Dollars (π^{com}) depends on world inflation and the world output gap. In the absence of shocks and with the world economy growing at potential, commodity price inflation will settle down to the world inflation rate (after adjusting for a constant "drift" term that captures the trend decline in real commodity prices). Modelling π^{com} as a function of the world output gap implies that if the world economy is growing at its potential rate then there will be no excess demand and no pressure on manufacturing capacity, and consequently no pressure on real commodity prices (whether they be commodities that are used as inputs to the production process, or commodities for final consumption). Several forms of asymmetry were tested in estimation to capture the apparent asymmetry in the commodity price cycle, including distinguishing between rises and falls in inflation, between positive and negative output gaps, and between positive and negative *changes* in the gap. There was little strong evidence to help choose between the alternatives but the following equation was chosen as the simplest econometrically sound equation that captures the key features:

$$\pi^{com} - \pi^{oecd} = 0.0082 + 0.467(\pi^{com} - \pi^{oecd})_{-1} + 4.18\langle \Delta wldgap/100 \rangle^{+} \qquad (8)$$
$$\quad\;\;(3.9) \quad\; (7.1) \qquad\qquad\qquad (4.2)$$

$$+0.577\Delta\pi^{com}_{-1} - 0.409\Delta\pi^{com}_{-2} + 0.358\Delta\pi^{c}_{-3} + 1.635\Delta\pi^{oecd} + 3.207\Delta\pi^{oecd}_{-1} + 3.925\Delta\pi^{oecd}_{-2}$$
$$\;\;(7.2) \qquad\quad (5.8) \qquad\quad (4.8) \qquad\;\; (1.9) \qquad\;\; (3.9) \qquad\quad (4.8)$$

Estimation period: 1970-2 – 1999-4. t-values in brackets.
$R^2 = 0.79$. Std. Error = 2.4%; DW = 1.9; AR(4) p-value = 0.59;
Jarque-Bera Normality p-value = 0.99

The single equation properties are shown in Figure 5. Changes in world output are estimated to have a large and statistically significant impact on commodity

Figure 5

Impacts on commodity price inflation (single equation properties)
Deviations from baseline (annual inflation rate, percentage points)

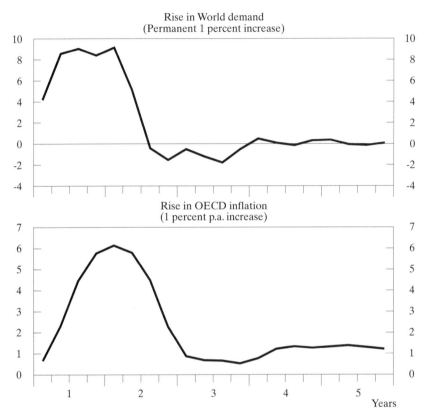

Authors' calculations. Explanations see text.

price inflation but only if world output growth *exceeds* potential (as denoted by the $\langle \Delta wldgap / 100 \rangle^+$ term). The OECD output gap was tested as an alternative measure of global excess demand but performed less well, the difference being most important during the recent Asian crisis. The OECD inflation rate excluding high inflation countries (π^{oecd}) is used to proxy world inflation, and the large coefficients imply a substantial degree of overshooting of commodity prices relative to consumer prices. Finally, the constant term implies that real commodity prices will fall by approximately 3 ½ per cent per annum, *ceteris paribus*.

2.5 Other variables

Monetary policy rules
The large recent literature on modelling monetary policy in small models of
this type has two branches: optimal rules; and the relative performance of
simple "rules of thumb" or interest rate reaction functions. Examples include
Drew/Hunt (1998), Ball (1998), Svensson (1998), Fair (2000), Rudebusch
(1999), and Smets (1998). Looking at optimal policy is certainly feasible in the
context of this model, but beyond the scope of this paper. Instead, some preliminary experiments have been performed using simple interest rate reaction
functions. A general précis of that branch of the literature suggest that policy
rules work better if: (a) interest rates respond to expected future inflation, rather than current inflation; (b) the current output gap is included; and (c) the
weights are higher than the simple Taylor rule. Experiments have been made
with the following rule:

$$r = r* + \alpha ygap + \beta\left(\Pi^e_{t+6} - \Pi*\right) \tag{9}$$

where $r = i - \Pi$ is the real short term interest rate, $r*$ is the equilibrium real interest rate, Π is the annual rate of core inflation, and Π^e and Π^* are the expected and target annual inflation rates respectively. In this way, interest rates
are increased if the output gap is currently above zero or if the expected core
inflation rate in eighteen months time is above its target level. A rule that
looks ahead eighteen months was chosen partly because the 18-months to
2-year period is typically regarded as the period over which monetary policy
has its greatest influence. In addition, it ensures that policy does not react to
short-term blips in inflation (i.e., those in the next 1 or 2 quarters) unless they
lead to longer lasting inflationary pressures. The weights chosen for the version of the model discussed here are $\alpha = 0.75$ and $\beta = 1.0$, although they are ex-
perimental and may be revised after further research. For comparison, the
"standard" Taylor rule depends on the output gap and current inflation, with
weights of 0.5 on each variable.[16] This rule is not intended to mimic actual central bank behaviour, but to approximate an optimal policy rule in the context
of this model.

Long-term interest rates
Long-term interest rates feed into domestic demand and can be modelled
using an approximation to the expectations theory of the term structure. The
bond rate (i^B) is assumed to be a weighted average of all future short rates (i^S)
where the weights decline geometrically in the future:

[16] Attempts to estimate the coefficients of the policy rule for the United States include Judd/Ru-
debusch (1998) and Clarida et al. (1998). Both papers include an interest rate smoothing term in
order to fit historical policy. Ball (1997) and Levin (1996) show that higher weights than implicit in
the Taylor rule are more successful at stabilising output and inflation in a small model of this sort
(Ball) and in the Fed's FRB model (Levin).

$$i_t^B = (1-\lambda)\sum_{i=0}^{\infty}\lambda^i E\big(i_{t+i}^S | t\big)+\varphi \qquad (10)$$

where λ determines the speed with which the weights decline and φ is an exogenous term or liquidity premium to capture the fact that the yield curve slopes up on average. With this formulation, bond rates are purely forward looking but put more weight on the near future than would be the case under the pure expectations theory. In contrast, the pure theory gives *equal* weight to next quarter's 90-day bill rate as it does to the 90-day rate in each of the next 39 quarters but zero weight to anything after 40 quarters. Aside from (10) being more a plausible guide to investment decisions in the domestic demand equation, it greatly simplifies the model solution. It can be rewritten by taking a Koyck lead:

$$i_t^B = (1-\lambda)E\big(i_{t+1}^B\big)+\lambda\big(i_t^S +\varphi\big) \qquad (11)$$

so that today's bond rate is a weighted average of next period's expected bond rate and the current short-term rate. The parameter λ is set to 0.9 to give a mean lead of 2 ½ years between short- and long-rates, which is approximately consistent with the observed relative volatility of bonds and bills.[17] The term premium (φ) has been set to 1 per cent.

Nominal exchange rates
Exchange rates against the United States Dollar (USD) (e_t) can be endogenised using uncovered interest rate parity (UIP).

$$\log e_t \approx E\big(\log e_{t+1}\big)+\big(i-i^f -\eta\big)/400 \qquad (12)$$

where i and i^f are the domestic and trade-weighted foreign short term interest rates respectively, and   is an exogenous risk premium. Since UIP assumes perfect capital markets, equilibrium requires that real interest rates in all regions be equal in the long run, adjusted for a risk premium. Under UIP the exchange rate is a jumping variable. A possible alternative that would reduce the degree of jumping is to model the exchange rate as a weighted average of the current rate and the UIP rate.

Rest of the world output gap
The output gap in the rest-of-the-world (i.e., the world minus the three major regions) is determined by a simple form of trade multiplier equation, but with an error-correction term to ensure that the rest-of-the-world gap returns to zero. The lag structure has been determined empirically:

[17] Bond rates appear to move "too much" to be consistent with the pure expectations theory, but the formulation used in the model will mimic the observed "excess" volatility because it puts more weight on the near future.

$$\Delta rowgap = 0.055 rowgap_{-1} + 0.300 \Delta rowgap_{-1} + 0.198 \Delta rowgap_{-2} \qquad (13)$$
$$\quad\quad\;\; (2.9) \qquad\qquad (3.2) \qquad\qquad (2.4)$$

$$0.114\Delta\left(usygap + usygap_{-1}\right) + 0.132\Delta eurygap + 0.047\Delta japygap_{-2}$$
$$(2.5) \qquad\qquad\qquad (2.5) \qquad\qquad (1.3)$$

Estimation period: 1974-3–1999-3; t-values in brackets;
$R^2 = 0.49$; Std. Error = 0.27; DW = 2.0

The coefficient estimates imply that output in the United States has the largest impact on demand in the rest-of-the-world, followed by the euro area and then Japan. The World Output Gap is then an accounting identity:

$$worldgap = 0.26\ usgap + 0.21\ eurgap + 0.19\ japgap + 0.34\ rowgap \quad (14)$$

3. Simulation properties

This section describes some simulations in order to demonstrate the major properties of the model. The simulations have been chosen specifically to emphasise the nature and size of the international linkages in the model. A range of "standard multiplier" shock results are reported in the Annex.

3.1 The inflationary consequences of a global boom

The first simulation illustrates the role of commodity prices in propagating a global demand shock. World domestic demand is assumed to be two per cent above base- line for two years. It is assumed that monetary policy does not re- act so that the demand and commodity price channels can be separated from the monetary policy channel as influences on global inflation.[18] The impacts are summarised in Figure 6. The thin line shows the impacts with commodity prices held at their baseline level, while the thick line assumes that commodity prices move according to equation (8).

Even with commodity prices held fixed at their baseline level, the demand shock has relatively large impacts on inflation. For example, United States headline inflation is 1.4 per cent higher after two years, and euro area inflation rises even higher but at a slightly slower pace. However, with endogenous commodity prices the increased demand pressure leads to a 20 per cent rise in commodity prices which pushes United States and euro inflation more than 2 per cent above baseline. Overall, the commodity price channel adds around half as much again to the inflationary consequences of a demand shock (slight- ly less than half in the euro area). The key to this result is that the demand

---

[18] More precisely, output in each region jumps by two per cent in the first quarter, stays at that level until quarter 8, then returns to baseline. Nominal interest rates and exchange rates are un- changed.

Figure 6

World demand shock – impacts on headline inflation

Annual rate, deviations from baseline in percent

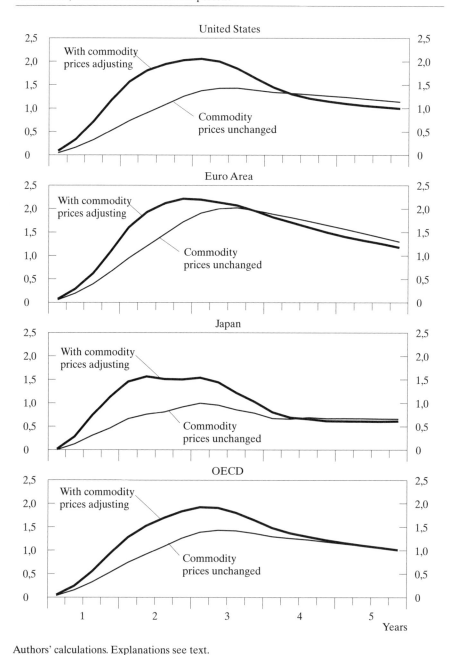

Authors' calculations. Explanations see text.

shock is genuinely global. A single-region shock will clearly have much smaller impacts on world demand, and therefore lead to perhaps marginal pressure on commodity prices. One policy implication concerns the recommendation in Stiglitz (1997) that monetary policy be used to "test the waters" because any inflation that results from excess demand will be slow in emerging. That may be reasonable for any individual country if the rest of the world remains sluggish. However, if a majority of OECD countries simultaneously move into a situation of excess demand, then the size of the pickup of inflation may be substantially increased. In addition, inflation picks up considerably more quickly if commodity prices are affected, implying that central banks will have much less time to react. Thus the view that "small mistakes have only small consequences" may need to be supplemented with "provided everybody doesn't make the same mistake at the same time".

3.2 United States domestic demand and monetary policy

This section describes an illustrative simulation to consider the role of international spillovers, the impact of monetary policy feedback rules, and the impact of floating exchange rates. The experiment is an immediate jump in United States domestic demand of 2 per cent. Half of this shock is then unwound the following year, leaving the remaining half to be unwound endogenously either by the economic feedbacks built into the model or by explicit monetary policy action.[19]

Figure 7 shows three variations on this simulation. The first (the thick line) assumes no monetary policy response (unchanged nominal interest rates) and therefore fixed nominal exchange rates. The second (the thin solid line) assumes that monetary policy adjust interest rates according to a rule of the type discussed in Section 2.5, but *still with fixed nominal exchange rates*. The third simulation (the dashed line) assumes that exchange rates are floating, being determined by uncovered interest rate parity. Note that the scales for the United States are different to those for the euro area and Japan.

Focussing first on the no-policy-response case (the thick line), the initial shock to United States domestic demand is amplified by the momentum or inertia effects in the domestic demand equation, so that the partial unwinding of the shock leaves the output gap still around 2 per cent above baseline after two years. United States inflation picks up strongly – 2 per cent above baseline after two years – and continues to climb so long as the output gap is positive. The main automatic equilibrating mechanism in the model works through trade. Higher inflation at a fixed nominal exchange rate implies an appreciating real exchange rate. The consequent reduction in net exports will reduce

---

[19] In this simulation, the demand shock is brought about by a residual adjustment to the domestic demand equation but keeping the equation endogenous.

Figure 7

US Demand shock

Deviations from baseline in percent

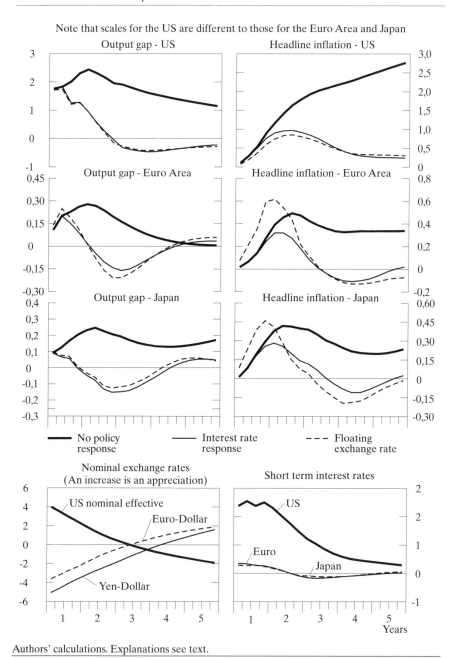

No policy response   Interest rate response   Floating exchange rate

Authors' calculations. Explanations see text.

the output gap directly and will also feed through to lower domestic demand. However, partly because the share of trade in total output is not large for the United States, this mechanism is comparatively weak. With no equilibrium correction mechanisms in the model, it will take many years for this trade channel to bring the economy back to equilibrium. Note also that the spill-overs to the euro area and Japan are not negligible. Output rises by around 0.3 per cent in both regions, and the inflation rate rises by 0.4 – 0.5 per cent per annum. The inflation impact will be partly due to stronger output and partly to imported inflation, including an effect from commodity prices.

An active interest rate response stabilises the system much more quickly (the thin line). The bottom-right panel of Figure 6 shows that short-term United States interest rates rise by 2 ½ per centage points in response to the higher output gap and the expected future inflation. Bond rates jump by less – a little over 1 per cent because the forward-looking nature of the bond market ex-pects short rates to come back in the future. This response is sufficient to close the United States output gap within two years, and to return United States in-flation towards target after three. Here almost all the monetary policy work is done by the United States; given that exchange rates are fixed, interest rates in the euro area and Japan rise by only 25 basis points or there- abouts.

The dashed lines show the impact of a floating exchange rate in transmitting the shock across regions. The United States nominal effective exchange rate jumps by 4 per cent in response to higher interest rates. This is not a large amount, but bear in mind that nominal interest rates do not stay high for long. The euro and Yen depreciate by 4–5 per cent against the dollar. The inter-esting result is that these depreciations have a significant effect on inflation in the euro area and Japan. Not only do they contribute at least as much as the di-rect trade-output channel, they also cause inflation to rise considerably faster. The implication here is that, at least as far as monetary policy is concerned, sig-nificantly misleading policy signals may be given if the exchange rate channel is ignored (see also Hall, Whitley 1999). This also illustrates one of the strengths of keeping a model small. The role of exchange rates in transmitting shocks between regions is often missed in large global models such as INTERLINK because it is technically difficult to solve them with for-ward-looking jumping variables.

4. Summary and future developments

This paper has described preliminary work on a short-term forecasting model of the major economic regions, with a particular focus on international linka-ges. With that in mind, there are several areas for potential further work. First, the impact of policy could be considered in greater depth by investigating al-ternative monetary policy reaction functions and alternative exchange rate rules. Second, the role of expectations as a transmission mechanism of policy both within and between regions could be developed. Third, closer scrutiny of differences in dynamics across regions may be warranted. For example, small differences in lag structures can imply large differences in the speed and magnitude with which an oil shock affects inflation in the three regions. Finally, the number of regions may need to be reconsidered. For example, the United States and Japan together account for less than 20 per cent of euro area trade, with the remainder accounted for by the "rest of the world" block. This is a particular weakness given the diversity of countries that make up this "residual" block and the likelihood that they are at different stages of the business cycle. A possible parsimonious solution would be to divide this block into more homogenous regions, each of which would explain the output gap as a single reduced form of the output gap in other regions.

Annex: Standard simulation results

Tables 6–8 present standard simulation results to illustrate the comparative properties of the three regional models plus the strength of interactions between regions. They are not intended to represent genuine policy simulations but are provided as simple diagnostics to document the properties of the model. The full model is run in each case (i.e., all three regional models plus the world block) with each table detailing the results of three separate simulations. For example, the first panel of Table A1 shows the impacts of a rise in US interest rates, assuming euro and Japanese rates are unchanged.

Table 6 shows a rise in short-term interest rates by 1 per cent for two years. Long-term interest rates are determined by the forward-looking equation in the model (see Section 2.5) and therefore rise by less than 1 per cent because financial markets anticipate that the tightening in monetary policy is temporary (in fact, long-term rates initially jump by around ½ per cent, then decline over the following two years). Nominal exchange rates are held fixed. Each region takes at least half a year to respond significantly to a tightening of monetary policy, with the peak response being around eighteen months after the tightening. Output in the euro area is the least sensitive of the three regions to the rise in interest rates. The full inflationary impact takes between two and three years to occur, although the slightly slow response is partly because the quicker-acting exchange rate channel has been neutralised in the simulations. The cross-country spillover effects are smaller than in INTERLINK.

Table 7 shows the impacts of a permanent increase in government spending of 1 per cent of potential GDP. Nominal exchange rates are again held fixed, as are nominal interest rates. Government spending initially crowds in private spending but crowding out occurs relatively quickly. Half of the impulse has gone within 4 quarters, and the spending increase has been fully crowded out within two years.

Table 8 shows the impacts of an exchange rate depreciation in each of the three regions, holding nominal interest rates fixed. Japanese activity is most sensitive to exchange rate movements, which is consistent with other evidence that Japan's exports are more price sensitive than most countries (Murata, Turner, Rae, and Le Fouler 2000). However, the euro area inflation rate is the most sensitive to a depreciation, partly because it is a "more open" economy than the other two.

Table 6

Impact of a rise in interest rates

1 percent increase of short term rates for two years; deviations from baseline in percent

	Quarters after shock						
	1	2	3	4	8	12	16
Rise in interest rates in the United States							
United States							
Output gap	0.0	0.0	−0.3	−0.4	−0.9	−0.8	−0.4
Inflation[1]	0.0	0.0	0.0	−0.1	−0.4	−0.7	−0.8
Net exports[2]	0.0	0.0	0.0	0.1	0.2	0.2	0.2
Euro Area							
Output gap	0.0	0.0	0.0	0.0	−0.1	−0.1	0.0
Inflation[1]	0.0	0.0	0.0	0.0	−0.1	−0.1	−0.1
Net exports[2]	0.0	0.0	0.0	0.0	−0.1	−0.1	0.0
Japan							
Output gap	0.0	0.0	0.0	0.0	−0.1	−0.1	0.0
Inflation[1]	0.0	0.0	0.0	0.0	−0.1	−0.1	0.0
Net exports[2]	0.0	0.0	0.0	0.0	−0.1	−0.1	0.0
Rise in interest rates in the Euro Area							
United States							
Output gap	0.0	0.0	0.0	0.0	0.0	0.0	0.0
Inflation[1]	0.0	0.0	0.0	0.0	0.0	−0.1	−0.1
Net exports[2]	0.0	0.0	0.0	0.0	0.0	0.0	0.0
Euro Area							
Output gap	0.0	0.0	−0.1	−0.2	−0.6	−0.5	−0.2
Inflation[1]	0.0	0.0	0.0	0.0	−0.3	−0.6	−0.7
Net exports[2]	0.0	0.0	0.0	0.1	0.2	0.2	0.2
Japan							
Output gap	0.0	0.0	0.0	0.0	0.0	0.0	0.0
Inflation[1]	0.0	0.0	0.0	0.0	0.0	−0.1	0.0
Net exports[2]	0.0	0.0	0.0	0.0	0.0	0.0	0.0
Rise in interest rates in Japan							
United States							
Output gap	0.0	0.0	0.0	0.0	−0.1	−0.1	0.0
Inflation[1]	0.0	0.0	0.0	0.0	−0.1	−0.1	−0.1
Net exports[2]	0.0	0.0	0.0	0.0	0.0	0.0	0.0
Euro Area							
Output gap	0.0	0.0	0.0	0.0	0.0	0.0	0.0
Inflation[1]	0.0	0.0	0.0	0.0	−0.1	−0.1	0.0
Net exports[2]	0.0	0.0	0.0	0.0	0.0	0.0	0.0
Japan							
Output gap	0.0	−0.2	−0.3	−0.6	−1.1	−0.9	−0.7
Inflation[1]	0.0	0.0	0.0	−0.1	−0.4	−0.6	−0.6
Net exports[2]	0.0	0.0	0.0	0.1	0.2	0.2	0.2

Authors' calculations. – [1]Annual rate of headline inflation. – [2]As a percent of potential output.

Table 7

Impact of a rise in government spending

Permanent increase of 1 percent of potential output; deviations from baseline in percent

	Quarters after shock						
	1	2	3	4	8	12	16
Rise in spending in the United States							
United States							
Output gap	0.8	0.9	0.7	0.4	0.2	0.0	−0.1
Inflation[1]	0.0	0.1	0.2	0.3	0.4	0.3	0.3
Net exports[2]	−0.1	−0.2	−0.2	−0.1	−0.1	−0.1	−0.1
Euro Area							
Output gap	0.0	0.1	0.1	0.1	0.0	0.0	0.0
Inflation[1]	0.0	0.0	0.1	0.1	0.1	0.0	0.0
Net exports[2]	0.0	0.1	0.1	0.1	0.0	0.0	0.0
Japan							
Output gap	0.0	0.1	0.1	0.1	0.0	0.0	0.0
Inflation[1]	0.0	0.0	0.1	0.1	0.1	0.0	0.0
Net exports[2]	0.0	0.1	0.1	0.0	0.0	0.0	0.0
Rise in spending in the Euro Area							
United States							
Output gap	0.0	0.1	0.1	0.1	0.0	0.0	0.0
Inflation[1]	0.0	0.0	0.1	0.1	0.1	0.1	0.0
Net exports[2]	0.0	0.1	0.1	0.1	0.0	0.0	0.0
Euro Area							
Output gap	1.2	0.7	0.9	0.8	0.1	−0.1	−0.1
Inflation[1]	0.1	0.2	0.3	0.5	0.6	0.5	0.4
Net exports[2]	−0.4	−0.2	−0.3	−0.2	−0.1	−0.1	−0.1
Japan							
Output gap	0.1	0.0	0.1	0.1	0.0	0.0	0.0
Inflation[1]	0.0	0.0	0.1	0.1	0.1	0.0	0.0
Net exports[2]	0.1	0.0	0.0	0.0	0.0	0.0	0.0
Rise in spending in Japan							
United States							
Output gap	0.0	0.0	0.0	0.0	0.0	0.0	0.0
Inflation[1]	0.0	0.0	0.1	0.1	0.1	0.0	0.0
Net exports[2]	0.0	0.0	0.0	0.0	0.0	0.0	0.0
Euro Area							
Output gap	0.0	0.0	0.0	0.0	0.0	0.0	0.0
Inflation[1]	0.0	0.0	0.0	0.1	0.1	0.0	0.0
Net exports[2]	0.0	0.0	0.0	0.0	0.0	0.0	0.0
Japan							
Output gap	0.6	1.3	0.4	0.5	0.3	0.1	0.0
Inflation[1]	0.0	0.1	0.3	0.3	0.3	0.2	0.2
Net exports[2]	−0.1	−0.2	−0.1	−0.1	−0.1	−0.1	−0.1

Authors' calculations. – [1]Annual rate of headline inflation. – [2]As a percent of potential output.

Table 8

Impact of an exchange rate depreciation

Permanent ten percent nominal depreciation; deviations from baseline in percent

	Quarters after shock						
	1	2	3	4	8	12	16
Depreciation of the United States Dollar							
United States							
Output gap	0.1	0.2	0.3	0.4	0.5	0.5	0.4
Inflation[1]	0.1	0.2	0.4	0.5	0.8	1.0	1.1
Net exports[2]	0.1	0.2	0.3	0.3	0.5	0.5	0.4
Euro Area							
Output gap	0.0	0.0	0.0	0.0	0.0	0.0	0.0
Inflation[1]	−0.1	−0.3	−0.4	−0.6	0.0	0.0	−0.1
Net exports[2]	0.0	0.0	0.0	0.0	0.0	0.0	0.0
Japan							
Output gap	0.0	−0.1	−0.1	−0.1	−0.2	−0.2	−0.1
Inflation[1]	−0.2	−0.4	−0.6	−0.7	−0.2	−0.1	−0.1
Net exports[2]	0.0	−0.1	−0.1	−0.1	−0.1	−0.1	−0.1
Depreciation of the Euro							
United States							
Output gap	0.0	0.0	0.0	0.0	−0.1	−0.1	0.0
Inflation[1]	0.0	0.0	0.0	0.0	0.1	0.0	−0.1
Net exports[2]	0.0	0.0	0.0	0.0	0.0	0.0	0.0
Euro Area							
Output gap	0.2	0.3	0.3	0.4	0.6	0.5	0.4
Inflation[1]	0.1	0.4	0.7	1.2	1.2	1.4	1.5
Net exports[2]	0.2	0.2	0.3	0.3	0.5	0.5	0.4
Japan							
Output gap	0.0	0.0	−0.1	−0.1	−0.1	−0.1	−0.1
Inflation[1]	0.0	0.0	0.0	0.0	0.1	0.0	−0.1
Net exports[2]	0.0	0.0	0.0	−0.1	−0.1	−0.1	−0.1
Depreciation of the Yen							
United States							
Output gap	0.0	0.0	0.0	0.0	−0.1	0.0	0.0
Inflation[1]	0.0	0.0	0.0	0.0	0.0	−0.1	−0.1
Net exports[2]	0.0	0.0	0.0	0.0	−0.1	0.0	0.0
Euro Area							
Output gap	0.0	0.0	0.0	0.0	0.0	0.0	0.0
Inflation[1]	0.0	0.0	0.0	0.0	0.0	−0.1	−0.1
Net exports[2]	0.0	0.0	0.0	0.0	0.0	0.0	0.0
Japan							
Output gap	0.1	0.2	0.3	0.5	0.8	0.9	0.7
Inflation[1]	0.3	0.5	0.9	1.0	0.6	0.6	0.7
Net exports[2]	0.1	0.2	0.3	0.4	0.6	0.7	0.6

Authors' calculations. – [1]Annual rate of headline inflation. – [2]As a percent of potential output.

Appendix – Data Definitions

All data is quarterly, seasonally adjusted, and is based on the OECD's Analytic Database (ADB). The euro area volume aggregates are calculated by aggregating the growth rates of individual countries, weighted by the previous period's share of nominal GDP at current exchange rates. Euro area financial aggregates are weighted averages of the levels of country variables, using the same GDP weights as above. A detailed description of ADB data can be found on the OECD's web site at www.oecd.org/eco(data/eoinv.pdf. A description of variables by category is given below (ADB mnemonics are in capitals).

Inflation, prices, exchange rates

Core inflation	$\pi = 100.\,\Delta\log(coreCPI)$
Core CPI	CPI excluding food and energy. Source: Main Economic Indicators (MEI)
Headline CPI	CPI all items, seasonally adjusted. Source: MEI. Euro area CPI is the harmonised CPI index from 1995, non-harmonised before that.
Import prices	π^{imp} = rate of change of implicit deflator for imports of manufactures and services, where the deflator has been detrended from 1980 using a time trend.
Weight on import prices	ω = (MM+MSR)/(GDP+MM+MSR) where MM and MSR are imports of manufactures and services respectively.
Commodity prices	WPHD: primary commodities excl. energy, world price, HWWA-index US-$
Weight on commodity prices	Weight of manufacturing output in GDP.
Oil prices	WPOIL: OECD crude oil import price, cif, US$ per barrel
Weight on oil prices	ν = oil intensity in output = production plus imports of oil relative to GDP. Source: OECD Energy Yearbook.
OECD Inflation	GDP weighted average of OECD consumer price inflation, excluding high inflation countries.
Real exchange rate	rer = log real exchange rate (CPIDR) based on relative CPIs. Weights based on manufacturing exports adjusting for third-country competitors. Euro area weights exclude intra-euro trade.

Output and Spending

Domestic demand gap	$ddgap$ = 100.(TDDV/GDPVTR-1) where TDDV is domestic demand and GDPVTR is potential output (both in volume terms).
Net export gap	$xmgap$ = 100.(XGSV-MGSV)/GDPVTR, where XGSV and MGSV are exports and imports of goods and services, volume, respectively.
Output gap	$ygap$ = 100.(GDPV/GDPVTR-1).
Government spending	$gspend$ = 100.(CGV+IGV)/GDPVTR
Government revenue	$grev$ = NLGQA + $gspend$, where NLGQA is the cyclically adjusted general government balance.
World gap and rest of world gap	$wldgap$ = GDP weighted world output gap. Based on Secretariat's estimates of output gaps for OECD members. The gap for the rest of the world is based on taking a Hodrick Prescott filter through an aggregate of rest-of-the-world GDP.
Relative gap	$relgap$ = $ddgap$ – foreign $ddgap$, where the foreign $ddgap$ is a trade weighted average of foreign domestic demand gaps.

Interest Rates

Short-term interest rate	IRS
Long-term interest rate	IRL
Real long-term interest rate (domestic demand eqn)	r = IRL – π^e where π^e is inflation expectations, proxied by very smooth Hodrick Prescott filter through actual inflation ($\lambda = 20{,}000$).
Real short-term interest rate (policy rule)	IRS - annual core inflation rate.

Other

US Sharemarket wealth	US household sharemarket wealth relative to disposable income. Wealth source: US Federal Reserve Board Flow of Funds Table L100.
Japanese land prices	Japanese urban land price index. Source: Japan real estate institute.

References

Ball, L. (1998), Policy Rules for Open Economies. Reserve Bank of Australia Research Discussion Paper 1998-06. Sydney.

Beechey, M., N. Bharucha, A. Cagliarini, D. Gruen and C. Thompson (2000), A Small Model of the Australian Macroeconomy. Reserve Bank of Australia Research Discussion Paper 2000-05. Sydney.

Bharucha, N. and C. Kent (1998), Inflation Targeting in a Small Open Economy. Reserve Bank of Australia Research Discussion Paper 1998-07. Sydney.

Coenen, G. and V. Wieland (2000), A Small Estimated Euro Area Model with Rational Expectations and Nominal Rigidities. ECB Working Paper 30. ECB, Frankfurt.

De Brouwer, G. and L. Ellis (1998), Forward-Looking Behaviour and Credibility: Some Evidence and Implications for Policy. Reserve Bank of Australia Research Discussion Paper 1998-03. Sydney.

Duguay, P. (1994), Empirical Evidence on the Strength of the Monetary Transmission Mechanism in Canada: An Aggregate Approach. *Journal of Monetary Economics* 33: 39–61.

Fair, R.C. (2000), Estimated, Calibrated, and Optimal Interest Rate Rules. http://fairmodel.econ.yale.edu/rayfair/pdf/1999D.PDF.

Giorno, C., P. Richardson, D. Roseveare and P. Van Den Noord (1995), Potential Output, Output Gaps and Structural Budget Balances. *OECD Economic Studies* 1995 (1): 167–209.

Hall, S.G. and J.D. Whitley (1999), *Linkages between Countries in International Models.* Unpublished.

Hargreaves, D. (1999), SDS-FPS: A Small Demand-side Version of the Forecasting and Policy System Core Model. Reserve Bank of New Zealand Discussion Paper G99/10. Reserve Bank of New Zealand, Wellington.

Hooker, M. (1999), Are Oil Shocks Inflationary? Asymmetric and Nonlinear Specifications versus Changes in Regime. Finance and Economics Discussion Paper 1999-65. Board of Governors of the Federal Reserve System, Washington, DC.

Meredith, G. (1997), *Effect of Equity Prices on Aggregate Demand.* Unpublished IMF Office Memorandum.

Murata, K., D. Turner, D. Rae and L. Le Fouler (2000), Modelling Manufacturing Export Volumes Equations – A System Estimation Approach. OECD Working Paper 235. OECD, Paris.

Richardson, P., L. Boone, C. Giorno, M. Meacci, D. Rae and D. Turner (2000), The Concept, Policy Use and Measurement of Structural Unemployment: Estimating a Time Varying NAIRU across 21 OECD Countries. OECD Working Paper 250. OECD, Paris.

Rudebusch, G. (1999), *Is the Fed Too Timid? Monetary Policy in an Uncertain World.* Federal Reserve Bank of San Francisco, mimeo.

Smets, F. (1998), Output Gap Uncertainty – Does it Matter for the Taylor Rule? BIS Working Paper 60. BIS, Basle.

Stiglitz, J. (1997), Reflections on the Natural Rate Hypothesis. *Journal of Economic Perspectives* 11(1): 3–10.

Turner, D. and E. Seghezza (1999), Testing for a Common OECD Phillips Curve. OECD Working Paper 219. OECD, Paris.

Gabriel Fagan, Jérôme Henry, and Ricardo Mestre

Structural Modelling of the Euro Area[1]

The econometric work on the euro area has already a long history at the European Central Bank. Indeed, much inspiration has been drawn from the analyses made ahead of monetary union by the European Monetary Institute (see e.g. EMI 1997), which indicated that the ECB would require a comprehensive econometric infrastructure. In order to meet this need in a timely way, given the standard and well-known lead times involved in the process of model-building, related work had therefore to start quite early (even before knowing precisely the country composition of the euro area). The first efforts, already at the EMI times, mostly concentrated on data collection for the EU countries and on tests on aggregation of country data. Estimation and simulation tasks conducted afterwards also implied successive rounds of amendments to the data and the model before publication of the first results obtained could be considered – see Fagan et al. (2001).

In line with suggestions made at the EMI times, the modelling of the euro area conducted at the ECB aims at producing a „suite of models", since, in principle, a variety of models would be better suited to address issues of different nature. In this respect, the type of models that were considered useful ranged from time-series ones – univariate, multivariate, trend-cycle, dynamic factor models – to structural models of various size, various country coverage, and various degree of disaggregation.

This objective has to be considered in a quite specific context, where issues to be faced go beyond those met when modelling single countries in isolation. In particular, aggregation across countries with possibly differing behaviour and conceptual data definitions is not a trivial issue. Another issue arises from the fact that structural breaks around the onset of EMU are more likely to occur than in other periods, so that the stability of relations estimated on past behaviour may be a less reliable feature than is normally the case.

---

[1] The opinions expressed in this paper are solely those of the authors and do not necessarily represent those of the ECB.

Against this background, this paper presents an overview of the work on the models which have been developed over the recent years by ECB staff, with a particular focus on the structural modelling of the euro area. In the first section, the history of modelling activities at the EMI and at the ECB is recalled, with a particular emphasis on the approach followed and the various tools developed/being developed. The second section concentrates on a illustration of this approach, based on the Area Wide Model (Fagan et al. 2001), presenting its structure, the key parameters, and how the model works in terms of both its long run steady state and the dynamic adjustement to it following a shock. Finally, the third section concludes and mentions further work to be envisaged on such models.

1. The story underlying the history of euro-area modelling at the ECB

It was mentioned early enough that, as a new central bank, the ECB should have at its disposal a refined econometric infrastructure, comprising in particular structural macro models for the euro area. For instance, the published EMI Report (1997) on the strategy for the single monetary policy put some clear emphasis on the need for such work to be conducted. Such tools were deemed necessary for tasks such as forecasting and the analysis of the „transmission mechanism" for the single currency area. Therefore, those tools would provide help to decision-making at the area level.

1.1 A specifically challenging context

When trying to cope with such a recommendation, EMI and later ECB modellers had to face a quite specific context, in terms of both data and economic issues. First, as regard data, measures of economic variables have not always been – and are still not fully – based on harmonised concepts across countries now constituting the euro area. Second, from a more purely economic standpoint, the heterogeneity of behaviour across countries may also complicate the understanding of the mechanisms driving the euro area as a whole.

In addition, econometric work on euro area data is likely to a particular extent to be affected by „structural" change. A first, albeit mechanical, example of such structural change relates to the number of new definitions that are employed for a number of key variables, the definition of which had to be changed because of the monetary union, such as money stocks (the ECB euro area new aggregates) and similarly the new Balance of Payments statistics. In addition, other series have been harmonised, such as the key consumer price indices (the Eurostat HICP), and also those affected by the overall changeover to a new system of National Accounts (the Eurostat ESA95). More fundamentally, from an economic viewpoint, monetary union is expected to also affect underlying behaviour, since a new central bank is created, implementing a new and single monetary policy for the whole area. This could have implications on the functioning of financial markets, on responses of agents to interest rate changes, on formation of expectations, etc.[2]

1.2 A suite of models, with priority on structural models

As a result of the above mentioned considerations, it was felt that a flexible framework was needed, in terms of data, country coverage, and also functions of models. Ideally, a „suite" of models would be constructed and become available, in the vein of e.g. the Bank of England approach, whereby specific tools could be built and used for specific purposes. Along these lines of thought, simple uni- or multi-variate time series models could first be used for forecasting. In addition, some more economic structure could be embedded in such models by resorting to Vector ECMs. Further, with a view to refining the policy analysis, small size macro models would be employed. Finally, at the end of this spectrum of econometric tools, medium size structural macro models would be designed and run to carry out policy analysis simulations and also back forecasts with an economic "story" consistent with recognised standard economic relations.

However, some prioritisation had to be defined, which led to priority being given to medium size structural models (such as the AWM, see Fagan et al. 2001). A number of reasons explain that. First, such modelling work clearly implies long lead times – in terms of data collection, estimation, test simulations, respecificaiton, etc. Second, there was a clear favourable spillover of database building on to other activities, by making the model data base available for other empirical work. Third, such models were thought to have a potential to understand and describe the transmission mechanism. Finally, the structure of such models is usually rich enough to document a forecast or a simulation with a sufficient degree of realistic detail whereas smaller models, albeit illustrative are not as useful in this respect.

In order to produce tools that could be employed in time, a number of early moves had to be made. First, as regard data, compilation of the database started as early as in 1996. Of course, at the time the list of EMU members was not yet known, hence the need to prepare data construction and aggregation routines that would work for any final list of participating countries, with no restriction ex ante. Second, alternative aggregation methodes were programmed, tested and compared (levels vs. indices / time-varying vs. fixed weights / simple sum with fixed vs. current exchange rates, etc.). The first product addressing those issues, namely a money demand study (Fagan, Henry 1998), could therefore be considered as our starting point for structural euro

---

[2] The approach followed is further documented in Henry 1999.

area modelling. Third, other central bank modellers, from both North America and Europe, were consulted to gather ideas on the appropriate specification for a euro area model, given the constraints faced.

1.3 Two structural models, the AWM and the MCM, supplemented with other tools

A number of econometric tools have been developed by ECB staff, among which structural models for the euro area as a whole or for the largest countries of the area, supplemented with a number of smaller size econometric tools. In most cases, research is still on-going on the devlopment of those various tools, and only some of the work has been published to date.

A first example of this modelling work is the AWM (cf. Fagan et al. 2001), which treats the whole of the euro area as a single economy. This quarterly model comprises 89 equations, of which 15 are behavioural – with mostly estimated and sometimes calibrated parameters. The sample period over which the estimation has been carried out spans over 1970 to 1998. The corresponding database – an original construction given the lack of official backdata for the euro area – is available on the ECB website.

Another example of such work is the ECB contribution to the construction of a quarterly multi country model (MCM) in collaboration with the National Central Banks of the ESCB. As the name indicates, this model will comprise models for each of the countries in the euro area, which then could be reconstructed by aggregation of those. In addition a trade link block is being developed at the ECB to connect the various countries when simulating the various country models jointly. Each of the country block is similar in size and structure to the the the AWM.[3] The period used for estimation at the ECB covers the sample 1980 to 1997.

In addition to these two examples of medium size structural macroeconometric models, a number of other ECB researchers have been working on a variety of projects. In some cases work is still in progress so that no publication has been undertaken. This is so, e.g. for time series models for both monthly and quarterly inflation forecasts, with a particular emphasis on the HICP. There are however other publications available which present work already well advanced on alternative tools. Starting from the less to the most structural models, a dynamic factor model for trend inflation and inflation forecasts is presented in Angelini et al. (2001a, 2001b). Different VARs based on standard money demand system (comprising money, inflation, interest rates, GDP) are documented in Coenen/Vega (1999), Brand/Cassola (2000) and such models can be used for forecasting purposes, as in Trecoci/Vega (2000) and Nicoletti

---

[3] The Central Bank of Ireland (see Mc Guire, Ryan 2000) and the National Bank of Belgium (see Jeanfils 2000) have already published material on their own contribution to the MCM.

Altimari (2001). Finally, small theoretical tools that are particularly tuned for dealing with monetary policy issues have been calibrated / estimated, an example of this approach being Coenen/Wieland (2000).

In view of this emerging literature, there seems to be two characteristic features. First, in spite of obvious difficulties, estimation techniques have been used mostly rather than calibration methods. Second, the implicit hypothesis whereby aggregation of countries would not deliver unplausible results at the area level seems to hold, although this appreacition may still be deemed controversial somewhat, see e.g. the discussions in Arnold (1996) and Fagan/Henry (1998) for the pros and cons of the aggregation across countries.

2. An illustration of the approach: the AWM[4]

2.1 The AWM Basic structure

The structure of the AWM is that of a standard structural macromodel, namely a long-run classical equilibrium with a vertical Phillips curve, with moreover some frictional and transitory Keynesian features in the short-run dynamics of the model. As a result, activity is determined in the short run by demand, since prices and wages do not adjust immediately to their long-run equilibrium levels. In the longer run, output is supply determined, employment having converged to a level consistent with the exogenously given level of equilibrium unemployment rate – which does not depend on interest rates. In addition, stock-flow adjustments are accounted for, e.g. by the inclusion of a wealth / cumulated saving term in the consumption equation. In all these respects, the model is fairly similar to those employed in e.g. the US Fed or the Bank of Canada. An importance difference in comparison with the latter two models is the treatment of expectations, which, albeit explicit, are strictly backward-looking in the Fagan et al. (2001) version of the model. However, the model can be adapted in a straightforward manner to incorporate forward-looking expectations in, in particular, price and wage behaviour.

Box 1 presents a simplified overview of the structure of the model, where only some stylised equations for key variables are reported and quickly described. Variables with a bar are exogenous (L^s labour force, G government consumption, Y_w world demand, P_w world prices). For behavioural equations, = sign is used, whereas other equations are accounting identities. The complete AWM framework comprises also additional variables such as a system of demand deflators, simplified accounts for households and the public sector – comprising in particular interest payments and income from profits, a limited number of items from the balance of payments, etc.

---

[4] This section is largely based on Fagan et al. 2001.

Box 1

A stylised overview of the AWM

Supply side	
$K \equiv (1-\delta)K_{-1} + I$	K CAPITAL stock accumulation, δ depreciation rate
$I = I(Y,r)$	I INVESTMENT classical function
$Ypot \equiv (1-\beta)K + \beta \overline{L}^S + Trend$	$Ypot$ POTENTIAL OUTPUT production function, β wage share
$Ogap \equiv Y / Ypot$	$Ogap$ OUTPUT GAP definition
$L = L(Y / Trend, K)$	L LABOUR inverted production function
$W = W(P / Trend, U)$	W WAGES function of productivity and unemployment
$U \equiv (\overline{L}^S - L) / \overline{L}^S$	U UNEMPLOYMENT definition
$P \equiv P(W / Trend, Ogap)$	P PRICES mark up on unit labour costs

Demand components (other than investment)	
$Y \equiv C + I + \overline{G} + X - M$	Y GDP definition
$X = X(\overline{Y}_w, P / e\overline{P}_w)$	X EXPORTS market share function of competiveness
$M = M(Y, P / e\overline{P}_w)$	M IMPORTS market share function of competitiveness
$C = C(Y_d, A)$	C CONSUMPTION income and wealth function
$Y_d \equiv W.L(1-t)$	Y_d INCOME – disposable, i.e. net of taxes, t tax rate
$dY \equiv t.Y - \overline{G}$	d DEFICIT in GDP pp's
$A - A_{-1} \equiv X - M + dY + I - \delta K_{-1}$	A WEALTH foreign assets + public debt + capital stock

Monetary side	
$\overline{M} = M^d(P.Y, IN)$	M^d MONEY DEMAND income and interest rate function
$r \equiv IN - \Delta P$	r REAL INTEREST RATE definition

In all cases, this theoretical framework has been used to estimate the model, estimations being based on ECM specifications reflecting those long-run relations. In general unrestricted short-run dynamics were employed – unless dynamic homogeneity was required e.g. in the wage dynamic equation to ensure there is no long-run unemployment/inflation trade off.

The employed framework permits some degree of flexibility of the framework as to policy modelling. As regards e.g. fiscal policy, taxes can adjust so as to ensure an exogenously fixed deficit to GDP ratio (as e.g. in Box 1). Alternatively tax rates can be set exogenous so that public deficit becomes endogenous. Also other fiscal rules can be considered, our preferred option being to express the changes in direct taxes levied on households as a function of the deviation of the debt to GDP ratio from its target (cf. Mitchell et al. 2000).

With respect to monetary policy, a number of alternative frameworks are also embedded in this model, e.g. the stock of money can be exogenously controlled, the inverted money demand function delivering the corresponding interest rate. Alternatively, the nominal interest rate can be set endogenously via an additional equation, namely a reaction function, so that money supply would then become endogenous, adjusting automatically to money demand. In particular a simple Taylor (1993) rule can be employed so as to assess the properties of the model in a standard environment.

As already mentioned, a key additional element is that the treatment of expectations in the full model is also flexible. Backward- or forward-looking specifications can be implemented with low „switching costs", by e.g. incorporating in the wage and price dynamics an explicit term in inflation expectations – which then can be assumed alternatively to be exogenous, backward-looking or forward-looking, with a specification very similar to e.g. Gerlach/Svensson (2000). In addition, a forward-looking exchange rate equation – on the basis of a standard UIP condition – can also be simulated along with the above mentioned set of equations, so that the resulting path of the economy would be sensitive to information on expected future interest rates.

2.2 Long run solution of the model: stylised facts

Although simplified, the version of the model reported in Box 1 suffices to describe with a relative degree of detail how the model can be solved, and what is the long-run solution to it. The supply, demand and monetary side are described in turn.

2.2.1 Supply side

Under the assumption that real interest rates are given, the capital to output ratio is then fixed (and so is the investment to output ratio). At equilibrium, moreover, both the output gap and the unemployment gaps are closed – via mechanisms to be described in the following section. Employment therefore equals the labour supply consistent with the exogenously given equilibrium unemployment rate – which is assumed to be 0 in Box 1, for simplicity.[5]

Under such conditions, and given the production function, the level of output is jointly given by the capital output ratio and the level of employment. In turn, the level of the capital stock can then determined. In addition, since unemployment reaches its long run level, the real wage has to equal labour trend productivity, so that the wage share in GDP-income is constant, in line with the assumption made of a Cobb Douglas production function. Both wages and prices share the same long-run restriction expressed in terms of a constant wage share.

2.2.2 Demand side

Since the equilibrium is supply-side determined, total aggregate demand has to adjust in its various components so that $Y^s = Y^d$, the investment and capital

---

[5] Details on computations employed to derive a time-varying equilibrium rate of unemployment for the euro area can be found in Fabiani/Mestre (2000), the AWM approach being that of Gordon (1997).

to GDP ratio being already pinned down by the real interest rate. Assume moreover that public debt is also at its equilibrium (desired) value in GDP points, so that the wealth held by consumers A has then only one unknown component, namely net foreign assets – the capital stock being already determined by the supply side.

Solving the demand side of the system (GDP identity, consumption function, trade volumes, wealth accumulation) for a given level of supply then leads to a relation between the real exchange rate and the real interest rate. Expressing all variables in GDP ratios, since at steady state the ratio foreign asset to GDP (denoted a) is constant, the following system obtains. It comprises 4 variables, trade balance, consumption, real exchange rate and net foreign assets (tb, c, R, a), with 4 bilateral relations, involving the real interest rate r:

$$
\begin{cases}
c \equiv 1 - tb - c_0(r) & \text{GDP identity, investment decreasing with r} \\
c = \gamma\alpha - \gamma_0(r) & \text{Consumption function with wealth effects, capital stock decreasing with r} \\
tb = -\tau R & \text{Net trade as a function of the real exchange rate, } \tau \text{ price elasticity} \\
tb = \alpha a - \alpha_0 & \text{Zero accumulation of foreign assets, } \alpha \text{ rate of return on the latter}
\end{cases}
$$

Solving for the foreign asset to GDP ratio and re-arranging leads to the following steady state expressions:

$$
\begin{cases}
a = \dfrac{1 + \alpha_0 - c_0(r) + \gamma_0(r)}{\gamma - \alpha} \\
c = \gamma a - \gamma_0(r) \\
tb \equiv \alpha a - \alpha_0 \\
R = \dfrac{\alpha a + \alpha_0}{\tau}
\end{cases}
$$

It then becomes clear that at steady state, an equilibrium relation appear between the real interest rate and the real exchange rate, through the interaction between trade, foreign asset accumulation and the wealth effect in private consumption. In case of a non-zero growth rate at steady state, however, the relation between trade balance, current account and net foreign asset would be less straightforward – however for our purpose, such an illustrative solution of the demand side is sufficient to understand the mechanisms at work in the model.

2.2.3 Monetary side

Turning to the monetary block, an additional assumption is needed to go beyond the above mentioned unique relation between real interest rates and real exchange rates. Assume e.g. that UIP holds, so that the change in nominal exchange rate equals the interest rate differential. It is then straightforward to check that, in order for the real exchange rate to reach some constant equilibrium value, the domestic real interest rate has in turn to be equal to the foreign one. As a result, the nominal exchange rate may have to continuously adjust to ensure PPP, the drift being exactly equal to the gap between domestic and external inflation (or similarly between the corresponding interest rates).

The long run of such a model determines however relative prices – and real magnitudes – but not the overall level of prices which has to be determined by some nominal anchor. Technically, a number of possibilities could be employed to achieve that goal.

First, under strict monetary targeting the long run price level would be given by the equilibrium condition for the demand for real money balances along with an exogenously fixed nominal money supply. Since the nominal money stock controlled by monetary policy pins down the price level, the nominal exchange rate has to adjust – given exogenous foreign prices – to ensure equilibrium between supply and demand.

Second, in case where short term interest rates were to depend on deviations of inflation or the price level from a given central bank's objective, the price level would be pinned down in the long run by the price objective. Again, since the domestic price level is pinned down, the nominal exchange rate would need to adjust. In case of an interest rate setting rule not explicitly taking into account the price level, the terminal price level would depend not only on the inflation objective, but also on initial conditions.

Third, under fixed nominal exchange rates, the level of prices would be pinned down by foreign prices in the long run. The steady state real exchange rate being given by the real side as discussed above, the (fixed) nominal exchange rate and exogenous foreign prices then determine the domestic price level consistent with real equilibrium. This latter configuration is however not relevant for a large and relatively close economy such as the euro area.

2.3 Long-run and short-run properties of some of the key equations

On the basis of the estimations conducted, some evidence of cointegration – although less than found in studies for euro area money demand – was found among the euro area variables defining the long-run of many equations. To some extent, these findings show that the theoretical long run restrictions, which were imposed a priori, were roughly consistent with the euro area data. All in all, there was moreover only a limited need for calibration since quite sensible parameter values were found. On the other hand, as evidenced by the generally low estimated ECM term, the speed of convergence to the implied long run of the equations is slow. This may come from behavioural heteroge-

Table 1

Responses of key variables to 10 % shocks on their determinants

	1 year	2 years	5 years	10 years	t-ECM
Employment					–4.7
Output	4.4	8.3	14.2	17.0	
Real wages	–1.8	–1.5	–0.6	–0.1	
Investment					–1.8
Output	10.0	9.9	9.0	6.3	
Real user cost of capital[1]	–0.5	–1.7	–5.3	–9.9	
Consumption deflator					–3.0
GDP deflator	6.4	8.7	9.4	9.4	
Import prices	0.8	1.0	0.8	0.6	
GDP deflator					–3.3
Unit labour costs	4.3	6.2	7.8	9.2	
Consumption					–3.3
Income	7.7	7.7	7.9	7.9	
Wealth	0.2	0.6	1.3	1.8	
Export volume					–2.6
World demand	10.0	10.0	10.0	10.0	
Competitiveness	4.8	8.9	8.7	8.0	
Import volume					–3.1
Domestic demand	19.8	16.8	11.6	10.4	
Competitiveness	–0.3	–1.1	–2.1	–2.6	
Export prices					–3.2
External prices	0.2	0.6	1.6	2.4	
Domestic prices	8.6	9.0	8.1	7.4	
Import prices					–2.0
External prices	2.7	2.6	1.8	1.2	
Domestic prices	4.4	5.3	5.8	6.2	

Authors' calculations. – [1]100 basis points to the real interest rate.

neity across countries or, perhaps, from the lack of variability – hence of information – contained in the aggregated euro area data.

Table 1 presents some of the key long-run and short-run responses to shocks for most of the behavioural equations in Box 1, supplemented with some additional information on other equations, such as those for deflators other than the one for GDP. Full details on estimation results are otherwise provided in an appendix to Fagan et al. (2001).

2.4 Adjustment to equilibrium and short-run mechanisms: an illustration

As to their short-run behaviour, prices and wages do not adjust instantaneously, hence the short-run equilibrium for output is demand-determined. As a result, transitory disequilibria appear in both goods and labour markets. In order to restore equilibrium, a number of mechanisms operate, involving disequilibrium terms and policy responses.

Assume for illustration purposes that the model is supplemented with a forward-looking UIP condition, a Taylor rule and a fiscal rule. The main mechanisms are then as follows (taking the example of a positive aggregate demand shock):

First, the shock mechanically increases output and employment, leading therefore to an increase in inflation via the Phillips curve. This triggers a rise in real short-term interest rates, since both arguments in the Taylor rule are deviating from their equilibrium or long-run values. This puts downward pressure on domestic demand, by weakening investment and therefore aggregate demand.

Second, some external channel will operate too, although limited it might be, for a relatively closed economy. In line with the expected change in interest rates, the UIP condition would lead to an initial jump in nominal exchange rate. There would be ceteris paribus an appreciation of the real exchange rate, therefore exerting downward pressures on both prices (via diminished imported inflation) and demand (via lower net trade and also lower net foreign assets).

Third, this initial nominal and real appreciation is reinforced by a further real appreciation and a crowding out via net trade caused by the additional inflation and growth resulting from the shock per se. First, the additional inflation induces a real appreciation of the exchange rate, which would tend to weaken net trade and, in part, offset the initial increase in output. Second, increased demand would boost imports, leading to a further weakening of trade contribution to growth.

Fourth, the "automatic stabilisers" of fiscal policy imply in the case at hand that transfers to households should fall on foot of lower unemployment, helping to further dampen the growth of disposable income. In addition, in the case where the shock emanated from a fiscal expansion, the fiscal solvency rule gradually "kicks-in" and the rise in direct taxes also dampens demand.

As an illustration we report one simulation to document the impact of the various adjustement mechanisms that are at play. In that exercise, a shock to public consumption amounting to 1% GDP is assumed. The shock is permanent – with monetary policy response and endogenous forward-looking exchange rate.

As can be seen in Figure 1, there is a positive response of GDP to the fiscal stimulus, with a multiplier however remaining small (close to one only the first year) and short lived (negative impact after 5 years). The various crowding out mechanisms tend to counteract the initial positive shock to demand, namely

Gabriel Fagan, Jérôme Henry, and Ricardo Mestre

Figure 1

Impact on GDP and prices of a permanent increase in real public consumption
deviation from baseline in %

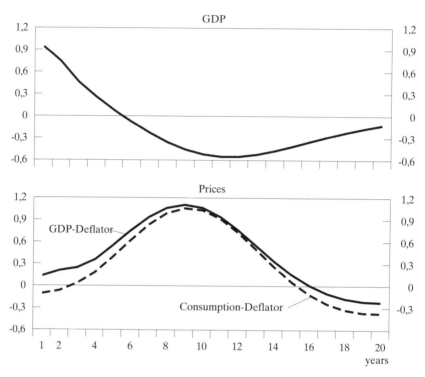

Authors' calculations. Explanations see text.

the competitiveness, fiscal stabilisers, and monetary policy response, as above mentioned. In particular, monetary policy has an effect on net trade through the initial appreciation in the exchange rate – reflecting future increases in the interest rate. Also investment is dampened by the impact of the changes in interest rates. Beyond the one year horizon, fiscal policy also adjusts, via taxes to ensure that the debt target is met, so that consumption is also affected. In addition, the price level albeit lower than baseline initially – thanks to the appreciation of the currency – very quicly increases beyond the baseline level, remaining higher than the latter for a substantial number of years. Inflation remains higher than baseline until about 8 years for both the GDP and consumption deflators. Eventually, let alone some cyclical fluctuations, inflation and the GDP level are consistent with their baseline values, both unemployment and output gaps being closed and the additional public demand compensated by other demand components being lower.

2.5 Evaluation and use of the model

Prior to finalising the published version, the model had been regularly evaluated, mostly via diagnostic simulations. Successive versions were tested, comparing the corresponding simulation results with a number of single country or multi country models. This led to successive rounds of respecification and additional and / or changed calibration for some of the parameters – such as e.g. the role of expectations in price and wage behaviour.

In its present version, the model can be used for a number of purposes, making the most of the flexibility of the framework. Diagnostic simulations are carried out, in and out of sample experiments, involving permanent or temporary shocks, both with respect to historical and steady state baseline, using either forward or backward looking formulations. Similarly, the simulation environment can be defined alternatively with endogenous or exogenous real interest rates, endogenous or exogenous nominal exchange rate, endogenous or exogenous fiscal policy variables. Shocks that could be analysed with the model affect public expenditure, world demand, world prices, exchange rate, interest rate, taxes, etc. Stochastic simulations can also be implemented with the model, as documented in Fagan et al. (2001).

3. Conclusions

A number of conclusions can be drawn from the experience already accumulated in terms of euro area structural econometric modelling:

- First of all, the investment, although quite heavy initially, appears worthwhile eventually, in view of the properties of the resulting model and also its potential use for a variety of purposes.

- Second, the new "object" which appeared in 1999, namely the „euro area" – strictly speaking the-countries-now-comprising-the-euro-area – is now better known. A first set of stylised facts can e.g. be derived from the estimation of standard relations on euro area data, which also contributes to focus the discussion on euro area level facts.

- Third, there are of course elements of uncertainty affecting those facts, that are clearly due to key factors, such as data quality and availability, structural change around EMU, the absence of long expertise, and also the issue of aggregation across a priori relatively heterogenous countries. The combination of country level analysis with the euro area one may there be a way forward.

- Fourth, a benchmark is now available, as against which to assess judgements. The process of modelling the euro area has only started; there is a clear need e.g. to systematically compare estimated standard behavioural equations based on synthetic euro-area data to those obtained on US or other countries' data.

- Fifth, more generally, such modelling work has to follow a continuous development and research process – already making plans for the next generation of our models, not having yet fully finalised the 1st one.

In any event, such structural models are only one among other tools, econometric or not, that can and have to be employed to assess the euro area economic situation.

References

Angelini, E., J. Henry and R. Mestre (2001a), A Multi-Country Trend Indicator for Euro Area Average Inflation: Computation and Properties. ECB Working Paper 60. European Central Bank, Frankfurt a.M.

Angelini, E., J. Henry and R. Mestre (2001b), Diffusion Index Based Inflation Forecast for the Euro Area. ECB Working Paper 61. European Central Bank, Frankfurt a.M.

Arnold, I. (1996), Money Demand Stability in the EMU: Lessons from the US. Working Paper. Nijenrode University.

Brand, C. and N. Cassola (2000), A Money Demand System for Euro Area M3. ECB Working Paper 39. European Central Bank, Frankfurt a.M.

Coenen, G. and J.-L. Vega (1999), The Demand for M3 in the Euro Area. ECB Working Paper 6. European Central Bank, Frankfurt a.M.

Coenen, G. and V. Wieland (2000), A Small Estimated Euro Area Model with Rational Expectations and Nominal Rigidities. ECB Working Paper 30. European Central Bank, Frankfurt a.M.

EMI (ed.) (1997), *The Single Monetary Policy in Stage Three: Elements of the Monetary Policy Strategy of the ESCB*. European Monetary Institute, Frankfurt a.M.

Fabiani, S. and R. Mestre (2000), Alternative Measures of the NAIRU in the Euro Area: Estimates and Assessment. ECB Working Paper 17. European Central Bank, Frankfurt a.M.

Fagan, G. and J. Henry (1998), Long Run Money Demand in the EU: Evidence for Area-Wide Aggregates. *Empirical Economics* 23 (3): 483–506.

Fagan G., J. Henry and R. Mestre (2001), An Area Wide Model (AWM) for the Euro Area. ECB Working Paper 42. European Central Bank, Frankfurt a.M.

Gerlach, S. and L. Svensson (2000), Money and Inflation in the Euro Area: A Case for Monetary Indicators? Mimeo, BIS, IIES, Basel, Stockholm.

Gordon, R. (1997), The Time-Varying NAIRU and its Implications for Economic Policy. *Journal of Economic Perspectives* 11 (1): 11–32.

Henry, J. (1999), Euro Area-Wide and Country Modelling at the Start of EMU. *Economic and Financial Modelling* 1999 (Autumn): 103–148.

Jeanfils, P. (2000), A Model with Explicit Expectations for Belgium. Working Paper 4. Banque Nationale de Belgique, Brussels.

Mc Guire, M. and M. Ryan (2000), Macroeconomic modelling developments in the Central Bank. Spring Bulletin. Central Bank of Ireland, Dublin.

Mitchell, P.R., J.E. Sault and K. Wallis (2000), Fiscal Policy Rules in Macroeconomic Models: Principles and Practices. *Economic Modelling* 13 (2): 169–184.

Nicoletti Altimari, S. (2001), Does Money Lead Inflation in the Euro Area? ECB Working Paper 63. European Central Bank, Frankfurt a.M.

Taylor, J.B. (1993), Discretion Versus Policy Rules in Practice. *Carnegie Rochester Conference Series on Public Policy* 39: 195–214.

Trecroci, C. and J.-L. Vega (2000), The Information Content of M3 for Future Inflation. ECB Working Paper 33. European Central Bank, Frankfurt a.M.

Jean Louis Brillet and Maria Dos Santos

The Consequences of EMU Entry for Spain and Portugal – Simulations Using the MacSim System

1. The model

We shall begin by a short description of the single country models, focusing on the originality of the two new countries. Then we shall describe, also shortly, the interactive system. A more detailed presentation of both single country behaviours and international interactions can be found in Augier et al. (1999).

1.1 Introduction

The Macsim package is based on a set of simplified models, associated with some of the main countries in the European Union. It brings together single-country mechanisms, including some financial elements, and international trade, represented by bilateral flows. It considers essentially the consequences of shocks, associated to fiscal and financial policies. For a single shock, the results will depend on the rules for determining the interest rate and the exchange rate, as well as the subset of countries belonging to the European Monetary Union.

The standard version of the model considers 6 countries: *France, Germany, Italy, Netherlands, Sweden, United Kingdom.*

In the present paper, simulations will use Spain and Portugal instead of Netherlands and Sweden. However, in our discussion on single country models, we shall consider tables for the whole set of 8 countries.

1.2 The single-country basic model

The single country model uses the structure of the MicroDMS model (Brillet 1997a) adding a few error correction mechanisms (Brillet 1997b). We have associated behaviours to the following concepts:

Figure 1
The single country model

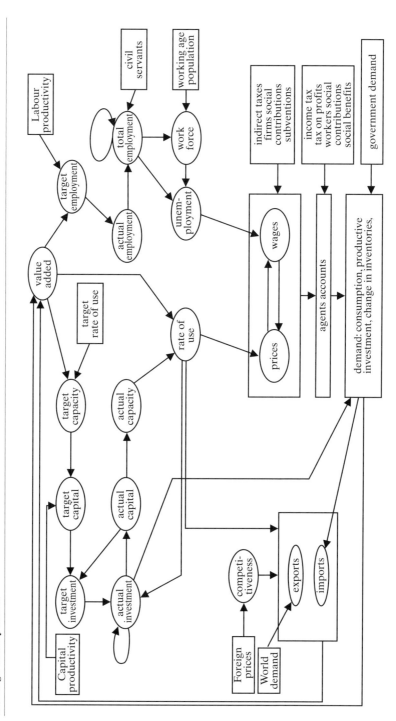

- Production factors: investment and employment, unemployment.
- Prices: wages, value added prices, export and import prices.
- Firms: Changes in inventories.
- Households: consumption.
- External trade: exports and imports.
- Interest rate: real exogenous value in the base version.
- Exchange rate: exogenous in the base version.

In all we shall estimate 11 equations per country. When country models are assembled, it is clear that some estimations concerning external trade will lead to over identifications, imports by one country being composed of exports by other countries, which introduces constraints on quantities and values exchanged. We shall present however the full set of equations, which were useful for testing individual models.

We shall now present the main behaviors, and the estimations for the eight countries selected.

1.2.1 Productive investment

$$i_t / k_{t-1} = c1 \cdot i_{t-1} / k_{t-2} + c2 \cdot \left[\left(q_t - q_{t-1} \right) / q_{t-1} + ut_t / 0.85 \right] + c3 \cdot tprob_t + c4. \quad (1)$$

We suppose here that firms set an investment target, depending on:

- the profits rate, representing both the expected profits on new investments, and the potential to finance them.
- a desire to adapt productive capacity at the next period to the expected demand. The last element implies the expected growth for the next period, but also the present adaptation of capacities to production.
- and that this process is affected by a strong inertia.

One can observe that the presence of the rate of use will ensure in the long run a full adaptation of capacity to production, at a level depending on the profitability of capital.

Results appear in table 1 (Appendix). If the lagged term and the "real" effect are almost always significant, the contribution of the profits rate shows often a poor quality. We have kept it nonetheless, and even fixed it for Italy.

1.2.2 Employment

We suppose that firms have a target labor productivity, associated with a structural trend. Knowing production this defines a target employment, to which actual employment adapts dynamically. Observing the graphs and using statistical breakpoint tests (such as the Chow or Perron tests) allows to identify two structural trends for labor productivity, with a negative break around 1973.

$$\Delta Log(le_t) = c1 \cdot \Delta Log(q_t) + c2 \cdot \left(Log(q_{t-1}/le_{t-1}) - c3 \cdot t - c4 \cdot t73 \right) + c5. \quad (2)$$

Where t73 is zero until 1972, then grows by 1 for each successive period. Results appear in table 2. They are always very significant, with rather similar results from one country to another (lower for Italy). The first coefficient (immediate response) is almost always higher, and our new countries present the highest values. The break is also identified for all countries.

1.2.3 Unemployment

The variations of employment do not translate fully into unemployment, as an improved employment situation will attract to the labour market previously inactive persons. The work force (employed + unemployed) will increase. As usual, we shall use an error correction framework.

$$\Delta cho_t = c1 \cdot \Delta le_t + c2 \cdot \Delta pop65_t + c3 \cdot \left(cho_{t-1} - c4 \cdot le_{t-1} - c5 \cdot pop65_{t-1} \right) - c6. \quad (3)$$

Results are presented in table 3. Results are generally good, with variable sensitivity to labor across countries. A little surprisingly, our two new countries present quite different short-term dynamics. While created jobs are mostly filled by the unemployed in Spain, they essentially increase the work force in Portugal.

1.2.4 The value added price

$$\Delta Log(pva_t) = c1 \cdot \Delta Log(c\sup_t) + c2 \cdot ut_t + c3 \cdot \left(Log(c\sup_{t-1}/pva_{t-1}) + c4 \right). \quad (4)$$

We suppose that firms use the price level to optimize between quantities sold (at a given capacity) and margins on each unit. This introduces a positive link between rate of use and margins. Going from one optimum to another due to changes in external conditions, firms will move both targets in the same direction. As usual, we shall apply an error-correction mechanism. Results are presented in table 4.

1.2.5 The trade prices

When defining their prices, exporters can take into account their own costs or the price of their competitors (in the same currency). The first behaviour will leave margins unchanged, but affect competitiveness. With the second behaviour, the reverse will happen. In our model, all exporters will apply both behaviors, but favour the first (70 % compared to 30 %). This is consistent with other models, whether single or multi-country. One can consider for instance INTERLINK (Richardson 1988), MIMOSA (MIMOSA Team 1997), or the models of the French administration (OFCE 1996).

1.2.6 The wage rate

$$\Delta Log(w_t) = c1 \cdot \Delta Log(pc_t) + c2 \cdot tcho_t + c4 + c3 \cdot Log(c\sup_{t-1} / pva_{t-1}). \quad (5)$$

The equation contains

- A dynamic indexation of the wage rate on inflation.
- A role of tensions on the labor market, represented by the unemployment rate.
- An error correction term, ensuring the convergence of the share of wages (actually, the wage cost) in production to a target, depending on the level of unemployment.

Results (table 5) are generally acceptable. But for our two additional countries, the error correction term is both low in value and not very significant. This will reduce the speed at which disequilibria on the price system will be reduced.

1.2.7 The changes in inventories

Firms try to maintain an inventory level proportional to production. This means changes in inventories will depend on changes in production. Based on the last two years, we get:

$$dstoc_t = c1 . \Delta q_t + c2 . \Delta q_{t-1}. \quad (6)$$

Results (table 6) are generally significant, with a rather stable coefficient. But for Spain, we had to fix it, as its estimated value was much too high, and quite unstable.

1.2.8 Household consumption

$$\Delta Log(co_t) = c1 \cdot \Delta Log(rdm_t / pc_t) + c2 \cdot [05 \Delta Log(pc_t) + 05 \Delta Log(pc_{t-1})] \quad (7)$$

$$+ c3 \cdot \Delta Log(tcho_t) + c4 \cdot Log[rdm_{t-1} / (pc_{t-1} \cdot co_{t-1})] + c5.$$

The formulation (error correcting) combines:

- Inertia in adapting to changes in purchasing power per capita.

- Inflation: financial savings are measured in (future) purchasing power, and must be increased with inflation.

- The fear of unemployment.

- A long term unitary elasticity of consumption to revenue.

Results (table 7) are on the whole rather satisfying, with our two new countries well within the range as to coefficient values. However the price effect is seldom significant, and had to be abandoned in three cases, including Spain.

1.2.9 Imports

Of course, particular attention must be given to this equation.

$$Log(m_t) = c1 \cdot Log(df_t \cdot ouv_t) + c2 \cdot Log(1 - ut_t) + c3 \cdot Log(pim_t / pp_t) + c4. \quad (8)$$

Imports are determined by:

- A constant elasticity to domestic demand, which we shall correct by the structural (smoothed) opening of borders. Actually we shall set this elasticity to 1.

- The capacity of local producers to face additional demand

- A comparison between local production and import prices.

Although this equation does not follow the error correction format, it is consistent with a long-term equilibrium. We can observe that it defines the share of imports in demand, as a function of terms that do reach a long-term target.

Results are presented in table 8. The capacity variable was seldom significant, but we have deemed its presence necessary, and set the same influence for all countries, to avoid not necessarily justified discrepancies. As to competitiveness, its coefficient is generally significant but rather low. One can observe that our two new countries present a rather low precision, and a high sensitivity to price competitiveness.

1.3 Integrating the financial variables

In the above version, the exchange rate and the real short-term interest rate are fixed, and the interest rates have almost no effect (only on the balances of agents). We shall now describe how we have given them a more important role, subject to a series of options. One will observe that some of the options have been chosen with European Monetary Union in mind.

1.3.1 The options for the interest rate

Actually, the options concern the short-term rate on new borrowings, from which the long-term and average rates are computed in a unique way. The *short-term rate* for one country can be defined as:

– a nominal exogenous value,
– a real exogenous value,
– a Taylor rule,
– the nominal rate of another country (Germany?),
– a common nominal interest rate with a set of countries (for the EMU).

Of course, the two last options can originate in any of the three first ones. In the Taylor rule, the rate will depend partly on inflation, partly on the output gap, measured by the capacity utilization rate:

$$TIC = 150 \cdot tx(PC) + 50 \cdot b \cdot (UT - UT^*) + c \qquad (9)$$

where $tx(PC)$ represents inflation, and the second term the output gap. In short, the rationale for this formulation is the following Taylor (1998)).

The National Bank (for instance, the Federal Reserve of the US or the European Central Bank) wants to control inflation, or the variability of inflation, or the variability of the couple inflation–growth. If it expects high inflation, it will increase the real interest rate. Symptoms for future inflation are: a present high rate, a high level of output compared to its potential value. In a backward looking framework, this leads to the above formula.

In the absence of potential output, we have introduced the rate of use of capacities. This option can be criticized, as it is constrained by the actual productive process, while potential output depends rather on human capital and resources.

Taylor has set the coefficients to the above values, which should represent the behaviour of the FED in the last two decades. However, they do not necessarily apply to other countries.

The *long-term interest rate* is a moving average:

$$TIL = c \cdot TIC + (1 - c)TIL_{-1}. \qquad (10)$$

The *mean borrowing rate* is and average of both:

$$TI = d \cdot TIL + (1 - d)TIC. \qquad (11)$$

The *mean rate paid* is a moving average:

$$TIM = e \cdot TIM_{-1} + (1 - e)TI. \qquad (12)$$

For simulations we shall use the values c: 0.5, d: 0.5 and e: 0.8.

1.3.2 The options for the exchange rate

The exchange rate can be defined as:

- Exogenous for a each country.
- Following purchasing power parity for the country (based on the consumption price)[1].
- Exogenous for a set of countries (actually the same as the first case, except that a single assumption is made).
- Following purchasing power parity for a set of countries (based on the weighted consumption price of the countries).
- Following uncovered interest rate parity for one country.
- Following uncovered interest rate parity for a set of countries.

Uncovered interest rate parity will make the exchange rate depend on the interest rate (both real, or both nominal). The rationale is the following: If the agents think that the currency of one country risks losing value in the future, they will ask for a higher interest rate than the international one. So the expected exchange rate will affect the present currency value. If returns are equalized, a one percent expected devaluation will increase the nominal rate by one point. In a backward looking framework, we shall use a simultaneous influence.

The sets of countries considered can be defined at simulation time. This allows in particular observing the consequences of a change in the composition of the EMU.

1.3.3 Summarizing the influences

The above influences can be summarized as in schedule 1. We can observe in particular:

- That combining a Taylor interest rate and Uncovered Interest Rate Parity leads to a 1.5 elasticity of the exchange rate to prices, representing devaluation in real terms. As the exchange rate itself has a highly positive influence on prices (imported inflation) this can lead (and actually will) to exploding properties. But one can question this juxtaposition, as the interpretation of the interest movements leading to UIP is quite different its the determination in the Taylor framework.
- That if the interest rate is fixed in real terms, PPP and UIP should give the same results (they will).

---

[1] To avoid underidentification of the system, the exchange rate of the Rest of the World is actually fixed, and the other currencies follow purchasing power parity compared to it.

Schedule 1

Interest rate

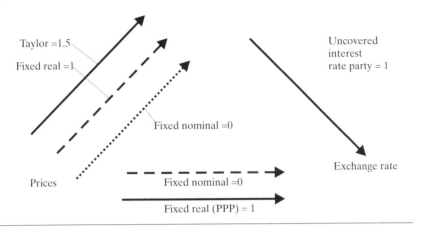

1.3.4 Enhancing the role of interest rates

Introducing a complex set of options for the interest rate was only efficient if its role was important, which was not the case in the base model. This led us to introduce it in two behaviors:

– Investment, through the long term real interest rate,

– Consumption, through the short-term real interest rate.

Unfortunately, every estimation we tried failed (which is apparently rather common for this case). This led us to check other models, and we decided to use coefficients that gave to the associated equations properties similar to the NiGEM model (produced by the National Institute for Economic Science and Research, UK). We have chosen the same value for all countries.

The equations become:

$$i_t / k_{t-1} = c1 \cdot i_{t-1} / k_{t-2} + c2 \cdot [(q_t - q_{t-1})/q_{t-1} + ut_t / 0.85] + \qquad (13)$$
$$-c3 \cdot tprob_t + c4 - 0.006 \cdot (til_t - 100(pc_t - pc_{t-1} / pc_{t-1}))$$

$$\Delta Log(co_t) = c1 \cdot \Delta Log(rdm_t / pc_t) + c2 \cdot [05\Delta Log(pc_t) + 05\Delta Log(pc_{t-1})] +$$

$$c3 \cdot \Delta Log(tcho_t) + c4 \cdot Log[rdm_{t-1} / (pc_{t-1} \cdot co_{t-1})] + \qquad (14)$$

$$c5 - 0.001 \cdot (tic_t - 100 * (pc_t - pc_{t-1}) / pc_{t-1}).$$

Of course, before applying these formulations, we have checked their influence, by observing the change in model properties with one addition or both (four cases). For this we have used two cases: an exogenous exchange rate with either a real interest rate or a Taylor rule, and applied shocks both to France and the full set. The results, which will appear in a separate paper, show a sizeable but reasonable influence.

From now on, we shall only consider both additions. The package will not propose any other option.

1.4 Merging the models

1.4.1 The exchange block

We shall start by establishing a coherent system for trade prices. We shall suppose that exporters base their price on their costs and the price of the target market:

$$Log\big(pex_{i,j}\big) = aLog\big(pp_i\big) + (1-a)\big(Log\big(pp_j ch_i / ch_j\big) + bt + c\big), \quad (15)$$

where i is the exporter and j the client, and ch_i the price of the currency of country i compared to the US dollar:

$$pim_{j,i} = pex_{i,j} ch_j / ch_i \quad (16)$$

$$pim_j = \sum_i m_{j,i} pim_{j,i} / \sum_i m_{j,i}. \quad (17)$$

For utilization rates, we use the same method:

$$utx_j = \sum_i m_{j,i} ut_i / \sum_i m_{j,i}. \quad (18)$$

We can now determine the global imports of country i, by modifying slightly the equation from the single country model, to take into account the capacity of exporters:

$$Log\big(m_i\big) = aLog\big(df_i ouv_i\big) + b\big\lfloor Log\big(ut_i\big) - cLog\big(utx_i\big)\big\rfloor + \quad (19)$$

$$dLog\big(pim_i / pp_i\big) + ...$$

This means that a general decrease in the available capacity of exporters will reduce exports, through a substitution effect. The coefficient 0.5 takes into account the larger associated capacities.

Finally, we separate imports into individual exports. Once again, we shall take into account relative competitiveness, and fluctuations in available capacities, relative to the above average. Actually, we shall again use set coefficients:

Figure 2

The trade block

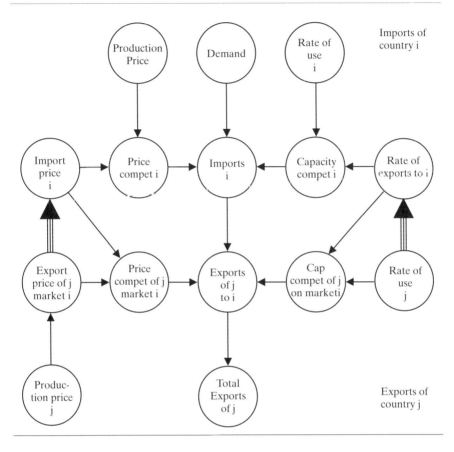

$$m_{i,j} = m_i . b_{i,j} \left[1 - a\left(pex_j ch_i / ch_j - pim_i \right) - b\left(ut_j - utx_i \right) \right] \qquad (20)$$

which means that (as for the single country models) exporters to one country will increase a "natural" share with competitiveness and available capacity, this time relative to their competitors.

One will observe that this technique guarantees the identity of the sum of individual exports with its global value, without any correction. Of course, the coefficients can be different from one market to another, but not within one market. The system can be summarized following figure 2.

In addition to the above, we have introduced some accounting equations:

– Exports from country *i* to *j*:

$$x_{i,j} = m_{j,i} \cdot usd0_j / usd0_i, \qquad (21)$$

where $usd0_i$ represents the base year value of the currency of country i, in US Dollars.

– Total exports computed as a sum

$$x_i = \sum x_{i,j}. \qquad (22)$$

– The average export price of country i:

$$pex_i = \sum b_{i,j} pex_{i,j}. \qquad (23)$$

1.4.2 The Rest of the World

The Rest of the World will not be associated with a model. Actually, we our goal will only be to give to its trade elements similar properties to the countries we consider. But this does not mean that we can keep its prices exogenous, or its capacities infinite: in case our six countries lead the same policy simultaneously (lowering the social contributions for example) we cannot assume that inflation and demand in the Rest of the World will remain unaffected.

We have chosen the following system, introducing the main mechanisms through a limited set of equations.

Production: We consider only production generated by exports. We start from the supply-demand equilibrium:

$$Q = D + X - M. \qquad (24)$$

Ex ante, X generates $Q = X$.

Ex post, an increase in production will generate revenue and demand:

$$D = a\,Q. \qquad (25)$$

Of which a share b will be imported:

$$M = b\,FD. \qquad (26)$$

Finally we get:

$$Q = 1/(1-a\,(1-b))\,X. \qquad (27)$$

Final demand will be defined as:

$$FD = c\,a\,Q + (1-c)\,FD0, \qquad (28)$$

where $FD0$ represents the part of final demand independent from trade.

In the absence of investment and capital, *the rate of use* follows an autoregressive behavior:

$Log(UT) = c \, [d \, Log(UT_{-1}) + e \, Log(Q/(Q_{-1}(1+txq)))) + (1{-}c) \, Log(UT0).$ (29)

As above, the share of production concerned with trade is treated endogenously. It separates two effects :

– the previous disequilibrium on capacities at a normal growth of production (it disappears gradually through additional investment);

– the present gap on production between the actual level and the one associated with a normal growth.

The production price differs from an exogenous track through the evolutions of the rate of use, and the import price (actually their deviations from a base track):

$$Log\big(pp_t\big) = Log\big(pp0_t\big) + f \cdot Log\big(ut_t \,/ut0\big) + g \cdot Log\big(pim_t \,/ pim0_t\big). \quad (30)$$

The *export price* will use exactly the same equation as country models.

Finally, the *import equation* uses the same framework as the single counties, except that it is not estimated:

$$Log\big(m_t\big) = c1 \cdot Log\big(df_t \cdot ouv_t\big) + c2 \cdot Log\big(1 - ut_t\big) + c3 \cdot Log\big(pim_t \,/ pp_t\big) - \ldots \quad (31)$$

2. The model properties

2.1 Simulation context

We shall now examine the properties of the full model. For this we need a base simulation. To make the diagnosis easier, we shall produce it on the future, using simplified assumptions. We shall suppose that the economy grows at structural rates, the same for each country:

– growth rate of population: 0.3 % per year,

– growth rate of labor productivity: 2.4 % per year,

– growth rate of prices: 2.4 % per year.

For this analytic simulation, we shall use a very long period, for several reasons:

– We want to control the presence of a long-term equilibrium, and of a steady state path. We do not necessarily believe conclusions drawn from the text of the equations.

– We want to free the results from any short-term fluctuations. As the model is not linear, an irregular base solution could disturb the sensitivities to shocks, and make the diagnosis less clear. If everything goes well, we should

Table 9

Export market shares by exporting country

Market	Germ	UK	Fran	Ital	Neth	Swed	RoW1	Port	Spai	RoW2
Exporter										
Germany	.	0.080	0.120	0.075	0.075	0.023	0.627	0.009	0.032	0.684
UK	0.121	.	0.094	0.047	0.066	0.025	0.647	0.009	0.035	0.683
France	0.168	0.097	.	0.092	0.045	0.011	0.587	0.015	0.070	0.558
Italy	0.190	0.065	0.131	.	0.029	0.009	0.576	0.014	0.047	0.553
Netherlands	0.281	0.093	0.105	0.052	.	0.017	0.452	.	.	.
Sweden	0.133	0.102	0.051	0.034	0.053	.	0.627		.	.
Rest of World 1	0.227	0.158	0.167	0.230	0.152	0.066	.	.	.	.
Portugal	0.187	0.117	0.147	0.034			.	.	0.146	0.369
Spain	0.142	0.082	0.201	0.092			.	0.078	.	0.405
Rest of World 2	0.370	0.204	0.191	0.139			.	0.083	0,.015	.

Authors' calculations.

get regular curves, easier to interpret. On the opposite, any irregular trajectory will be attributed to the model.

Our simulations will be conducted on a 200 years period, which appear to guarantee long term convergence. In the same way, shocks will start in 2101. Of course, we have checked that the general conclusions drawn from these shocks can also be applied to the period we shall actually use: 2000 and the following periods.

A definition of the "structural" shares of partner countries in imports and exports of a given country. We have used the definition equations for the foreign markets of one country, presented by the NiGEM model, and the global imports from the year 1995. The shares of partners in the exports of our six countries (and of the Rest of the World by difference) give in turn:

– imports by the Rest of the World from each country, then total imports of the Rest of the World,

– imports of countries from each single country, then individual imports from the Rest of the World (by difference), then total exports of the Rest of the World.

In table 9, each line gives the share of each market in the exports of the associated country. Of course, only the lines and columns associated to the new countries and the rest of the world will be affected.

2.2 The shocks

We shall now consider how the composition of the Euro zone affects out two countries through the consequences of policy shocks. We shall concentrate on asymmetric shocks, affecting either Spain or Portugal. Indeed, we have already observed (see Augier et al. 1999) that symmetric shocks had very similar properties notwithstanding the composition of the zone.

For simplicity, we shall suppose that the rest of the countries follow the actual status: Germany, France and Italy belong to EMU, while UK does not. We shall only consider four cases, with Spain and Portugal in or out of the system, independently from each other. Logic will lead us to start as a basic case with both countries outside EMU. This will allow us to observe what happens when they join, and not when they quit, which is actually almost unfeasible.

2.2.1 A demand shock in Spain

We shall increase Government demand in Spain by one full GDP percentage point. As stand earlier, shocks will begin in 2101, when the steady state is almost reached, but we have checked that conclusions apply to the present situation.

Spain and Portugal do not belong to EMU
As this is our basic case, we shall have first to give some basic explanations on the macroeconomic effects of such a decision. But we shall be quite short, as the issues are well known, and our model does not present very particular features, compared to the previous MacSim system or to any model of this family.

Figure 3 shows that under the assumption of a fixed nominal exchange rate and a fixed real exchange rate, the short-term multiplier for Spain is well above 1, but decreases with time to about 0.4, due to losses in competitiveness, as shown in figure 4. We have seen that for Spain, the sensitivity of imports to prices was very strong; actually not much lower the one. In the short-medium term, we observe the usual cycles, coming from the inertia on capacity adjustment (figure 5). The trade balance deteriorates significantly, even in current terms (figure 6). The PPP assumption eliminates the loss in competitiveness, and stabilizes the multiplier at a much higher level (1.5), with the same medium term cycles.

The Taylor rule almost eliminates the cycles, by going against the accelerator as to the influence of the output gap: higher tensions increase investment directly but also increase the interest rate. In practical terms, if a pursuer keeps the same inertia on its previous speed, but can close the present gap much faster, he is more likely to overshoot.

The evolution of the Portuguese economy is perhaps more interesting, as some elements were not necessarily obvious. Of course, it profits a lot from the Spanish demand, as it represents about 15 % of its exports (see table 8). It will be noted that Spanish imports from Portugal account only for 8 % of the total, due to the difference in country size.

We can see (figure 7) that in the short medium term, the Portuguese trade balance actually deteriorates. This comes from several sources. First, to supply the Spanish demand, it has to import equipment goods (about 2 units per additional output unit), and the jobs created will create additional consumption. Second, the limits on capacity will reduce the exports to the other countries, and the satisfaction of local demand, which leads to imports.

As capacities build up, these effects will disappear, but Portuguese inflation will increase more than the rest (except for Spain, of course) (figure 8). This country will lose competitiveness compared to EMU+UK, and even on average if we include Spain. And we have seen that Portuguese imports are quite sensitive to prices. This loss in competitiveness reduces the need for additional capacity, leading investment down and GDP further down. This accounts for the fact that in the long run Portugal does not profit from the Spanish policy, while Spain itself does (but at some cost) (figure 9).

But we have still to explain the higher inflation itself, in the absence of local growth. It actually comes from the lingering effects of initial tensions on capacities and labour, and from the inflation imported from Spain, as the change in the relative prices has a limited substitution effect on import shares.

The changes in rules bring logical results. With PPP the GDP increase reappears, to a normal level (0.2 is about 15 % of the Spanish 1.5 multiplier), which shows that the loss in competitiveness was indeed to blame. The Taylor rule with a fixed exchange rate smoothes the profile without bringing any long term growth, and with PPP it the additional inflation increases the real rate and limits the growth.

Spain does not belong to EMU, but Portugal does (figures 10 to 12)
From now on, we shall present the differences with the previous case. First, let us remark that the Spanish situation is not significantly affected. This will always be the case: the properties for one country depend essentially from the conditions of that country. This is truer of course for Portugal, considering its size.

Considering the basic case, we can observe that Portuguese growth is somewhat improved. The reason lies in the (disputable) fact that the interest rate is decided at the EMU level, and that the higher Portuguese inflation reduces the local real rate, bringing more growth (and more inflation). With the other rules, we can observe interesting evolutions:

– First, PPP reduces inflation, compared to a fixed rate. In the previous case, Portuguese inflation increased more than the average of its partners, due to local tensions and the Spanish influence. Now we consider EMU as a whole: in EMU (including Portugal), inflation increases a little more than at its partners. Weighted by the specific Portuguese trade (in which the devaluated Spanish peseta plays a large role), the Portuguese exchange rate actually improves, bringing deflation. Of course, this brings also a loss in competitiveness, and eliminates any GDP growth.

– Second, the Taylor rule is less efficient in its dampening effects. The rate of use, and the over indexation on inflation, are computed at the EMU level.

Spain belongs to EMU, but Portugal does not (figures 13 and 14)
Comparing results with the basic model shows the usual effects. With fixed nominal exchange rate and real interest rate determined at EMU level, growth is improved by the decrease of the real Spanish rate. With PPP, the loss in competitiveness is only very partially limited, as the Euro adapts to the evolution of EMU inflation. The increase in inflation is only a little higher. This means that the Taylor rule will have similar effects in both cases, close to the previous fixed exchange rate case. Defined at the EMU level, its dampening effects are a little lower, but do not affect growth on average.

For Portugal, it is interesting to note that local inflation being higher than in the EMU zone, PPP actually devaluates the currency relative to the Euro and brings large competitiveness gains compared to Spain, which has devaluated much lower than its own inflation. The long run GDP increase stabilizes at a much higher level.

Spain and Portugal belong to EMU
This case is less interesting, as it gives the usual results of any asymmetric shock inside EMU. PPP gets closer to the fixed rate assumption, the Taylor rule stabilizes less, and does not differentiate between exchange rate rules. We can observe however that Portugal profits from the decrease of its real interest rate, and the lower inflationary effect compared to Spain. The improvement of growth is quite significant.

2.2.2 A supply shock in Spain

We shall now decrease the rate of firms' social contributions by one percentage point. This reduces ex ante the wage cost by around 0.75 %.

Spain and Portugal do not belong to EMU (figures 15 and 16)
The base assumption produces the usual results. Firms decrease their prices, gaining competitiveness, and invest as profitability increases. Both effects improve GDP, but take some time in reaching their full impact, as the investment decisions are rather inert, and capacity is needed for external trade to profit from competitiveness.

In the first period, the long-term interest rate follows only partially the reduction in inflation, especially in the "real" case. Its real value increases, leading to a globally negative effect on GDP in the first period. As usual, PPP reduces the efficiency with this elimination of competitiveness gains. But the effect is almost compensated by the higher disinflation, and the decrease in the price of imports, which improves profitability through the price of capital. And the Taylor rule mixes an over indexation on reduced prices with a decrease of the output gap, with uncertain results.

In our particular case, the most interesting observations come from Portugal. But this time results are less clear, even in the basic case. As a main partner of Spain, Portugal suffers higher losses in competitiveness, but not too important as the reduced price of products imported from Spain lowers local inflation. And at the same time Spanish imports increase, a large share coming from Portugal.

On the whole, Portuguese GDP does increase in the short-medium term, but by a small amount. In later periods, the variations coming from strong cyclical effects are quite higher than the small average improvement. PPP leads to a significant improvement of GDP. If Spain loses its competitiveness gains, the shock brings still growth through capital profitability and the increase in the real holdings of households. Portugal profits from it, the more so as competitiveness is maintained. And the Taylor rule, as usual, stabilizes the cycles, and reduces the efficiency in the PPP case.

Spain does not belong to EMU, but Portugal does
Now Portugal has to follow the interest rate and exchange rate of the Euro zone. As its deflationary effect was higher than its partners, the real interest rate increases, and PPP maintains some competitiveness gains.

The basic case leads to a decrease of activity in the short run, and the interest rate plays again a stabilizing role, through quite different channels than the Taylor rule. This is somewhat compensated somewhat by PPP. But all these effects are not very high, as we have not changed the option for Spain. And the size of Portugal limits the backward effects of the new assumption on the Spanish economy.

In the long run, the shock becomes demand-oriented, and the situation improves as the EMU weighted inflation is lower than the Portuguese one, in particular in the PPP case. But this also brings down the Portuguese real interest rate.

Spain belongs to EMU, but Portugal does not (figure 17)
Now things will be quite different, as the origin of GDP growth in Spain, the improvement of price competitiveness, is maintained for all options, including PPP. But at the same time, we observe an increase in the real interest rate, as inflation decreases more in Spain than in its partner countries. But as these options showed very comparable efficiencies in the non-EMU case, this does not

have a significant effect, at least in the short and medium term. We observe only a small improvement of the efficiency for Spain.

Spain and Portugal belong to EMU
As the consequences from each entry were not individually very important, combining them gives results comparable to their sum.

2.2.3 A demand shock in Portugal

Spain and Portugal do not belong to EMU (figure 18)
Considering the basic case, the results are consistent with the Spanish equivalent. But we can observe that the multiplier is quite lower. Being a much smaller country (about 7 times in GDP terms) the share of imports in demand is much higher, and tensions on capacities appear much faster. The cycles are stronger, as the importance of external trade increases the role of the rate of use of capacities.

It is also interesting to note that the gains from the Spanish demand shock were actually higher. Ex ante, the share of Spain in Portuguese exports is around 15 %, and Portugal was not submitted, as in the present case, to inflationary and capacity effects.

Finally, the consequences for Spain are symmetrical to the previous case. We observe a short term loss on the real trade balance, as the need to supply the Portuguese demand leads to investment and consumption, and the Portuguese inflation is transmitted though imports. But the effect is somewhat lower, as Portugal is less important for Spain than the reverse.

Spain does not belong to EMU, but Portugal does (figure 19)
We observe the usual consequences of EMU participation for a country producing an asymmetric shock. But now the size of the country means that the effects of the shock on the interest rate and the exchange rate are very small. The results are almost identical to the basic case, for all the assumptions. This is what we already observed for Spain, where the consequences of a local shock converged to the real exchange rate case. The reason for the limited convergence was the weight of Spain in the determination of the exchange rate. With a weight 7 times smaller, the convergence is now almost full.

This was not the case when the shock originated in Spain, as the assumptions used affected directly the consequences for Portugal. As a comparatively important partner of Spain, the shock created disequilibria between Portugal and its partners as to inflation and tensions, and the consequences of these disequilibria on the exchange and interest rates changed a lot with participation to the EMU. Moreover, the exchange rate affected directly the source of the Portuguese growth, exports to Spain.

In the present case, the same disequilibria are produced, but they do not significantly affect the nominal EMU rates, leading all cases to the basic one.

Spain belongs to EMU, but Portugal does not
Belonging to the EMU allows Spain to reduce the increase of interest rates,
improving growth. The exchange rate keeps close to the fixed assumption, introducing permanent losses in competitiveness. But this also limits the inflationary effect, with positive consequences.

Spain and Portugal belong to EMU
As seen earlier, the entry of Portugal in EMU leads all assumptions to the
basic case. Again, we find here the consequences of Portugal's small size. Even
with a five-country EMU, the change in rules has virtually no effect on GDP
improvement, in the case of a local shock. This is at least partly due to the fact
that local inflation has a small effect on the Euro rate; moreover, as its main
partner has strong inflationary properties, the fixed exchange rate assumption
had properties closer to PPP.

2.2.4 A supply shock in Portugal

For simplicity, we shall not address this issue individually. The main observa-
tion is that the small size of the country precludes any sizable backward effect,
including the changes in the interest rate and the exchange rate. Once this is
considered, we get the same conclusions as for Spain, but with a higher efficiency, due to the weight of external trade in the Portuguese economy. However, this is countered by the lower Portuguese disinflation, coming from the
smaller dynamic coefficients of the price-wage loop.

2.3 General conclusion

This study has confirmed some elements observed in the previous papers, and
some new ones.

General consequences of the rules in a single country framework
Facing an asymmetric demand shock, PPP stabilizes competitiveness, but
leads to higher inflationary effects. The change in GDP increases in the original country, while the diagnosis is less clear for its partners, with contrary effects of a larger external market and the disappearance of competitiveness
gains. The Taylor rule stabilizes the shocks, by delaying investment, but does
not affect the average efficiency. Combined with PPP, the higher inflation and
activity increases the real interest rate and exert a permanent downward effect. For supply shocks, PPP limits gains but improvement still comes from the
profitability of capital. The Taylor rule has a limited role, as disinflation and
tensions have opposite effects.

Consequences of external trade in the basic case
We are studying the case of two countries of very different size, with strong
economic links. For the small country, a local shock can have smaller effects
than the same shock (in GDP terms) in the large one. This applies to both
GDP and inflation. In the short-medium term, a shock in the large country can
deteriorate the trade balance in the small one, due to the need to increase capacities, and the loss in competitiveness to other countries. This also applies, to
a lesser degree, to the large country for a shock in the small one.

Consequences of EMU participation for the shocked country
In the basic case, the only consequence is the adoption of a common interest
rate. If inflationary effects in the country are higher than for its partners, the
real interest rate will decrease, which will profit growth (this effect looks somewhat dubious). The main changes affect the other options. The role of PPP
is limited, as the exchange rate is unaffected in the zone, and the effective devaluation applies to the global inflation, which increases much less at the
EMU level.

As the effect of the local inflation on the Euro rate depends on the weight of
the country, the smaller the country, the lower the devaluation. A shock in Portugal will leave the Euro almost unchanged, while in Spain we observe a slight
devaluation, leading to a higher efficiency of the PPP assumption. As to the
Taylor rule, it brings much smaller variations to the interest rate, and we have
again to consider the weight of the country to determine if the over indexation
on global (limited) inflation, and the influence of global tensions, are enough
to make the real interest grow. It actually grows for Spain, but again the small
size of Portugal brings it down, around an average negative value. The varia-
tion of the real interest rate comes mainly from local inflation, and much less
from the nominal interest rate, which follows usual, but small, variations. Combining PPP and the Taylor rule, the higher inflation brings down the efficiency
of the shock.

Consequences of EMU participation for the other countries
In a way, the consequences of EMU participation are more important for the
non-shocked countries, as the increase in GDP come through imports, which
are relatively more sensitive to the assumption than local GDP. Also, the size
of the country will increase the convergence of options.

Figure 3

Demand shock in Spain, 3-country EMU: Spanish rate of use of capacities

2100 to 2150; deviation from basic case in percentage points

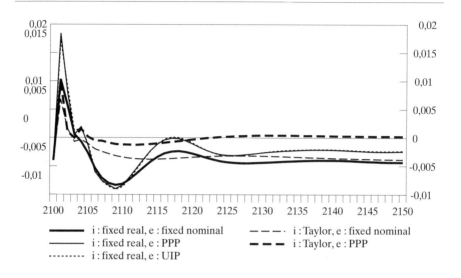

Authors' calculations. Explanations see text.

Figure 4

Demand shock in Spain, 3-country EMU: Spanish value added deflator

2100 to 2150; deviation from basic case in percentage points

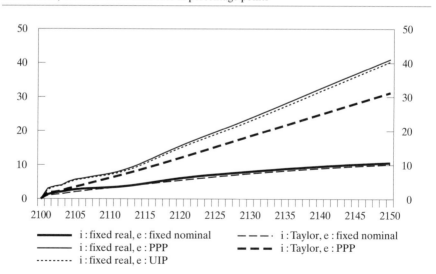

Authors' calculations. Explanations see text.

Figure 5

Demand shock in Spain, 3-country EMU: Spanish rate of use of capacities

2100 to 2150; deviation from basic case in percentage points

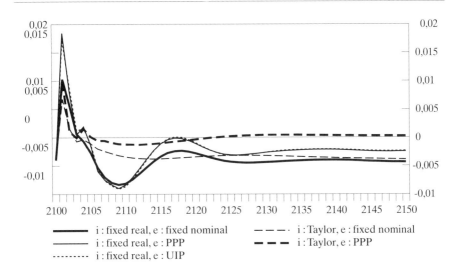

Authors' calculations. Explanations see text.

Figure 6

Demand shock in Spain, 3-country EMU: Spanish export-import ratio in current terms

2100 to 2150; deviation from basic case in percentage points

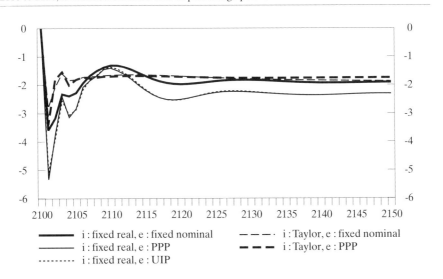

Authors' calculations. Explanations see text.

Figure 7

Demand shock in Spain, 3-country EMU: Portuguese export-import ratio in current terms

2100 to 2150; deviation from basic case in percentage points

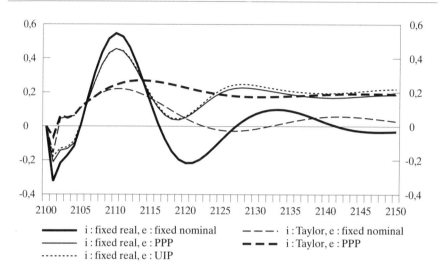

Authors' calculations. Explanations see text.

Figure 8

Demand shock in Spain, 3-country EMU: Portuguese value added deflator

2100 to 2150; deviation from basic case in percentage points

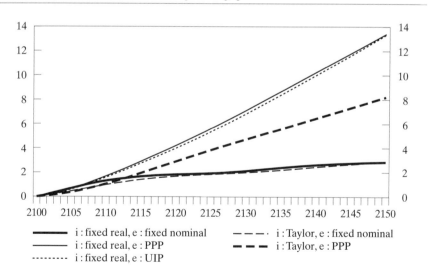

Authors' calculations. Explanations see text.

Figure 9

Demand shock in Spain, 3-country EMU: Portuguese market GDP

2100 to 2150; deviation from basic case in percentage points

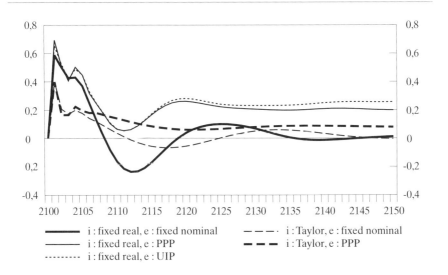

Authors' calculations. Explanations see text.

Figure 10

Demand shock in Spain, 4-country EMU with Portugal: Portuguese market GDP

2100 to 2150; deviation from basic case in percentage points

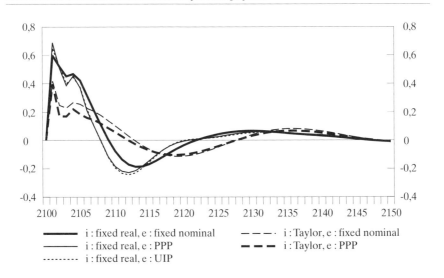

Authors' calculations. Explanations see text.

Figure 11

Demand shock in Spain, 4-country EMU with Portugal: Portuguese value added deflator

2100 to 2150; deviation from basic case in percentage points

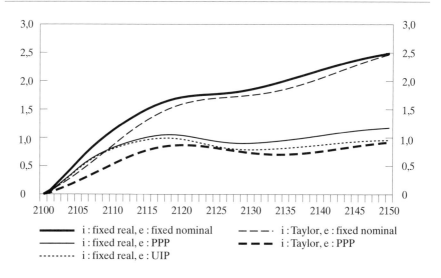

Authors' calculations. Explanations see text.

Figure 12

Demand shock in Spain, 4-country EMU with Portugal: Portuguese export-import ratio in current terms

2100 to 2150; deviation from basic case in percentage points

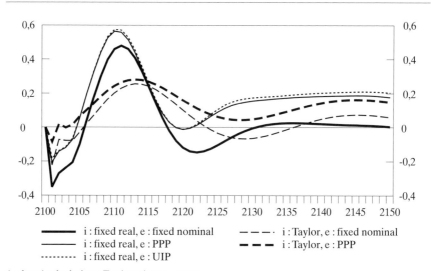

Authors' calculations. Explanations see text.

Figure 13

Demand shock in Spain, 4-country EMU with Spain: Spanish market GDP

2100 to 2150; deviation from basic case in percentage points

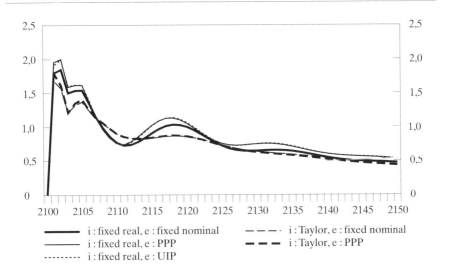

Authors' calculations. Explanations see text.

Figure 14

Demand shock in Spain, 4-country EMU with Spain: Spanish value added deflator

2100 to 2150; deviation from basic case in percentage points

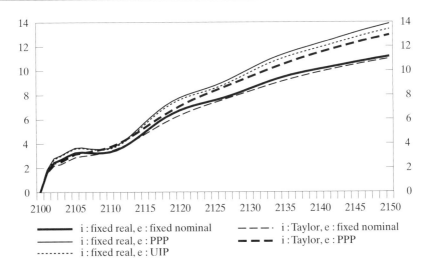

Authors' calculations. Explanations see text.

Figure 15

Supply shock in Spain, 3-country EMU: Spanish market GDP

2100 to 2150; deviation from basic case in percentage points

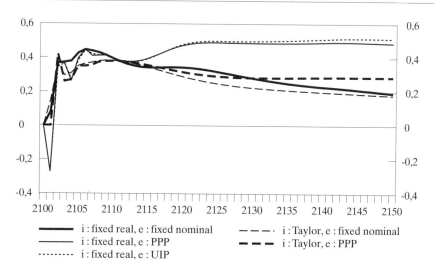

Authors' calculations. Explanations see text.

Figure 16

Supply shock in Spain, 3-country EMU: Portuguese market GDP

2100 to 2150; deviation from basic case in percentage points

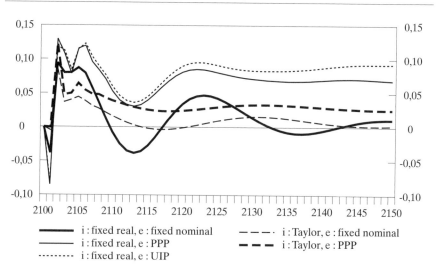

Authors' calculations. Explanations see text.

Figure 17

Supply shock in Spain, 4-country EMU with Spain: Spanish market GDP

2100 to 2150; deviation from basic case in percentage points

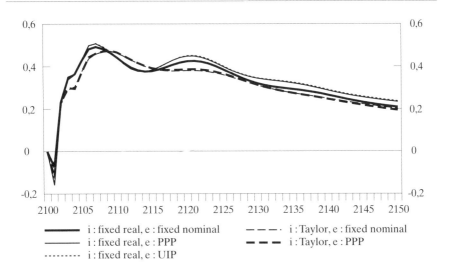

Authors' calculations. Explanations see text.

Figure 18

Demand shock in Portugal, 3-country EMU: Portuguese market GDP

2100 to 2150; deviation from basic case in percentage points

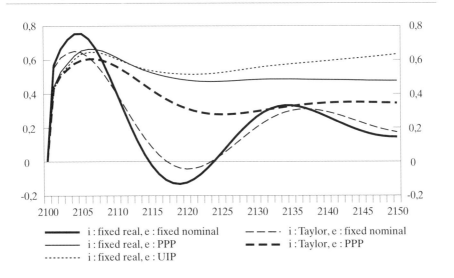

Authors' calculations. Explanations see text.

Figure 19

Demand shock in Portugal, 4-country EMU with Portugal: Portuguese market GDP

2100 to 2150; deviation from basic case in percentage points

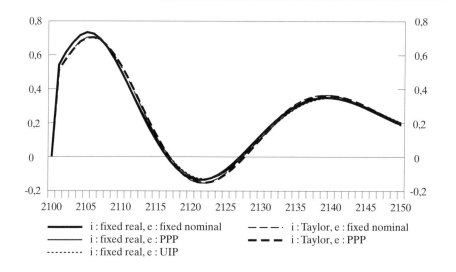

i : fixed real, e : fixed nominal   — — — · i : Taylor, e : fixed nominal
i : fixed real, e : PPP   ▬ ▬ ▬ i : Taylor, e : PPP
········· i : fixed real, e : UIP

Authors' calculations. Explanations see text.

Table 1

Productive investment

$I/K\{-1\}=a*I\{-1\}/K\{-2\}+b*(Q-Q\{-1\})/Q\{-1\}+c* UT/.85+d*TPROB+e$

countries	a	b	c	d	see/DW
Germany	0.769 (8.44)	0.062 (2.68)	0.088 (1.01)	–0.055 (–2.89)	0.311 1.170
United Kingdom	0.803 (12.31)	0.040 (3.25)	0.109 (1.57)	–0.038 (–3.30)	0.207 1.670
France	0.730 (15.31)	0.089 (6.12)	0.060 (2.22)	–0.080 (–6.21)	0.193 1.610
Italy	0.682 (6.87)	0.104 (5.96)	0.050 set	–0.086 (–6.01)	0.245 2.067
Netherlands	0.600 (4.42)	0.080 (2.31)	0.058 (1.00)	–0.062 (-2.04)	0.385 1.880
Portugal	0.650 (15.31)	0.089 (6.12)	0.060 (2.22)	–0.080 (–6.21)	0.193 1.610
Spain	0.682 (6.87)	0.104 (5.96)	0.050 sez	–0.086 (–6.01)	0.245 2.067
Sweden	0.764 (10.59)	0.053 (1.47)	0.272 (2.38)	–0.066 (-2.22)	0.408 1.980

Authors' calculations. t-values in brackets.

Table 2

Employment

$\Delta Log(LE)=a\Delta Log(Q)+b(Log(Q\{-1\}/LE\{-1\}))-ct-d*(t+7)*(t>7))+e$

countries	a	b	c	d	e	see/DW
Germany	0.390 (4.82)	0.324 (3.76)	0.053 (8.15)	–0.035 (–4.78)	–3.632 (–3.80)	0.760 1.020
United Kingdom	0.424 (5.68)	0.398 (4.88)	0.038 (20.02)	–0.022 (–8.64)	–3.780 (–4.91)	1.155 1.240
France	0.514 (9.17)	0.247 (2.92)	0.046 (15.66)	–0.024 (–7.87)	–3.064 (–2.78)	0.466 1.668
Italy	0.264 (3.26)	0.240 (2.68)	0.054 (13.31)	–0.029 (–6.01)	–4.266 (–2.68)	0.997 1.400
Netherlands	0.487 (3.88)	0.254 (3.26)	0.079 (5.68)	–0.070 (–4.74)	–2.955 (–3.29)	1.038 1.460
Portugal	0.650 (9.17)	0.247 (2.92)	0.037 (15.66)	–0.021 (–7.87)	–3.064 (–2.78)	1.950 1.530
Spain	0.703 (3.26)	0.260 (2.68)	0.040 (19.40)	–0.021 (–2.57)	–0.001 (–2.68)	1.360 1.310
Sweden	0.354 (3.23)	0.451 (4.13)	0.039 (19.67)	–0.021 (–8.09)	–5.604 (–4.13)	1.359 1.053

Authors' calculations. t-values in brackets.

Table 3

Unemployment

$DCHO=a*DLT+b*DPOP65+c*(CHO(-1)-d*LT(-1)-e*POP65(-1))+f$

Country	a	b	c	d	e	f	see/DW
Germany	−0.561 (−13.07)	0.434 (5.64)	−0.184 (−1.80)	−0.474 (−9.99)	0.475 (32.36)	−5.440E+06 (−63.25)	65469 1.325
United Kingdom	−0.642 (−12.88)	0.733 (3.82)	−0.037 (−0.33)	−0.627 (−10.87)	0.917 (27.31)	−1.580E+07 (6,92)	113137 1.210
France	−0.749 (−8.99)	0.253 (1.937)	−0.124 (−1.13)	−0.456 (−6.34)	0.478 (23.32)	−4.390E+06 (−5.92)	65101 1.859
Italy	−0.315 (−3.71)	0.111 (1.11)	−0.223 (−2.92)	−0.004 (−0.048)	0.285 (12.16)	−8.684E+06 (−73.91)	101919 1.136
Netherlands	−0.785 (−9.23)	0.000	−0.332 (−3.78)	−0.293 (−5.72)	0.278 (11.76)	−5.075E+05 (−5.04)	26017 1.997
Portugal	−0.192 (−2.57)	0.251 (2.73)	−0.086 (−1.21)	−0.501 (−0.82)	0.355 (0.93)	−6.146E+04 (−4.66)	35907 1.130
Spain	−0.809 (−9.23)	0.273 (1.11)	−0.172 (−1.99)	−0.854 (−4.38)	0.738 (8.32)	−4.481E+06 (−2.25)	61603 1.992
Sweden	−0.413 (−12.36)	0.109 (0.79)	−0.205 (−3.29)	−0.252 (−7.29)	0.614 (12.24)	−2.083E+06 (−5.59)	13326 1.815

Authors' calculations. t-values in brackets.

Table 4

Value added price

$\Delta log(PVA)=a*(\Delta Log(CSUP)+b\Delta UT)+c*(Log(CSUP\{-1\}/PVA\{-1\})+b*UT\{-1\})+d$

countries	a	b	c	d	see/DW
Germany	0.654 (6.60)	0.485 (1.61)	0.060 (0.90)	0.002 (0.10)	1.267 1.308
United Kingdom	0.822 (12.64)	0.827 (2.99)	0.193 (2.19)	−0.087 (−1.190)	1.910 1.193
France	0.515 (10.82)	0.784 (2.97)	0.213 (6.52)	−0.042 (−0.88)	0.702 2.102
Italy	0.805 (12.59)	1.312 (5.36)	0.089 (1.68)	−0.043 (−0.88)	1.384 0.854
Netherlands	0.481 (4.60)	0.933 (1.51)	0.277 (3.74)	−0.118 (−0.76)	1.347 1.248
Portugal	0.310 (4.44)	0.283 (5.39)	0.312 (1.09)	−0.114 (−0.47)	3.511 0.800
Spain	0.646 (10.10)	0.171 (3.39)	0.199 (1.48)	−0.093 (−0.85)	1.500 1.430
Sweden	0.629 (7.56)	1.450 (3.20)	0.064 (0.58)	−0.038 (−0.31)	1.791 1.568

Authors' calculations. t-values in brackets.

Table 5

Wage rate

$\Delta log(W)=a*\Delta Log(PC)+b* TCHO+c*Log(W\{-1\}* LE\{-1\}*(1+ TCSE\{-1\})/$
$(PVA\{-1\}* Q\{-1\}))+d$

countries	a	b	c	d	see/DW
Germany	0.539	−0.026	−0.084	0.194	1.446
	(3.51)	(7.46)	(−3.26)	(2.12)	1.431
United Kingdom	0.960	−0.017	−0.064	0.225	1.952
	(12.21)	(−2.56)	(−1.87)	(2.24)	2.150
France[1]	0.628	−0.037	−0.111	0.100	0.635
	(7.64)	(10.91)	(−7.50)	(3.96)	2.412
Italy	0.831	−0.076	−0.201	0.126	2.073
	(11.00)	(−3.06)	(−2.14)	(1.14)	1.710
Netherlands	1.000	−0.036	−0.155	0.210	1.824
	set	(−4.47)	(−3.43)	(2.30)	1 830
Portugal	1.000	0.089	−0.111	−0.251	4.370
	set	(−2.33)	(−1.21)	(−2.75)	1.210
Spain	1.000	−0.027	−0.070	−0.060	2.020
	set	(−4.38)	(−1.21)	(−2.49)	2.100
Sweden	0.764	−0.027	−0.115	0.297	1.991
	(4.36)	(−3.43)	(−3.31)	(2.39)	1.812

Authors' calculations. – [1]Unitary indexation over 2 periods. t-values in brackets.

Table 6

Change in inventories

$\Delta STOC=a*\Delta Q+b \ Q\{-1\}$

countries	a	b	see/DW
Germany	0.317		9113
	(6.51)		0.990
United Kingdom	0.207	0.102	1034
	(4.44)	(2.15)	1.190
France	0.404		15606
	(8.69)		1.160
Italy	0.270		6746550
	(5.93)		0.800
Netherlands	0.370		2640
	(8.20)		0.710
Portugal	0.300		
	set		
Spain	0.300		
	set		
Sweden[1]	0.764	−0.017	11437
	(2.03)	(−5.40)	0.870

Authors' calculations. t-values in brackets. – [1]The first term represents the level of final demand.

Table 7

Household consumption

$\Delta log(CO)=a*\Delta Log(RDM/PC)+b*(.5*\Delta Log(PC)+(1-.5)*\Delta Log(\ PC\{-1\}))+c*D(TCHO)$
$+d*Log(\ RDM\{-1\}/(\ CO\{-1\}*\ PC\{-1\}))+e$

countries	a	b	c	d	e	see/DW
Germany	0.696	−0.236	−0.371	0.590	−0.063	0.698
	(8.80)	(−1.72)	(−1.24)	(3.25)	(−2.90)	1.160
United Kingdom	0.740	−0.073	−0.614	0.374	−0.034	1.161
	(6.76)	(−1.30)	(−2.34)	(2.77)	(−2.03)	1.240
France	0.386	−0.141	−0.834	0.265	−0.016	0.947
	(4.36)	(−1.67)	(−2.21)	(3.04)	(−1.41)	1.610
Italy	0.503	0.000	−0.343	0.073	0.002	1.245
	(4.86)	set	(−0.76)	(2.21)	(0.22)	1.990
Netherlands	0.375	0.000	−0.622	0.445	0.004	1.002
	(3.49)	set	(−2.36)	(4.18)	(0.91)	1.140
Portugal	0.649	−0.355	−0.500	0.384	−0.008	2.780
	(4.96)	(−3.75)	set	(3.46)	(−0.512)	1.840
Spain	0.608	0.000	−0.496	0.418	0.076	1.000
	(8.15)	set	(−3.31)	(4.07)	(4.88)	2.090
Sweden	0.764	−0.185	−1.597	0.110	0.024	1.343
	(2.23)	(−1.96)	(−4.91)	(1.36)	(2.60)	1.870

Authors' calculations. t-values in brackets.

Table 8

Imports

$Log(M)=a*Log(\ F*OUV)+b*(Log(UT)-0,5*Log(UTX))+c*Log(COMPM)+d$

countries	a	b	c	d	see/DW
Germany	1.000	0.500	−0.225	−1.302	0.055
	set	set	(−1.58)	(−75.59)	0.528
United Kingdom	1.000	0.500	−0.150	−1.348	0.055
	set	set	set	(−125.31)	0.288
France	1.000	0.500	−0.244	−1.554	0.036
	set	set	(−4.29)	−192.719	0.974
Italy	1.000	0.500	−0.208	−1.709	0.062
	set	set	(−3.43)	(−87.83)	0.379
Netherlands	1.000	0.500	−0.090	−0.755	0.040
	set	set	(−1.17)	(−77.09)	0.400
Portugal	1.000	0.500	−0.717	−1.441	0.096
	set	set	(−8.89)	(−90.05)	0.500
Spain	1.000	0.500	−0.998	−2.028	0.117
	set	set	(−9.87)	(−70.27)	0.430
Sweden	1.000	0.500	−0.272	−1.134	0.058
	set	set	(−2.58)	(−83.43)	0.593

Authors' calculations. t-values in brackets.

References

Augier, P., J.L. Brillet, G. Cette and R. Gambini (1999), *The MACSIM Project*. Full Economic Description. Paper presented at the 1999 LINK Conference in Athens, 4-8 November 1999.

Augier, P., J.L. Brillet, G. Cette and R. Gambini (2000), *The Financial Rules and EMU*. A Study Using the MACSIM System. Paper presented at the 2000 LINK Conference in Oslo, 2-6 October 2000.

Ball, L. (1998), Efficient Rules for Monetary Policy. NBER Working Paper 5952. NBER, Cambridge, MA.

Brillet, J.L. (1997a), WinMCD, utilisation sous Windows du modèle MicroDMS. INSEE Guides 5–6. INSEE, Paris.

Brillet, J.L. (1997b), Analysing a Small French ECM Model. INSEE Working Paper G9709. INSEE, Paris.

Gabay, D., P. Nepomiaschy, M. Rachdi et A. Ravellli (1978), Etude, résolution et optimisation de modèles macroéconomiques. INRIA Rapport R312. Institut National de Recherche en Informatique et en Automatique, Le Chesnay.

MIMOSA Team (1997), La nouvelle version de MIMOSA, modèle de l'économie mondiale. CEPII-OFCE Working Paper M-97-01. Paris.

OFCE – Office Français de Conjoncture Economique (ed.) (1996), Structure et propriétés de cinq modèles macroéconomiques français. OFCE Working Paper 96-04. Paris.

Penot, A. et J.P. Pollin (1999), Construction d'une règle monétaire pour la zone Euro. *Revue économique* 50 (May): 535–546.

Richardson, P. (1988), The Structure and Simulation Properties of OECD's INTERLINK Model. Economic Studies 10. OECD, Paris.

Tanner, E. (1998), Deviations from Uncovered Interest Rate Parity: A Global Guide to where the Action Is. IMF Working Paper 98,117. IMF, Washington, DC.

Taylor, J.B. (1998), An Historical Analysis of Monetary Policy Rules. NBER Working Paper 6768. NBER, Cambridge, MA.

Ullrich Heilemann, György Barabas, and Hiltrud Nehls

Shifts or Breaks? – West German Macroeconomic Parameters and European Integration[1]

Ever since the Treaty of Rome was signed in 1957, the process of European integration has had a substantial influence on the economic development of the participating countries. With trade-barriers diminishing, economic linkage has reached a considerable level; moreover, to a growing extent, member states' economies had to submit to common rules, and political authority was shifted to the European Commission. With the start of the European Monetary Union (EMU) on January 1, 1999, a new plateau has been reached.

Certainly this will, to a certain extent, change the conduct of economic policy. But it raises the question whether the EMU will induce fundamental shifts in economic preferences, behaviour, and structures. Consequences of this evolution may show up in the parameters as well as in the stability of relationships between economic aggregates. From an analytical point of view, one outcome would be that the long time series would no longer be consistent/coherent, and the quality of forecasts or simulations would suffer in the new regime. Despite their importance, these issues have been ignored so far, or, at best, been addressed in a loose, qualitative way. Most of the studies of European Integration[2] (i.e., the consequences of the single market in terms of trade creation/trade diversion) argued in a framework of fixed parameters derived from the "old regimes". As a first approximation, this may well have been justified. However, there should have been an interest in ex-post examination of the validity of the assumption of stable parameters, particularly after the *Lucas critique* had started to question parameter stability for less far-reaching and final changes of regime. As a consequence, our knowledge about integration-related shifts in behaviour on the micro, as well as on the macro level, is to put it mildly, very modest.

---

[1] We thank *Stephen Hall*, *Lawrence Klein* and *Peter Pauly* for helpful comments.

[2] For an overview see Ohly 1993.

There are reasons to believe that even large steps toward European integration might not have changed macroeconomic reactions immediately in a fundamental way, *Marshall's natura non facit saltum* is always a comforting promise[3]. The main reason is that in many cases the "new" institutional settings such as the Common Market and the EMU, though large steps in themselves, are implemented only gradually, starting with the commitment to the respective innovation, continuing with a slow decline in the autonomy of national policies until the rules of the new institution are incorporated in the behaviour of economic agents.[4] For instance, when in 1957 the goal of free trade in Europe was announced, tariffs were cut step by step until finally in 1967, the customs union was formally implemented. But it still took more than 30 years to remove the remaining (non-tariff) barriers to trade. Most of the changes to be expected in the behaviour of investors and consumers stretched over a long period.

To clarify these questions for the German case, the present paper studies the behavioural consequences of previous integration steps, finally suggesting an analogy to the EMU. For methodical reasons, as well as because of policy relevance, it concentrates on the macro level.

The examination is done in the context of the RWI-macroeconometric model, which ensures the necessary broad perspective on economic reactions and allows us to portray the macroeconomic consequences of any identified changes on the single-equation/parameter level. To test for parameter-shifts resulting from integration and quantifying their macroeconomic effects, we choose two ways: First, with the (40 quarter) moving window technique we analyse the evolution of some of the model's pivotal parameters over the last 30 years, concentrating on the trade sector and on investment. In a second step, we extend the sample period of the model from 1960-I to 1994-IV, add dummy variables to control for impulses in integration and, finally, quantify their overall macroeconomic effects by simulation of the "new" model.

Section 1 gives a short description of European integration, highlighting events of major macroeconomic importance and the consequences attributed to them in the literature. Section 2 elaborates the theoretical and methodical procedures of the study, followed, in section 3 by the presentation of the results of "moving windows", of the dummy variable approach in the single-equation analysis, and in the complete macroeconometric model framework. The last section (4) summarises the findings and draws conclusions for policy and further research.

---

[3] The question of „revolutionary" or „evolutionary" changes in economics is, of course, much older (Easterlin 1998: 25ff).

[4] As to policy, recently Ballabriga/Martinez-Mongay (2002: 37) analyse empirically pre-EMU fiscal and monetary policy rules and conclude that they differ not much from those of EMU.

Table 1

Major steps to economic integration in Europe

Date	Measure	Effects
1950	Ratification of the Schumann-Plan ("Treaty of Paris"): Inauguration of the European Coal and Steel Community (ECSC) (Benelux, France, Germany, Italy)	Political signalling, sectoral effects
1957	Treaties of Rome: ECSC	
	European Economic Community (EEC "EC") comprising a *common market* in the long run and *common agricultural policy* (CAP)	Rapid expansion of intra-EC trade in agricultural goods (trade diversion)
	European Atomic Energy Community (EAEC)	
1960–1968	Successive reduction of tariffs	Mainly trade creation
1968	*Customs Union* (abolishment of internal tariffs and quantitative restrictions), introduction of common external tariffs	All customs revenue is diverted to the EEC, trade creation
1968	Unrestricted movement of labour within the EEC is established	Factor movements
1969	Hague Summit: Formal consent to "completion, deepening and enlargement", meaning mainly the readiness to open for new members (in particular UK), to provide Community's own resources and to envision a Monetary Union in the long run	
1970	EC receives "own resources": apart from receipts from customs duties and agricultural levies VAT resources are introduced	
1972	First attempts to stabilise exchange rates	
1973	Accession of UK, Denmark, and Ireland	Major trade partners enter the EEC
1975–1977	Greece, Spain, and Portugal apply for membership	
1979	Introduction of the ECU	Germany gains leading role in monetary policy
1981/1986	First Greece, then Spain and Portugal join the EC	
1986	First revision of contracts, "Single European Act" targets 1992 as the date for the completion of the internal market	New push for integration
1988	Fully liberalised capital movements	
1992	Second revision of contracts ("Maastricht Treaty") formation of the *European Union* (EU). Main innovations: Timetable towards an *EMU*, settling the criteria of sufficient convergence. Apart from that, a closer co-operation in several fields of policy	Dynamic effects: Higher competition, reduction of costs and therefore lower prices, stronger technical progress and more innovation
1993	Start of European *Single Market*	
1995	Accession of Austria, Finland and Sweden	
1998	Decision on the founding members of the EMU (AT, BE, ESP, FIN, FR, GER, IRL, IT, L, NL, POR)	
1999	EMU is inplemented	
2002	Euro becomes the European currency	

RWI
ESSEN

Authors' compilation from various sources.

1. Major fields of European integration and their macroeconomic consequences

European economic integration on the macroeconomic level can be assigned to three main categories: *trade liberalisation, fiscal co-ordination, and monetary integration* (an overview is given in Table 1). This section lists the main steps in these three fields and relates them to their effects on the real economy as reported in previous studies.

1.1 Trade liberalisation

Until the early sixties, although economic integration in the European Community (EC) was of pre-eminent relevance for the political system in post-war Europe (van der Wee 1984: 424ff), its direct effects on macroeconomic aggregates were negligible. This is mainly because during its first years, European attempts to co-operate were limited to certain sectors of the economy (such as the Treaty on Coal and Steel in 1950) or fell far short of being put into practice (e.g., the common market). In addition, only a very limited number of partner countries, *Belgium, France, Germany, Italy, Luxembourg and the Netherlands,* joined the EC.

With the adoption of general trade liberalisation as its main goal, the impact of economic integration increased considerably. First, tariffs were cut on a unilateral basis, then these cuts were extended systematically to selected sectors and, with the creation of the customs union, they were abolished completely. All this happened in an environment of increasing international linkage and a global attempt to foster free trade by the institution of GATT.

From the EC's perspective, the aim of dropping trade barriers was to realise welfare gains from free trade. Therefore, trade creation, not trade diversion, should be the driving factor in the shift of trade-patterns in the EC – with perhaps the exception of agriculture (Jacquemin, Sapir 1988: 135). The *Common Agricultural Policy* (CAP) was based on the idea of sheltering European agriculture, to some extent, from international competition. Therefore, in the trade of farming products, one would expect effects of trade diversion rather than trade creation.

Many empirical studies, scrutinising the effects of lowering trade barriers within the European framework, confirm a realisation of these expectations (e.g., Verdoorn, Schwarz 1972, European Commission 1996). They all find a close link between the progress of EC integration and the growth of trade; and by far the largest component of the latter is attributed to trade creation. By the end of the sixties, the trade creation effect, according to a paper by *Mayes* (1978:6) accounted for between USD 1.8 and USD 20.8 billion, depending on method and author. Trade diversion was estimated to be between USD –4.0

and USD 2.4 billion, compared to total exports of the six EC-countries of roughly USD 65 billion. The wide range of results demonstrates the difficulties in registering these effects. In addition, *Mayes* (1978:21) states the problem that models are rarely captive of isolating trade creation/diversion from dynamic effects, as trade flows are not only induced by comparative advantages and terms of trade as viewed by *Viner*. On the contrary, efficiency of firms, the exploitation of economies of scale, the abolition of non-tariff barriers, and changes in the rate of economic growth gain major importance as motives for changing international trade patterns.

The customs union, completed in 1968, was still far from being the *final* step towards European trade liberalisation. Besides the strategy of multilateral liberalisation, trade policy was pursued also by regional integration; i.e., by various enlargements (Table 1).

Starting in 1985, and perhaps even more significant, were the political attempts to reduce the remaining barriers to trade listed in the so-called White Paper (European Commission 1985). In the following years, myriad hindrances to trade such as remaining quantitative restrictions for imports, licences and national quotas for intra-EC transport and differences in standards and technical regulations were tackled. By 1 January 1993, the official start of the European single market, most of them were removed.[5] Empirical studies tried to capture not only the direct impact on trade, but also the repercussions from induced income. For example, the "Ceccini-Report" (European Commission 1988: 19), based on a multitude of assumptions, expected a gain of ECU 125–190 billion (4–6.5% of GDP) from the abolishment of all still-existing trade-barriers in the EC – but it remained rather vague in which time period these gains would be realised. Other estimations were more explicit: Prognos AG (1990: 111, 404) expected gains in additional real GDP growth during the period 1988 to 2000 for the EC as well as for Germany, in the range of 0.4 percentage points per year. In terms of employment, the expected number of unemployed in Germany in 2000 was (in the most optimistic scenario) 33 per cent lower with the common market completed than in the reference scenario without the program. However, all these calculations suffer from two major caveats: First, a more analytical one, the lack of a convincing "yardstick"; the distance of the actual trade regime from the "ideal" of free trade cannot be measured when there is a complex system of multilateral and bilateral agreements with a multitude of other countries. Any counterfactual or "antimonde" simulation of trade liberalisation has to consider not only the links to EU-countries but also remaining barriers to trade with non-EU-countries[6].

---

[5] For a detailed review see European Commission 1996.

[6] A newly established method to construct such a yardstick are gravity models (e.g., Bayoumi, Eichengreen 1995, or Soloaga, Winters 2001). But they, too, suffer from the lack of completely free-trade examples.

Figure 1

Germany's EU-trade

1976 to 2000; Intra-EU trade as percentage of total

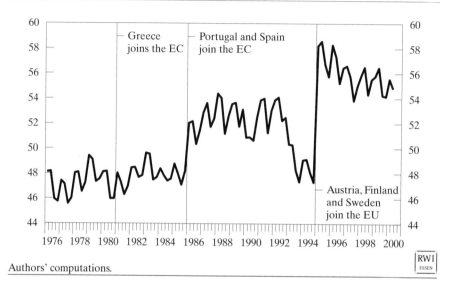

Authors' computations.

Second, changes other than trade liberalisation within Europe cannot be anticipated and therefore are difficult to account for. For instance, the sudden rise of the Newly Industrialising Countries (NICs) as well as the fall of the "iron curtain" boosted German exports to Asia and Eastern Europe, thereby reducing the relative importance of European trading partners.

Figure 1 gives an idea of these effects by putting German exports to EU-partners in relation to the total German exports[7], which lies between 45 and 60 percent. The shift in 1995 marks the statistical relocation of Austria, Finland and Sweden from extra-EU-trading partners to EU-members. Interestingly, the jumps in 1986 and 1994 are followed by a downward trend, hardly conform to the concept of continuous integration and growing inter-linkage of the economies. It rather indicates that trade effects induced by EU-integration were dominated by other influences on trade, so that even if the intra-EU trade rarely declined in absolute terms, in the years after the accession of new EU-members the respective trade share fell.

A more detailed look on bilateral trade between Germany and other EU-countries (Table 2) confirms this: The structural coefficients of most of the

---

[7] The share of German imports from EU-countries develops generally in line with the share of Germany's exports to the EU, within the same range with a similarly falling trend after the accession of additional countries.

Table 2

Integration effects of the European Union
Structural coefficients[1] of German exports to EU-countries,1960 to 1999

	1960/1972	1973/1985	1986/1994	1995/1999
Belgium	1,4	0,8	1,1	0,8
France	1,4	0,8	1,2	0,9
Italy	1,4	0,9	1,0	1,0
Netherlands	1,2	0,8	1,0	0,8
Denmark	0,7	1,1	0,9	0,9
Ireland	1,3	1,2	1,0	1,0
UK	1,4	1,9	1,0	1,0
Greece	1,2	0,9	0,9	0,9
Portugal	0,9	0,7	1,4	1,2
Spain	1,8	0,9	1,6	1,3
Austria	0,9	1,0	1,1	0,9
Finland	0,6	0,9	0,9	1,4
Sweden	0,7	0,9	0,9	1,0

Source: Authors' calculations. – [1]Structural Coefficient: actual to hypothetical export. Hypothetical export: exports to an EU-country in the base-year (year of accession) multiplied with the geometric mean of German export expansion to all countries and import growth of all imports of the EU-country. Structural coefficient > 1 = positive integration effect, < 1 = no integration effect. - Shaded: Country has not yet entered EU.   RWI ESSEN

countries are superior to unity – indicating a higher than average growth of German trade volumes in the years directly after their accession; in later periods, however, they often decline, indicating a lower than average trade expansion. Obviously, after some years the "integration booms" wore off.

This leads to three conclusions: First, the impact of regional enlargements was not as long-lasting as had been initially assumed; second, there is barely evidence that the efforts of lowering trade barriers within the EU resulted in a "fortress Europe"[8] that suppressed trade with other countries; third, the accession of new EU-members had significant one-off-effects in Germany's regional trade structure.

1.2 Fiscal co-ordination

After trade liberalisation, fiscal issues became a major item on the European integration agenda. Here, we concentrate on the financing of the *direct costs* of the new administration in Brussels (and elsewhere), and the *Maastricht-treaty* succeeded by the *Stability and Growth Pact*. Both issues were widely discussed in their times and seen as major losses of national sovereignty.

---

[8] Of course, without regarding adjustments in exchange rates, disaggregation of goods, and other factors, the analysis of trade volumes can only give a first hint.

Until 1970, the EC-budget was financed by small contributions from the member countries, ranging between 0.05 and 0.07 per cent of GDP. In 1970, the EC was given its own financial resources; starting with the revenues by import tariffs and levies of the EC-members, and later receiving part of the VAT revenues (the "VAT-own-resources") as its own "tax". As to the former, in a trade union all duties are collected at its outer frontiers without regard to their local incidence. Because it is impossible to identify the true target country (country of incidence), it seemed appropriate to use these revenues for the common institutions. As to the latter, they were politically motivated and expressed the willingness of transferring some mandatory rights to the EC. One consequence was a harmonisation process of the VAT in Europe. The modalities of calculating the VAT-own-resources were changed several times; nevertheless, in quantitative terms, they never were of macroeconomic relevance. Since 1992, the fixed upper band for EU-income has been 1.27 per cent of EU-GDP – however with much smaller net flows.

In contrast to the nearly negligible influence of these direct costs, the fiscal criteria established by the Maastricht-treaty in 1992 represent a major change of future EMU members' fiscal policy. Though there is no way to separate the global trend for *budget consolidation* from the efforts made in order to meet the Maastricht-rules, it is obvious that the distinct decline of public deficit (in Germany, it shrank from 3.4 (1996) to 1.2 (1999) per cent of GDP) is a direct consequence of this process of fiscal co-ordination. The total effects on real economic behaviour are controversial, because the immediate consequences of fiscal tightening are certainly contractionary, but in the long run, the argumentation of "crowding in-effects" may hold: by discharging financial markets, the interest rate may fall, inducing demand and growth. Econometric results show that while the loss of tariff- and tax revenues seem to have been of minor macroeconomic impact, consolidation may have reduced EU-GDP in the short run by 0.3 to 0.4 percentage points per year (Barrell et al. 1996, Horn, Zwiener 1996). For Germany, the loss in GDP due to fiscal policy between 1993 and 1997 is estimated at around 1.5 per cent in 1997 (Rheinisch-Westfälisches Institut für Wirtschaftsforschung 1996).

1.3 Monetary integration

Monetary integration was triggered by the breakdown of the *Bretton Woods* system and the consequent desire for exchange rate stabilisation. The creation of a European "snake" in the Bretton Woods "tunnel" in the turbulent early seventies can be seen as a first attempt of monetary integration. But the success was rather limited, as after numerous devaluations, some currencies dropped out, and the system was reduced more or less to the "Deutschmark zone"[9]. The first concrete step toward monetary integration of EC-members was taken in 1979 with the introduction of the European Monetary System (EMS) and its new synthetic currency ECU. This led to some stabilisation of the exchange rates between the member countries. Despite the heavy setback of its crisis in 1992/93, the path to monetary integration has been successful in the sense that, in 1999, it culminated in the EMU with its common currency unit, the Euro.

For the private sector, the fixation of exchange rates means a reduction of exchange-rate risk and, therefore, more planning certainty and lower costs of hedging. In "One market, one money", (European Commission 1990:21) the sum of transaction costs was calculated to reach 0.5 per cent of GDP. On the policy level, however, the decision over devaluations and monetary policy is given to the European Central Bank (ECB). The consequences of this are hard to quantify. In addition, there is no reference scenario, as European exchange rates never floated but were, with few exceptions, always more or less fixed. In principle, the EMU should bring about considerable changes in macroeconomic reactions on the demand side as well as structural reactions and factor supply. But it shouldbe remembered that the step in the direction of irrevocably fixed rates and the common currency is, for most EMU participants, only a change from a national central bank bound to German monetary policy towards membership in the ECB-council. For Germany, the loss of autonomy might have been largest.

2. Examining European integration – theoretical and methodical issues

Until now, European integration has been a process affecting many different fields of activity in the private and in the public sector. It has taken place in a broad context of similarly directed policies, e.g., the several GATT-rounds or the liberalisation of capital movements, and was stretched over a long period of time. A multitude of reinforcing as well as of compensating influences makes it very difficult to identify accurately the pure effects of single measures or policies of integration.[10] Furthermore, there are analytical difficulties. Although the economic theory of integration is, in principle, rather straightforward (Krugman, Obstfeld 1991: 231ff), it is still unclear, how the determinants of exports, imports, private consumption, investment etc. are affected. Economic theory is more concerned with shifts in "impulses" than in "propagation". To illustrate this point, take the example of a national export equation (a

---

[9] Including Benelux and Denmark as EC-members, but also Austria, Norway and Sweden.

[10] Establishing an "anti-monde" (Mayes 1978: 4) is therefore not possible. Hence, it is not surprising that the macroeconomic effects of fundamental changes of the institutional setting such as NAFTA or EMU are usually derived from computable general equilibrium (GE) models in which the parameters are *calibrated*, i.e. more or less assumed.

kind of reduced model itself): will integration increase/reduce the *elasticity* of world trade, terms of trade, and capacity utilisation? If so: How quickly will they change? Will there be compensational shifts in other sectors/parameters etc.? Certainly these questions are beyond the still simple cases addressed, for example, in the framework of the *Heckscher-Ohlin* model with variable coefficients (Krugman, Obstfeld 1991: 87f) – not to mention recent doubts concerning the explanatory power of classical trade theory (see Krugman 1993). In other words, the present macroeconomic framework allows only a rather phenomenological analysis and even then conclusions have to be drawn cautiously.

Of the three fields of integration, we concentrate on the first one; i.e., trade liberalisation. Judging from magnitudes involved, fiscal co-ordination cannot have caused major shifts in parameters, at least not when accounting for the net flows, that are most often less than 0.5 per cent of GDP; the Maastricht-treaty and its consequences are not yet captured by our sample period. Monetary integration is still a new experience and within the context of national macroeconomic models, hard to deal with. In addition, within the traditional system of European currencies, the Deutschmark was the anchor-currency (Tsoukalis 2000: 143ff), and therefore, the German monetary framework was changed least by the fixation of exchange rates in the EMS and the introduction of the Euro.

Our study is restricted to the national context. At first glance, a European framework would be of greater interest, somewhat reducing the role of assumptions and increasing the role of parameters. A closer look, however, reveals that the national perspective might not be limiting: First, a multi-country model would affect the size of the impulses and their repercussions and not the reaction parameters; second, the financial sphere (international capital movements) plays a major role in the international context, but have not yet been modelled in a satisfactory way (Bryant et al. 1988, Döhrn, Schira 1998). Therefore, especially as we focus on Germany, our approach might well be justified (see also below).

The following short description of the RWI-model informs about the theoretical and empirical environment in which the examined equations are imbedded; of course, a more integration-specific model of the foreign sector is easily conceivable. The overview also gives an idea about the channels which generate model effects/multipliers and about their magnitudes.[11]

2.1 The RWI-business cycle model

The RWI-business cycle model is a medium-sized, quarterly model, which has been used for short-term forecasting (six to eight quarters) and simulation

---

[11] More detailed descriptions of the models used and the results are available from the authors.

since the late 1970s. The version used here consists of 41 stochastic equations and 86 identities, which together form an interdependent, weakly non-linear model (for details on this and the following see Heilemann 1998). From a macroeconomic perspective, it can be partitioned into five sectors: GDP-origin (5 stochastic equations; 17 definitions), demand (8; 24), prices (8; 12), income distribution (6; 13), and government (14; 20). The list of major exogenous variables includes policy-determined variables, such as the social *security contribution rate, government construction outlays*, and interest rates, and internationally determined variables, such as *world trade* (volume index) and *import prices*. The architecture of the model follows the *Keynes/Klein* tradition; its reactions are governed by the income/expenditure approach with supply side elements being of minor importance. Expectations are formed in an adaptive way, though with rather low mean lags ("weakly rational"). The specification of the equations of particular interest for this paper is shown below.

The model is re-estimated (OLS) twice a year from seasonally unadjusted data. The sample period covers only the last 40 quarters of the available data ("moving window") in order to avoid cyclical bias as well as problems generated by the inclusion of a no-longer-relevant past. The model's forecasting accuracy has been continuously examined, ex post and ex ante, in general as well as in particular situations (e.g., Rheinisch-Westfälisches Institut für Wirtschaftsforschung 2000). When compared to other forecasts, the model's performance has been found satisfactory.

It should be emphasised that in terms of its general structure, specification of the single equations and their selection, the model is basically short-term oriented. The model's long-term properties and its determinants are of minor interest but when examined have been found to be "stable". As with most short-run models, impact and interim multipliers are of greater importance.

As with most models of this type, reactions are driven by the exogenous variables. Their weight is different for the various policy goals. Regarding growth, world trade, and interest rates are the most important ones, while import prices strongly influence domestic prices. Sooner or later, exogenous and endogenous impulses propagate through the system in the same way, i.e., the income/expenditure links. The government investment multiplier[12] reaches 1.6 in the first, and 2.3 in the third year; corresponding figures for the interest rate multiplier (impulse: -1 percentage point of short- and long-term interest rates) are 2.4 bill DEM and 6.8 bill DEM. In general, the model reacts rather quickly: about 90 percent of the lags are not longer than 4 quarters and only few mean lags (Koyck-lag) are longer than two quarters.

---

[12] These results are taken from the model version spring 1993 (no. 37).

2.2 Methods of analysis

To test the influence of integration on the behaviour of the foreign sector and investors, two paths are followed. The first examines *equations* taken from the RWI-business cycle model: on the basis of subsequent 40 quarter sample periods their parameters were calculated and shifts in these parameters were scrutinised for possible associations with the institutional changes/policies in the EC described above.[13] This procedure has the advantage of using parameters derived from a reasoned empirical base. On the other hand, the moving window technique implies, by construction, a smooth reaction to data innovations, as every estimation has got (here) 39 sets of (quarterly) data in common with its predecessor. Even in the case that a particular step towards further integration had caused an immediate response, only the fortieth part of it would be captured in the subsequent estimation.[14] In contrast, out-of-sample errors as presented below, might react quickly to such changes.[15] Therefore, we did not only check the parameters and elasticities for shifts, but also quality of fit.

The second, more conventional path, uses dummy variables for detecting structural breaks. This procedure starts with an extension of the model's sample period to 1960-I (actually 1964–I because of lags) to 1994–IV when the *Federal Statistical Office* ceased producing West German quarterly national accounts (NA) data. Then, for the major steps of European integration dummy variables are introduced into the tested equations:

- D68: on the formation of the customs union,
- D73: the first enlargement of the EC,
- D79: the introduction of EMS and
- D87: the announcement of the single market.

We use only 0/1 dummy variables (e.g., D68: until 1967–IV = 0, thereafter 1). There are a number of more refined techniques, such as temporary or step-wise dummies, however, their proper application requires more information than available.

Both approaches are affected by a lack of coherence in NA-data with regard to the length of the time span. New concepts of data collection[16], major general structural changes in the economy, not to mention attempts to harmonise data

---

[13] For earlier studies using the moving window technique see e.g., Heilemann, Münch 1984, or Barabas, Heilemann 1999.

[14] Recursive estimates solve this problem only in parts.

[15] Bear in mind that the moving window estimates have been assigned to the last quarter of the sample period in figure 1 and 2.

[16] For instance, there is a break in trade statistics in 1993 when customs documentation for intra-EU trade stopped, and any data collection since then has had to rely on companies' reports.

within Europe or degradation of data quality can all cause changes that are not easily distinguished from changes in the economy that result from integration.

In the end, trade liberalisation may affect all activities and actors of an economy, depending on the economy's integration in world markets and time. Examining the macroeconomic reactions as incorporated in the RWI-model – as a good representative of most models of this size – the equations for exports, export prices, imports, and investment in machinery and equipment are the most likely ones to be affected. A natural candidate for examination would also be, of course, wages, but here we restrict ourselves to the four variables specified above. Integration changes economic relationships: First of all, through the intensified competition enhanced by more transparency; which should reduce opportunities to pass on higher costs of production. Secondly, the growing inter-linkage in the production processes should alter the elasticities with ongoing integration.

Taking this into consideration, one might be tempted to formulate *ad-hoc* hypotheses about the directions in which the parameters might change. A closer examination, however, reveals that strong assumptions about the economic structures within Europe would be necessary. Whether more transparency leads to more price competition or rather to segmentation/specialisation; whether German exports profit from lower exchange rate risks or are dampened because European competitors gain the same advantage; to what degree German unit labour costs are influenced by Europe – the answer to these and more questions are preconditions to economic reasoning about shifts in the behaviour of German economic agents. In the light of this, the character of this study is of rather explorative nature.

3. Results

3.1 Single-equation context

As has been elaborated by, for example, *Pesaran, Smith, Yeo* (1985), behavioural change might not only be found in the equation's parameters (elasticities) but also in the statistical quality, in particular the fit quality, or in both. Declines in fit quality may hint at explanatory deficits. It should also be remembered that changes of parameters are not always able to catch large movements in the explaining variable (co-factor). Again, the interpretation of results has to be cautious.

Exports and export prices
The (logarithmic) equation for real exports follows the so-called "export push"-hypothesis, linking West German exports inversely to capacity utilisation. The main influences, however, are the two traditional determinants of ex-

Table 3

Macroeconomic reactions and European integration – Regression results of four equations[1]
1964–I to 1994–IV

Regressor[1]/ statistics	Regression parameters (t-statistics) Dummy variables for the European integration included:											
	no		D68		D73		D79		D87		all four	
Equation 1: Exports, real, log ()												
log(World_)	1.009	(122.3)	1.001	(95.8)	1.037	(71.8)	1.053	(54.3)	1.010	(88.5)	1.114	(30.6)
Tot	0.473	(7.9)	0.494	(8.0)	0.506	(8.4)	0.616	(7.5)	0.472	(7.5)	0.700	(7.9)
D68			0.021	(1.4)							0.011	(0.6)
D73					−0.034	(2.3)					−0.057	(3.2)
D79							−0.044	(2.5)			−0.056	(3.1)
D87									−0.001	(0.1)	−0.015	(0.7)
R^2, corr.	0.993		0.993		0.993		0.993		0.993		0.993	
DW	0.59		0.60		0.62		0.65		0.59		0.75	
SEE	0.042		0.042		0.041		0.041		0.042		0.040	
Equation 2: Export prices												
Pim	0.117	(8.3)	0.117	(8.4)	0.107	(8.1)	0.128	(8.3)	0.116	(7.1)	0.127	(7.4)
Ulc	32.986	(6.4)	29.925	(5.5)	25.590	(5.1)	33.117	(6.4)	32.888	(6.2)	23.220	(23.2)
Capa	0.036	(1.7)	0.045	(2.1)	0.052	(2.7)	0.042	(2.0)	0.037	(1.7)	0.044	(2.2)
World_	0.047	(2.8)	0.044	(2.6)	0.052	(3.3)	0.050	(3.0)	0.047	(2.7)	0.039	(2.5)
Pex(−1)	0.678	(16.5)	0.693	(16.7)	0.716	(18.5)	0.676	(16.6)	0.680	(15.2)	0.689	(17.1)
D68			0.353	(1.7)							0.365	(1.8)
D73					0.965	(4.7)					1.230	(4.9)
D79							−0.482	(1.7)			0.133	(0.5)
D87									−0.026	(0.1)	0.724	(2.8)
R^2, corr.	0.999		0.999		0.999		0.999		0.999		0.999	
DW	1.29		1.40		1.64		1.31		1.30		1.79	
SEE %	0.78		0.77		0.72		0.77		0.78		0.70	
Equation 3: Imports, real												
Cp_	0.235	(8.4)	0.261	(8.1)	0.324	(9.4)	0.253	(9.2)	0.246	(8.2)	0.379	(10.8)
Nocp_	0.385	(15.8)	0.368	(13.9)	0.331	(12.5)	0.389	(16.7)	0.369	(13.0)	0.333	(12.4)
D68			−1.996	(1.6)							−3.747	(3.1)
D73					−4.815	(4.0)					−5.422	(4.5)
D79							-3.562	(3.5)			−4.438	(4.5)
D87									1.31	(1.0)	−3.035	(2.3)
R^2, corr.	0.994		0.994		0.995		0.995		0.994		0.996	
DW	0.85		0.88		0.99		0.95		0.85		1.29	
SEE %	3.2		3.2		3.1		3.1		3.2		2.8	
Equation 4: Investment in machinery and equipment, real												
Demand_	0.117	(14.6)	0.117	(14.5)	0.114	(13.5)	0.121	(15.9)	0.107	(10.2)	0.107	(10.4)
Ulc	−43.575	(5.1)	−43.366	(4.9)	−37.101	(3.4)	−64.873	(6.8)	−37.732	(4.0)	−71.840	(5.5)
Interest_	−0.018	(0.1)	−0.026	(0.1)	−0.164	(0.1)	−0.357	(1.4)	−0.086	(0.3)	−0.467	(1.8)
D68			−0.137	(0.1)							1.658	(1.3)
D73					−1.327	(1.0)					2.061	(1.4)
D79							5.549	(4.1)			6.889	(4.6)
D87									1.953	(1.5)	3.594	(2.5)
R^2, corr.	0.912		0.911		0.912		0.922		0.913		0.925	
DW	0.44		0.44		0.47		0.51		0.47		0.57	
SEE %	8.9		8.9		8.9		8.4		8.9		8.2	

Authors' computations. – [1]Seasonal dummies and intercept are not exhibited. Abbreviation of the regressors: Capa – Capacity utilization; Cp_ – Private consumption, real; Demand_ – Sum of private consumption, investments and exports, real; Interest_ – Real long-term interest rate; Nocp_ – Final demand excluding private consumption, real; Pex – Export prices; Pim – Import prices; Tot – Terms of trade = Pim/Pex; Ulc – Unit labour cost; World_ – World trade volume, real.

Figure 2

Consequences of European integration

Elasticities and out-of-sample errors[1] of selected equations; 40 quarter moving window[2]
West Germany, 1960-I to 1994-IV

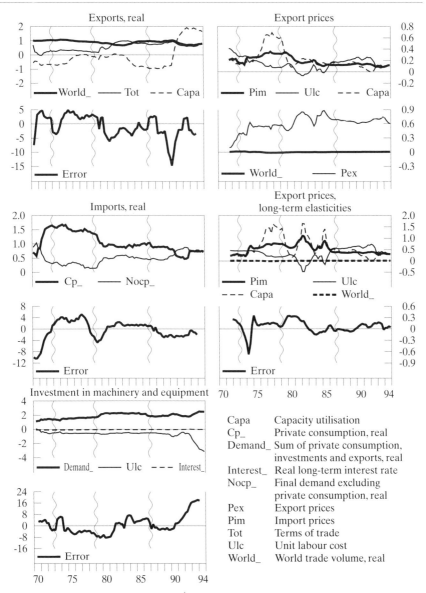

Authors' calculations. Dates marked by ⟩ indicate important trade liberalisations (1973, 1979 and 1987). – [1]Mean absolute percentage error over four quarters; sign corresponds to that of the mean error (forecast minus observed value). – [2]Elasticities and errors are assigned to the last quarter of the sample period.

Figure 3

German economy and European integration

Selected aggregates and their determinants West Germany, 1960-I to 1994-IV; annual rates of change

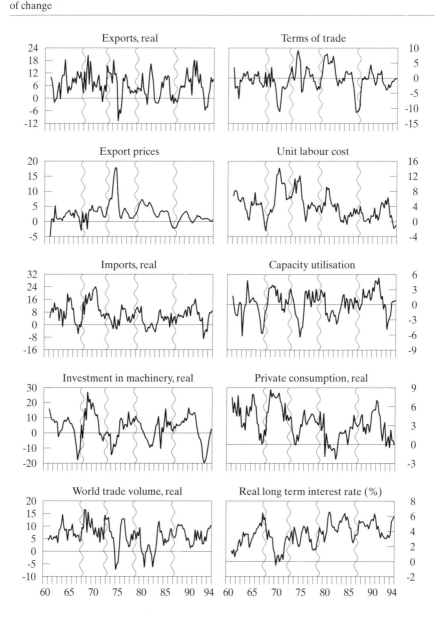

Source: Federal Statistical Office, Bundesbank, UNO. Dates marked by $\rangle$ indicate important trade liberalisations (1973, 1979 and 1987).

RWI
ESSEN

ports: World trade and terms of trade. (The specification of this and the other equations examined is given in Table 3.)

The evolution of elasticities is shown in Figure 2, time-series in Figure 3, fit-statistics and error measures for the long sample period version of the model in Table 3. The results are both disappointing and encouraging at the same time. They are disappointing insofar as none of the three parameters (ignoring seasonal dummies and intercept) show any evidence of integration effects, even if a long spread of these effects is allowed for. Encouraging is the fact that observed shifts of the elasticities can be explained, even though mainly by other economic events.

The decrease of the world trade elasticity and the implicit loss of world market share during the 1970s may be a consequence of regional shifts in world trade, i.e., the rapidly rising trade-volumes in Asia, which had only a small direct effect on German exports. The increase of the terms of trade-influence starting at the end of the 1970s might be seen in connection with a shift in trade-patterns in the sense that *intra*-industrial trade gained more and more importance compared to *inter*-industrial trade, which intensified competition. The shifts of all three elasticities in the beginning of the 1990s are the result of German unification since West German deliveries to East Germany of about DEM 180 billion (about 5 per cent of GDP and 25 per cent of exports) were in NA counted as exports.

The statistical quality ($\overline{R}^2$, DW not shown here) is somewhat deteriorating and reflects breaks to be observed with the elasticities. The *dummy-variable approach* (Table 3) largely confirms these findings. Both the D68 ("customs union") as well as the D87 ("announcement of the single market") are insignificant; D73 ("first enlargement") and D79 ("introduction of the EMS") are significant and raise the world trade- and terms of trade-elasticity of exports (at the expense of the intercept). The increases however are small, in particular when compared to the reaction shifts of the 40 quarter window detected earlier. (For the effects on multipliers, see below.) Moreover, capacity utilisation is missing, since its parameter does not take the expected (negative) sign for the long sample period, especially because of the 1990s. Tests for structural breaks (CUSUM, CUSUM square, and, after autoregressive correction, various *Chow* tests) did not affect these results and hence are not reported here.

Export prices are explained by a demand/import-price augmented version of the *mark up*-hypothesis. Until the early eighties short-term elasticity – based on the Koyck-model – appears to be rather stable. Only the capacity term shows a large increase in the mid-seventies, probably a reflex of the high capacity utilisation rates of this period. The results for the early 1990s again mirror unification, though here they are more modest. The long term elasticities reflect these changes, but are more pronounced. Again, while the development of the elasticities shows some remarkable changes, they can hardly be associated with European integration.

The results of the dummy variable approach are not very enlightening. Though D73 is found to be significant, at the same time its effect on the economic variables explaining the deflator are rather widespread: the influence of unit labour cost is increased by more than 40 per cent, while that of capacity utilisation is reduced by more than 20 per cent – the same holds for the elasticities.

Imports
Real imports are – in this model – determined by demand, represented by private consumption and the rest of final demand. No explicit price effects are included, because parameters of terms of trade in most of the sample periods do not have the expected sign. The evolution of the import-parameters can be divided into three stages: Until the end of the 1970s, the import-elasticity of private consumption is largely above unity, and that of the aggregates with German competitive advantages (exports, investments) below unity. Probably both reflect the undervalued Deutschmark; corresponding to the evolution of parameters of the Export equation. During the 1980s, the elasticity declines considerably but still remains close to one, denoting a nearly constant share of imported goods in consumption. The elasticities remain on these levels until the advent of German unification that has, for similar reasons as with exports, a distorting effect. Again, direct evidence for influences of European integration is hard to find[17]. On the contrary, the results lead to the counter-intuitive proposition that despite the intensified integration in Europe and in the world, import-elasticity declines. At least the various test statistics do not display large movements.

The experience with the dummy variable approach corresponds to that of exports: D68 and D87 do not indicate influence of the corresponding integration steps. D73 allows the consumption reaction of imports to increase considerably while that of the other demand aggregates is reduced; an outcome which is hard to explain economically. However, the parameter/elasticity changes seem to be largely offsetting each other as already experienced with the moving window results. Interestingly, the effects seem to have been of a transitory nature, since the D79-results are reversing to a large degree both effects, as is again confirmed by the moving window results.

---

[17] Barrell/te Velde (2002: 290) do not find convincing evidence for changing parameters caused by the Single Market Programme in German import equations, either. They argue that differing results might suffer from omitted variables, i.e. effects of foreign direct investment and technology.

Investment in machinery and equipment

Though investment in machinery and equipment was rarely expected to be directly affected by the various integration steps, the completion of the internal market is one of the few, though prominent exceptions: The increased competition enhanced investment in order to rationalise and to enlarge the production capacity. The explanation follows a neoclassically modified accelerator approach, combining final demand, unit labour cost, and the real (long-term) interest rate. The elasticity of the demand component gets a slight boost at the end of the 1970s and again in the early 1990s. While the latter might be seen as indicating internal market effects, the increasingly negative elasticity of unit labour cost does not fit into this picture. Again, the new reactions, with rapidly deteriorating $\bar{R}^2$ may primarily reflect the effects of German unification. The dummy-approach yields significant influences only for the period after 1979, though these are impressive. The unit labour cost parameter and the interest rate parameter are now much higher. Comparing them with the elasticities calculated using the moving window technique, the former achieves nearly the mean value of all sample periods of the moving windows, whereas the elasticity of the interest rate is still much lower.

3.2 The complete macroeconomic model context

While the effects of European integration on the four aggregates examined here may have changed, at least transitorily, the influence of some explanatory variables in the single-equation context, their macroeconomic impact remains open. We therefore calculated multipliers for world trade and import price in the model context. The comparison between the multipliers of a model without dummies (base line) and of the same model with dummies should give an idea of how much the economy's overall reaction patterns have been altered.

The base line model is developed following the specifications of the 1999 all-German version of the RWI-model, ignoring all but seasonal dummy variables. The sample period is 1964-I to 1994-IV. With the exception of the equation explaining indirect taxes (now log-linear), no changes of the functional forms are made. In some cases, variables have to be dropped and lag structures have to be modified. In general, all parameters keep their (correct) sign and fit quality is satisfying. This holds also for the alternative (dummy) model.

As usual with this type of model, general deliberations and single equation results point to autocorrelation. To get an idea of its influence on parameters and model reactions, the equations are re-estimated using the *Hildreth-Lu* procedure (Greene 2000: 546ff). This leads – in most cases – to small differences in parameters (though, a few times, the sign changes), but the model's reactions, compared to the original model, are hardly affected. Since our long experience relies on the version without the modification, the modifications are not used here.

Table 4

Macroeconomic effects of European integration
Differences to the baseline multipliers, two-year mean

Impulse[1]	World trade	Import prices	World trade	Import prices	World trade	Import prices	World trade	Import prices
Dummies applied[2]	single (D73)		all four		single (D79)		all four	
Solution period	1973/74				1979/80			
Employment	0.1	0.0	0.1	0.1	0.0	0.1	0.1	0.2
Investment in machinery and equipment, real	−0.1	0.1	0.8	0.6	0.6	0.4	0.6	0.6
Exports, real	−0.1	0.1	0.3	0.7	0.0	0.4	0.3	0.7
Imports, real	−0.4	−0.2	0.1	0.1	0.2	0.3	-0.1	0.1
GDP, real	0.0	0.1	0.2	0.2	0.0	0.2	0.2	0.3
GDP deflator	0.1	0.1	0.1	0.2	0.0	0.1	0.1	0.2
Government deficit as % of GDP	−0.1	−0.1	−0.2	−0.2	0.0	−0.1	−0.1	−0.2

Authors' computation, for details see text. – [1] Increases of the rates of change of World trade or Import prices by 10 percentage points in the first year. – [2]No dummy variables applied in the base line solution; in the alternative solution, the four equations (see Table 3 for details) include either single (D73 or D79) or all four dummy variables (D68, D73, D79, D87).

RWI
ESSEN

To test for the various integration policies, dummy variables representing the implementation of the measures (Table 3) are inserted and the multipliers of world trade and import prices for two periods, 1973/74 and 1979/80, are calculated and compared to the model without the dummies. As mentioned before, the periods of 1968 and 1987 are of minor interest, because the dummies for these years are not significant.[18]

The multipliers are calculated by inserting impulses on both world trade and import prices of 10 percentage points in the first year (rates of change). The difference between the multiplier of the baseline solution and the version applying the dummies are shown in Table 4. It is notable, that some differences between the results of two solution periods even in the same model without dummy-modification occur because of the type of multiplier (rate of change) and particular non-linearities of the model.

As Table 4 reveals, the multipliers of the dummy-version are generally higher than in the baseline model, particularly when using the full set of dummy variables. Of course, the three demand categories display the most visible effects. Interestingly, the results do not have the same sign within their aggregates, nei-

---

[18] In an additional procedure, we started to check slope dummies like (simplified)
$y = \alpha_0 + \alpha_1 {}^* x_1 + \alpha_2 {}^* dummy_1 + \alpha_3 {}^* (x_1 {}^* dummy_1) + ... + \varepsilon$.
The results hint at breaks in several parameters, in particular in 1979 and 1987. For 1979, this confirms the results mentioned above. The period captured by the 1987 dummy (1987-1994) is distorted by the effects of German unification.

ther in investment, exports nor imports; the sign does not change in employment, real GDP, the GDP deflator and in government deficit. However, measured by GDP growth or in terms of employment, with up to 0.2 or 0.3 percentage points in a two-year mean, the effects are still not very impressive.

Overall, the simulation results suggest that the reactions to European integration captured by the dummy variables changed the reactions as to be expected from the single-equation results. The shifts are not limited to the response of the foreign trade sphere but obviously also had some effects on investment and other demand aggregates. Given the small size of the effects, we did not see the necessity to isolate direct from indirect effects.

4. Summary and conclusions

The paper attempts to trace and quantify the consequences of European integration on German macroeconomic behaviour since the early 1960s. The study concentrates on the effects of trade liberalisation, without controlling for other realms of European integration, or other trade liberalisation policies such as general tariff reductions in the wake of GATT. The analysis is restricted to four variables – and their equations – most likely to be affected by trade liberalisation, i.e., exports (real and export prices), imports, and investment in machinery and equipment. The equations under examination are those employed in the RWI macroeconometric short-term model.

In one sense, the results are rather disillusioning. While there are clear theoretical expectations about trade creating and trade diverting effects of integration – to name the two most prominent effects of this process – they are hardly discernible in the parameters, and in the macroeconomic reactions. The parameter development (moving windows) and the dummy approach give no substantiation of changes in the four equations. While some dummy variables are significant in the early and late 1970s, as with the changes in parameters, one has to be cautious in ascribing them to European integration. In a broader perspective this raises the question of how and where the often cited macroeconomic effects – the impulses – were generated. As usual, the answer may lie in more rigorous testing of alternative explanations on the single-equation level. A second answer might be found in the level of analysis, arguing that many of the integration effects took place on the meso or micro levels and obviously were not important enough to show up on the macro level. Finally, it can be argued that the effects stretched over such a long period of time – starting long before the measures were enacted – and hence were, at each time, so small that they could not be identified here.

One motive for our analysis was to identify possible consequences of the EMU for future model building and use. Because of the lack of long experience with the new monetary regime, we took trade liberalisation as an example of the effects of European integration. Of course, the creation of the EMU, the loss of monetary autonomy and of the exchange rate instrument, is of a quite different nature and importance and one may doubt the relevance of such a comparison. Nevertheless, the lesson of our study suggesting that the successive steps towards the single market did not cause noteworthy parameter instability, is rather reassuring. Two arguments cause us to be hopeful about a similar outcome for the EMU: First, the immediate changes concern two policy instruments, and do not directly affect attitudes or actions of economic agents. Given the presumably similar goals of European and the former Bundesbank policy, the "innovation" appears not to be overwhelming. In addition, most of the EMU-members have not used these policy instruments for a long time but stabilised exchange rates vis-à-vis the DM. In the case of Germany, there was no need to bring down inflation or interest rates in order to fulfil the Maastricht-criteria. While the present results may hold for Germany, they should not be applied to, say, Italy or Spain. Second, macroeconomic as well as structural consequences of the process will, again, remain in effect over a long period and hence be rather modest at any one time.[19]

As to future research, the main conclusion might be that highly aggregated macroeconomics is not a promising turf for further study of the problem. What is needed is an internationally and regionally detailed examination. However, international macroeconometric models with exports and imports deeply disaggregated by regions are still not only rare, but contain their own inherent caveats, like the always questionable treatment of exchange rates, and will not produce indisputable results either.

Literature

Ballabriga, F. and C. Martinez-Mongay (2002), Has EMU shifted policy? Economic Papers 166. European Commission, Brussels.

Barabas, G. and U. Heilemann (1999), *Sample Selection Problems in a Macroeconometric Model Context – Some Further Results*. Paper presented at the November 1999 *Project* LINK meeting, Athens, Greece, 1–5 November 1999.

Barrell, R., J. Morgan and N. Pain (1996), *The Impact of the Maastricht Fiscal Criteria on Employment in Europe*. NIESR, London.

Barrell, R. and D.W. te Velde (2002), European Integration and Manufactures Import Demand: An Empirical Investigation of Ten European Countries. *German Economic Review* 3 (3): 263–293.

---

[19] Toolsema et al. (2001) analysing possible convergence of monetary transmission in EMU come to the same conclusion.

Bayoumi, T. and B. Eichengreen (1995), Is Regionalism Simply a Diversion? Evidence from the Evolution of the EC and EFTA. NBER Working Paper 5283. National Bureau of Economic Research, Cambridge, MA.

Bryant, R.C. et al. (eds.) (1988), *Empirical Macroeconomics for Interdependent Economies*. Brookings Institution, Washington, DC.

Döhrn, R. and J. Schira (1998), Internationale Perspektive: Zur Leistungsfähigkeit von Mehrländer-Modellen. In U. Heilemann and J. Wolters (eds.), 255–274.

Easterlin, R.A. (1998), *Growth triumphant – The twenty-first century in historical perspective*. Ann Arbor: University of Michigan Press.

European Commission (ed.) (1985), *Completing the Internal Market*. White Paper from the Commission to the European Council. Office for Official Publications of the European Communities, Luxembourg.

European Commission (ed.) (1988), The economics of 1992. *European Economy* 35: 17–243.

European Commission (ed.) (1990), One market one money. *European Economy* 44: 7–381

European Commission (ed.) (1996), Economic Evaluation of the Internal Market. *European Economy* 4.

Greene, W.H. (2000), *Econometric Analysis*. 4th Edition. Prentice Hall, New Jersey.

Heilemann, U. (1998), Erfahrungen mit dem RWI-Konjunkturmodell 1974 bis 1994. In U. Heilemann and J. Wolters (eds.), 61–92.

Heilemann, U. and H.J. Münch (1984), The Great Recession: A Crisis in Parameters? In P. Thoft-Christensen (ed.), System Modelling and Optimization. Proceedings of the 11th IFIP Conference 1983. Lecture Notes in Control and Information Sciences 59. Berlin, Heidelberg, New York: Springer, 71–82.

Heilemann, U. and J. Wolters (eds.) (1998), Gesamtwirtschaftliche Modelle in der Bundesrepublik Deutschland: Erfahrungen und Perspektiven. Schriftenreihe des RWI 61. Berlin: Duncker & Humblot.

Horn, G.A. and R. Zwiener (1996), *Beschäftigungsentwicklung im Zuge der Europäischen Währungsunion*. Gutachten im Auftrag des DGB und der Hans-Böckler-Stiftung. DIW, Berlin.

Jacquemin, A. and A. Sapir (1988), European Integration or World Integration? *Weltwirtschaftliches Archiv* 1988 (1): 127–139.

Krugman, P.R. (1993), *Geography and Trade*. Cambridge, MA: MIT Press.

Krugman, P.R. and M. Obstfeld. (1991), *International Economics* – Theory and Policy. 2nd ed. New York: Harper Collins.

Mayes, D.G. (1978), The Effects of Economic Integration on Trade. *Journal of Common Market Studies* 17 (1): 1–25.

Ohly, C. (1993), What Have We Learned About the Economic Effects of EC Integration? Economic Papers 103. European Commission, Brussels.

Pesaran, M.H., R.P. Smith and J.S. Yeo (1985), Testing Structural Stability and Predictive Failure: A Review. *Manchester School of Economic Studies* 53: 280–295.

Prognos AG (1990), Die Arbeitsmärkte im EG-Binnenmarkt bis zum Jahr 2000. Beiträge zur Arbeitsmarkt- und Berufsforschung 138.1. IAB, Nürnberg.

Rheinisch-Westfälisches Institut für Wirtschaftsforschung (ed.) (1996), Die wirtschaftliche Entwicklung im Inland. *RWI-Konjunkturberichte* 47 (2): 123–163.

Rheinisch-Westfälisches Institut für Wirtschaftsforschung (ed.) (2000), Vierteljährliche Prognose mit dem RWI-Konjunkturmodell 2000-1 bis 2001-4. Nr. 51. RWI, Essen.

Soloaga, I. and A. Winters, (2001), Regionalism in the Nineties: What effect on trade? *North American Journal of Economics and Finance* 12: 1–29.

Toolsema, L.A., J.E. Sturm, J. de Haan (2001), Convergence of Monetary Transmission in EMU. CESifo Working Paper No. 465.

Tsoukalis, L., (2000), The New European Economy Revisited. 2nd edition, New York: Oxford University Press.

Verdoorn, P.J., A.N.R. Schwartz (1972), Two Alternative Estimates of the Effects of EEC and EFTA on the Pattern of Trade. *European Economic Review* 3: 291 – 335.

Wee, H. van der (1984), *Der gebremste Wohlstand – Wiederaufbau, Wachstum und Strukturwandel der Weltwirtschaft seit 1945.* Geschichte der Weltwirtschaft im 20. Jahrhundert 6. München: dtv.

Ray Barrell, Karen Dury, and Ian Hurst[1]

Decision Making within the ECB: Simple Monetary Policy Rules Evaluated in an Encompassing Framework

1. Introduction

The purpose of this paper is to examine the merits of different monetary policy rules for the European Central Bank (ECB) by using stochastic simulation
techniques on the National Institutes Global Econometric Model, NiGEM.
The paper investigates the stabilisation properties of these rules in terms of reduced variability in certain major economic time series, such as output and inflation for individual member countries and for the Euroland aggregate as a
whole. The best policy rule for individual member economies may not be the
best policy rule for the Euroland aggregate and we investigate this by analysing the covariance structure of inflation within Euroland. We examine the
choice of policy rule and ask whether there is a potential conflict between the
decision making bodies within the ECB.

Large-scale macro-models of the economy need monetary closure rules even
more than they need fiscal closure rules, as many analyses cannot be sensibly
undertaken without some knowledge of the response of the monetary authorities. There are two classes of monetary policy rule that can be used in large models and by policy makers, and they have different implications for the stability
of the economy. There are those that tie a nominal magnitude or variable
down in the long run, including fixed exchange rate rules, money stock guidelines and nominal GDP targeting[2]. There are others that feed back on the inflation rate, and stabilise that in the long run. The latter class in general imply
that the price level will follow a random walk whilst the former class do not.
The distinction between these two classes of rules is brought out in a related
paper (Barrell et al. 1999). In this paper we analyse a set of rules that are fully

[1] The support of the ESRC under grant R022250166 Do small differences matter? is gratefully
acknowledged. We would like to thank Andy Blake for many helpful comments on this paper. All
errors remain ours.

[2] The class also includes using the change in the interest rate to target the level of inflation.

nested within one general framework in terms of their impact on stabilising inflation and output. We find that a combination of both these types of rules is the best policy rule for the ECB to follow in terms of reducing output and inflation variability.

Since Taylor's paper (1993), there has been much interest in the evaluation of different monetary policy rules. A substantial part of this literature concentrates on the use of simple policy rules on small stylised models many of which are backward looking closed economy models (see Rudebusch, Svensson 1999; Svensson 1997; Ball 1997). They argue that the optimal policy is some form of inflation targeting through a Taylor type rule in which interest rates are adjusted in response to deviations of output and inflation from their desired path. Many have advocated that interest feedback rules that respond to increases in inflation with more than a one for one increase in the nominal interest rate, are stabilising (see Clarida et al. 2000; Christiano, Gust 1999). Taylor (1999a) finds that there is historical evidence in the US that shows there is an unambiguous correlation between monetary policy rules and macroeconomic stability. Three eras of US monetary history were analysed. First, 1879–1914, where rates were unresponsive to fluctuations in output and inflation. Second, 1960–1979, where short term interest rates were more responsive, but the response on interest rates to changes in inflation were less than 1, and third 1986–1997, where the interest rate response was greater than 1. The latter period proved to be the most stable period. However, Orphanides (1998) casts doubt on these results using contemporary data rather than the final revision.

Taylor (1999b) suggests that the ECB should follow such a rule where the response coefficient on the inflation target is greater than one. However a recent paper by Benhabib et al. (1998) has argued that such an "active" policy rule can lead to instability. They show in an optimisation framework that even if there exists a unique steady state equilibrium for this rule, there will exist an infinite number of equilibrium trajectories lying near the active steady state. They advocate that using local techniques to analyse the stability of the system may lead to inappropriate policy regimes. We find that for individual member countries and for Euroland as a whole, increasing the feedback coefficient on a pure inflation targeting rule can help stabilise both output and inflation variability. However, it is still not the preferred rule in terms of minimising the variability of output and inflation.

Monetary policy also affects the economy through exchange rate channels as well as through the interest rate effects on domestic demand. Therefore the choice of a "best" monetary policy rule may change when working in an open economy framework. Svensson (2000) extends the analysis of inflation targeting to a small open economy model where the exchange rate plays a prominent role in the transmission mechanism of monetary policy and shows that by targeting variables other than just inflation, the variability of other economic variables is reduced. In order to take account of the variability of these other variables it is necessary that small models are expanded to include them, and that we work in an open economy framework. Hence there is a strong case for analysing the ECB's problems using a large open macro–economic model. Taylor (1999b) uses stochastic simulations on a seven country open economy macro–economic model to calculate the variability of certain economic variables under a Taylor rule. However, he does not analyse how the economic stability is affected by changing the parameters of the rule. We aim to build on this work by taking a class of monetary policy rules considered in the general framework that we have developed and apply different parameterisations of the rules to ascertain whether these small model findings hold on a large open–economy macro–econometric model.

We use stochastic simulation techniques on the National Institutes Global Econometric Model, NiGEM, in order to evaluate the performance of the policy rules. The best way to evaluate the stabilisation properties of the rules is to apply a sequence of random shocks to the model. Analysing policy rules using deterministic shocks is useful as it can give a clear comparison of the effects under a very specific shock to the economy (Barrell et al. 1998). However, the overall performance of a policy rule will depend on its ability to stabilise economic variables given a variety of shocks. To conclude that one rule is superior to another, we must apply a number of random shocks to the model and measure their overall performance, and hence the most effective way to evaluate rules is to use stochastic simulation techniques as we do in this paper. We also build on existing work in this area by including exchange rate uncertainty in the simulations as in the past it has been standard practice to exclude them in stochastic simulations. This issue is discussed in Section 4.

The format of the paper is as follows: In section 2 we develop the framework for analysing a class of monetary policy rules. We discuss four types of rules that are nested within that general framework. Section 3 provides a brief overview of NiGEM and Section 4 gives a summary of the techniques used to undertake stochastic simulations on NiGEM. Section 5 reports the results of the simulations on the variability of certain economic variables. Section 6 discusses the European aggregates and the covariance structure of inflation among the Euroland countries and Section 7 concludes.

2. An encompassing framework

We concentrate on the use of various simple policy rules as opposed to deriving the policy rule from an optimal control perspective. One of the main reasons for the widespread use of simple rules on large macro-economic models is that they are easy to understand and interpret. Advocates of simple policy rules argue that they are helpful in monitoring the performance of the authorities (see, for instance, Taylor 1985).

In this section we provide a general framework for evaluating different monetary policy rules. We compare four possible feedback rules for the interest rate that are nested within one general policy rule. We focus on a standard monetary policy rule, where the central bank targets some monetary or nominal aggregate, a combined nominal aggregate and inflation targeting rule and also a pure inflation targeting rule with different feedback coefficients. It appears from Duisenberg (1998), that the ECB has adopted a combination of money base targeting and inflation targeting and so in this paper we evaluate this rule against other rules nested within it.

In order to investigate the performance of these regimes we need to give an explicit form to the policy rule that is to be followed. The four interest rate rules we investigate are encompassed by[3]:

$$r_t = \gamma_1 \left(y_t - y_t^* \right) + \gamma_2 \left(\pi_t - \pi_t^* \right) \tag{1}$$

where r is the short term interest rate, is the annualised domestic inflation rate, y is log of nominal output and $_1$ and $_2$ are feedback parameters. An astrix denotes target variables. The policy rule that the ECB follows will depend on the Euro wide aggregates and interest rates react to Euroland aggregates. Various types of rules are nested within this general framework. The table below summarises the policy rules and the value of the feedback parameters.

Type of rule		Parameter values	
		γ_1	γ_2
NOM	Nominal GDP targeting rule	50	0
CR	Combined nominal GDP and inflation targeting rule	50	1
INFT1	Inflation targeting rule	0	1
INFT1.5	Inflation targeting rule	0	1.5

The nominal GDP rule, NOM, the combined rule, CR, and the pure inflation targeting rule, INFT1 are fully nested. Rules INFT1 and INFT1.5 are directly comparable in that the coefficient on the inflation target is increased from 1 to 1.5.

We use the terms, nominal GDP and monetary aggregate, as substitutes for each other, as a velocity de-trended monetary aggregate will move in line with nominal GDP in the medium term. We are also not assuming that the authorities wish to hit their target period by period so responses will be similar with

---

[3] For further details on policy rules that are encompassed within a general framework see Barrell et al. 1999.

either target. The rules used in this paper use the Consumer Price Index (CPI) inflation rate as a target.[4] The rules target the current rate of inflation and the current level of a nominal magnitude. It is sometimes argued that a measure of forecast inflation is more appropriate due to the lag in monetary policy affecting the economy (see Svensson 1997; Batini, Haldane 1999). But as Blake (2000) shows, the inclusion of a forward looking term is not significantly different from the use of a current term in forward looking models, as current conditions will reflect future out–turns. We also believe it is likely that the ECB is actually reacting to what it perceives as current conditions, which are endogenous in our framework. For these reasons we concentrate on using current deviations from target in our rules.

3. The model

NiGEM is an estimated model, which uses a "New-Keynesian" framework in that agents are presumed to be forward-looking but nominal rigidities slow the process of adjustment to external events. The theoretical structure and the relevant simulation properties of NiGEM are described in Barell/Sefton (1997), Barrell et al. (2001b) and NIESR (2001). The model has a full description of all the economies of the OECD, including South Korea[5]. Each economy has a supply side, a demand side, and a full set of asset accumulation relationships including a complete set of government sector, foreign sector and private sector financial accounts· All equations have been tested for structural stability and the most recent stable relationships are used. Labour market descriptions contain wage equations based on a bargaining framework where there is no nominal inertia, but also where forward looking expectations for prices have an influence on wage setting.

Exchange rates follow the forward looking open arbitrage condition, and hence they can "jump" when there is news, and long term interest rates are the forward convolution of expected future short rates and they can also "jump" in the first period. These "rational expectations" elements are augmented by labour market relationships that look forward and backward. Hence, we can claim we have addressed the "Lucas Critique" of policy analysis on large models especially as all relationships are tested for structural changes and the most recent, stable, description of behaviour is always used. We discuss below how the exchange rates are shocked in the stochastic simulations.

---

[4] Issues arising from targeting the domestic inflation rate (where only inflation in the domestic component of the CPI, or GDP deflator) is targeted are dealt with in Svensson 2000.

[5] China is also modelled separately and there are regional blocks for East Asia, Latin America, Africa , Miscellaneous Developing countries and Developing Europe.

4. Stochastic simulations

The world is constantly faced with shocks; they can be large and infrequent or small and frequent. It is impossible to know where the next major surprise will come from. One obvious example of a major surprise in the recent past is the collapse of the East Asian economies in 1997 and 1998. By repeatedly shocking the model with different sets of shocks it is possible to evaluate the range over which a variable may move. Stochastic simulations require that shocks are taken at random from a particular distribution and repeatedly applied to the model. From this the moments of the solution of the endogenous variables can be calculated and variability investigated. Stochastic simulations can be done either in respect to the error terms, coefficient estimates or both. In this paper we assume that the coefficient estimates are known with certainty and the stochastic shocks to the model are only applied to the error terms, much as in the rest of the economic literature.

We use the boot strap method where the shocks are generated by repeatedly drawing random errors for individual time periods for all equations from the matrix of single equation residuals (SER), as in Blake (1996). The shocks drawn will have the same contemporaneous distribution as the empirical distribution of the SER, which are assumed to be normally distributed, $N(0,\sigma^2)$. In this way the historical correlation of the error terms are maintained across variables, but not through time. We have taken our model NiGEM, and calculated the historical shocks to all the structural equations for all 1000 estimated relationships. We draw our shocks from the period 1993q1 to 1997q4 on the assumption that the near future will be similar to the near past. See Barrell et al. (1999) for a detailed discussion of the model solution algorithm and the procedure used for shocking and solving the model under stochastic simulations[6].

These unexplained events have then been applied repeatedly to our forecast (which runs 24 years into the future) to produce a new future history. We have applied the shocks over the period 1999 to 2003, running the model "forward" to calculate the expectations that would be a reasonable response to the news. The model is solved far enough into the future to ensure the results are independent of the end points of the run. One stochastic simulation consists of shocking the model in the first quarter, solving forward for 18 years, retaining results from that quarter and then repeating this exercise for each of the following quarters we are shocking using the projections from the previous run as a baseline. We use the outcome from the previous run as the baseline for the current run in order to update expectational variables that change in the current period and in the future in response to news. We do this 200 times for each regime. This means we have a total of 4000 simulations per regime. We show in

---

[6] See also chapter 5 of Clements/Hendry (1999) contains a clear description of the technique used in this paper.

a previous paper that after roughly 100 stochastic simulations the results settle down (see Barrell et al. 2000). A good assessment of the variabilities can hence be made with 200 trial runs and further simulations would not change the results noticeably.

Shocking the Exchange rate
In this paper we include shocks to exchange rates however this is not standard practice in these exercises (see Fair 1998). Shocks to the exchange rate have been excluded in the previous literature as the exchange rates are often used as policy reaction functions in the model. They are therefore treated as rules with no stochastic errors i.e. they are deterministic. In our analysis we assume that the market sets the exchange rate and so it is therefore not in any sense a policy instrument. The equation therefore has a random error associated with it and there is no reason to exclude this variable from being shocked. In our model the interest rate is the policy instrument and so we do not apply shocks to this equation[7].

The construction of historical shocks to sterling is clear, as the bilateral rate against the dollar existed in the past, as did the rates for Japan, Canada, Sweden and so on. However, we are simulating the model with an exchange rate equation for the Euro, a currency that did not exist in the past. Moving from the a regime where individual Euro area countries have their own exchange rates to one where there is single exchange rate for EMU members introduces some uncertainties as to what shocks to apply to the Euro. We could construct a set of shocks to the Euro that was the weighted average of shocks to the individual currencies over the past. However, this would not necessarily be the correct strategy, as EMU has been set up, and hence shocks across bilateral rates within the Union are no longer possible. A better strategy would be to apply the shocks that occurred to the core of EMU (Germany, Belgium, Netherlands, France (and Austria)) over the 1993 to 1997 period, and we adopt this for the Euro. However, this means that we are applying a subset of historical shocks, especially to the European Monetary Union and to the US, as in the latter case shocks to the exchange rate are the result of shocks to all US dollar bilateral rates.

Stochastic experiments on NiGEM
This paper seeks to use the method of stochastic simulations to evaluate the different types of monetary policy rules discussed in Section 2 on a large econometric open economy model. We focus on the implications of the results for interest rate determination at the ECB. We examine the degree to which output, inflation and some other key economic variables fluctuate around the forecast baseline or target path. We examine the variability of individual time

---

[7] For a more detailed discussion of the issues involved and the importance of shocking the exchange rate see Barrell et al. 2001a.

series across the different policy rules for each member country and for the Euro area as a whole. A policy that reduces the variability of these economic series will be judged to be more effective. In the following section we report the results of the stochastic simulations across the four different rules. In Section 6 we go on to discuss the implications the different rules have for the covariance structure of inflation in the Euro area and the implications this has for decision making in the ECB.

5. Results

There are a number of potential patterns of results that we might observe. In this section we show that when we include a direct inflation target with a nominal GDP targeting rule, output and inflation variability are both reduced for virtually all individual member economies and for the Euro area as a whole. Removing the nominal aggregate from the rule so that the ECB follows a pure inflation targeting rule results in higher output and inflation variability for individual economies and for the Euro aggregate. However, when we increase the feedback on the pure inflation target, both output and inflation variability fall but they are still greater than under the combined rule.

Our results indicate that the best policy rule for the ECB to follow is a combined nominal GDP and inflation targeting rule as both output and inflation variability are lowest under this rule. We also show that individual country performances, in terms of the changes in inflation variabilities across the rules, are different to the behaviour of the Euroland aggregate, implying a changing covariance structure across the Euroland area. We explore this in Section 6.

In this section we present the results for each Euroland member country under the four policy rules. Following the analysis of Bryant et al. (1993), the results from the stochastic simulations are reported as Root Mean Squared Deviations (RMSDs) from their target path[8]. This summary statistic shown in tables 1 and 2 gives a simple average of the deviations from target over the whole time period considered. The tables also contains an index value for the variability of results under the combined rule (CR), the inflation targeting rule with a feedback coefficient of 1 (INF1) and 1.5 (INF1.5), respectively, compared to the nominal GDP targeting rule (NOM). Where stochastic simulation results give a lower variability than under the Nominal GDP targeting rule, the box is shaded. The tables also indicate the statistical significance

---

8

$$RMSD = \sqrt{(1/N)\sum_{t=1}^{N}\left\{(1/J)\sum_{j=1}^{J}\left[\frac{\left(x^j_{it} - x^B_{it}\right)}{x^B_{it}}\right]^2\right\}}$$ where x^j_{it} is the value of variable i in period t from

the jth trial, x^B_{it} is the value of the variable i on the base in period t, J is the number of trials taken. For variables such as interest rates and inflation rates, absolute deviations are measured.

Table 1

Variability of output, index value for the combined rule (CR),
and inflation targeting rules (INFT1 and INFT1.5)

Country	NOM	CR	INFT1	INFT1.5	NOM = 100		
					CR	INFT1	INFT1.5
GE	3.17	3.10	3.29	3.28	98	104[a]	103[a]
FR	1.25	1.19	1.36	1.28	95[c]	109[a]	103[a,b]
SP	1.89	1.87	2.07	1.98	99	110[a]	105[a,b]
IT	1.12	1.11	1.20	1.18	99	107[a]	105[a]
NL	2.21	2.18	2.25	2.24	99	102[a]	101
BG	1.67	1.67	1.72	1.73	100	102	103
PT	2.35	2.33	2.41	2.39	99	102[a]	101
IR	3.06	3.07	3.13	3.14	100	102	103
FN	1.13	1.06	1.22	1.15	94[c]	108[a]	102[a,b]
OE	3.08	3.07	3.15	3.13	100	102	102
EL	1.76	1.73	1.85	1.82	98	105[a]	103[a]

Authors' calculations. – [a]Indicates variance is significantly different to the variance under CR. – [b]Indicates variance is significantly different to the variance under INFT1 (only the comparison of INFT1.5 to INFT is shown). – [c]Indicates variance is significantly different to the variance under NOM.

between variances[9]. Tables 1 and 2 present results for output and inflation variability for individual member countries and for the Euroland aggregate. Superscripts indicate whether one rule is significantly different to another at the 5 % level.

Output variability

– Rule NOM→ CR
    The majority of EMU member states benefit from reduced output variability under the combined rule compared with a nominal targeting rule (although this is only significant for France and Finland). The variability for Euroland output also falls.

– Rule CR → INFT1
    A pure inflation targeting rule increases output variability for all European countries compared to the combined rule. The increase is significant for all countries with the exception of Belgium, Ireland and Austria. Euroland output variability also increases significantly as the nominal aggregate is removed.

– Rule INFT1 → INFT1.5
    All EMU member states experience a fall in output variability as the in-

[9] The F–ratio to be tested is formed by taking the larger variance (not the RMSD as shown in the tables) divided by the smaller variance with the degrees of freedom associated with the number of sample points. This will give a value greater than unity. We may say that if variances differ by more than 6 to 7 percent then they are significantly different from each other at the 5 % level. A related paper gives results for the UK and the US, see Barrell et al. 2001a.

Table 2

**Variability of inflation, index value for the combined rule (CR),
and inflation targeting rules (INFT1 and INFT1.5)**

Country	NOM	CR	INFT1	INFT1.5	NOM = 100		
					CR	INFT1	INFT1.5
GE	1.11	1.08	1.16	1.14	97	105[a]	103[a]
FR	0.59	0.56	0.66	0.64	95[c]	111[a]	108[a,b]
SP	0.97	0.95	1.04	1.00	97	108[a]	103[a,b]
IT	0.98	0.98	1.06	1.03	100	109[a]	105[a,b]
NL	0.97	0.95	1.00	0.99	98	104[a]	103[a]
BG	1.91	1.89	1.91	1.92	99	100	101
PT	1.61	1.64	1.61	1.62	102	100	101
IR	1.01	0.97	1.05	0.97	96c	104[a]	96[b]
FN	0.61	0.61	0.67	0.65	100	109[a]	106[a]
OE	1.73	1.72	1.77	1.74	100	102	101
EL	0.59	0.56	0.68	0.63	94[c]	115[a]	106[a,b]

Authors' calculations. – [a]Indicates variance is significantly different to the variance under CR. – [b]Indicates variance is significantly different to the variance under INFT1 (only the comparison of INFT1.5 to INFT is shown). – [c]Indicates variance is significantly different to the variance under NOM.

flation coefficient is increased from 1 to 1.5, (except for Belgium and Ireland who experience a slight rise, although this is insignificant, and Austria who sees no change in output variability). However, output variability is higher than under either the nominal or the combined rule. The difference from the unit coefficient rule is only significant for France, Spain and Finland. The Euro area as a whole also sees a fall of 2% in output variability but this is not significant.

Inflation variability

– Rule NOM → CR
Most of EMU member countries see a fall in inflation variability under the combined rule compared to the nominal aggregate rule. Out of the 4 largest economies it is only Italian inflation variability that does not fall. It is interesting that for EMU as a whole, inflation variability falls by more than in any individual country. We return to this issue below.

– Rule CR → INFT1
Moving to a pure inflation targeting rule with a feedback coefficient of 1 raises inflation variability for all countries (with the exception of Portugal), and for virtually all countries this is significant. For EMU as a whole there is a rise in inflation variability of over 20% as compared to the combined rule, however no individual country experiences such a large increase.

– Rule INFT → INFT1.5
All countries see a fall in inflation variability when the feedback coefficient

on inflation is increased in the pure inflation targeting case (with the exception of Belgium and Portugal). For EMU as a whole the fall in inflation variability between these two rules is significant.

If the ECB were to follow a pure inflation targeting rule, then output variability would increase for every country and for the aggregate as a whole. This is not surprising as nominal GDP is the product of real GDP and the price level and any rule involving a nominal aggregate therefore contains an implicit target on the level of real GDP. We thus see a rise in output variability when this target is removed from the rule. Svensson (1999) also shows that in a simple model with a rational expectations based Lucas supply curve, nominal targeting may reduce both output and inflation variability. With a Phillips curve relationship in a new-Keynesian framework it is possible that output variability might be higher under a nominal targeting rule than an inflation targeting rule. However our model, NiGEM, has a Taylor style bargaining framework where both past and future expectations of inflation are included and hence it is a compromise between the two extremes. As Vestin (2000) shows it is possible to design a policy rule that weights output so that inflation is more stable under nominal targeting when the supply side displays forward looking behaviour but also exhibits nominal inertia. Hence our results are fully consistent with the predictions of these papers.

The combined rule with a coefficient of 1.0 on inflation is the best rule for the Euro Area as a whole as both output and inflation variability are lower than in any of the other rules considered. Pure inflation targeting with a coefficient of 1 appears to be the least effective at stabilising the Euro area aggregates. However, increasing the feedback coefficient from 1 to 1.5 does help to reduce both output and inflation variability, although it still leaves output and inflation variability significantly higher than that achieved under the combined rule.

It is interesting to examine individual country performance and compare it to that of the Euro aggregate. In terms of inflation, the majority of individual countries see a fall in variability under the combined rule compared to the nominal aggregate rule. However, for the Euroland as a whole inflation variability falls by more than in any individual country. This implies that the covariance structure of inflation in the Euro area changes across the rules. The same pattern emerges when moving to a pure inflation targeting rule. The change in the variability of the Euroland aggregate is larger than in any individual country.

The variabilities of output and inflation can be compared to that we have seen over the five years from which we draw shocks. The standard deviation of output as compared to a time trend over this period for the Euro Area is 0.41 as compared 1.73 to 1.85 in the stochastic simulations. Our simple policy responses do not include any active fiscal feedbacks, and hence it is not surprising that output is more volatile than over the past when policy has been used in this way. Inflation volatility over the same period is 1.1 for the Euro Area as compared to 0.56 to 0.68 in the stochastic simulations. As inflation variabilities in our stochastic simulations are below "actuals" for the Euro area it is not surprising that output is more variable in the simulations. This implies that in the past output took a greater weight in policy reactions as compared to inflation in these countries than in our simple rules.

6. Euroland aggregates

In this section we examine the apparent discrepancy between the changes in the variability of individual country inflation rates and the changes in the variability of inflation for the Euro area as a whole. We show that the reason for this discrepancy is that the covariance structure of inflation in the Euro area changes over the rules and that this may have important implications for decision making at the ECB.

The ECB has stated that its concern is to minimise the variability of Euroland inflation rather than the variability of inflation in individual member countries. The former entails calculating the weighted average of individual country inflation rates and *then* examining the variability of this measure from its target path. The latter entails weighting each member country's inflation rate variances. The two measures of Euroland inflation are not the same – the variance of a sum is different to the sum of variances. The ECB will therefore be concerned with the covariances between individual country inflation rates and this can be seen below. The variance of Euroland inflation at time t is

$$Var\left(EMU \inf_t\right) = \left[\sum \alpha_i \pi_{it} - \sum \alpha_i \pi^*_{it}\right]^2 \qquad (1)$$

where i is country at time t, and   is country i's inflation rate at time t. An astrix denotes target variables. This can be rearranged to give:

$$Var\left(EMU \inf_t\right) = \left[\sum \alpha_i^2 \left\{\pi_{it} - \pi^*_{it}\right\}^2 + 2\sum_{i \neq k} \alpha_i \alpha_k \left\{\pi_{it} - \pi^*_{it}\right\}\left\{\pi_{kt} - \pi^*_{kt}\right\}\right] \qquad (2)$$

or simply

$$Var\left(EMU \inf_t\right) = \left[\sum \alpha_i^2 \, var(i)_i + 2\sum_{i \neq k} \alpha_i \alpha_k \, cov \, ariances\,(i, k)\right] \qquad (3)$$

The first element is the sum of individual country variances multiplied by the square of the individual country weights. The second is the sum of twice the covariance between countries multiplied by the corresponding country weights. Table 3 shows the breakdown of Euroland inflation variability as a whole.

Table 3

Components of total Euroland inflation variability

	NOM	CR	INFT1	INFT1.5
$\sum \alpha_l^2$ VAR	0.19	0.18	0.21	0.20
$2 * \sum \alpha_i \alpha_k$ COV(i,k)	0.16	0.13	0.25	0.19
Mean squared deviation[1]	0.35	0.31	0.46	0.39
RMSD	0.59	0.56	0.68	0.63

Authors' calculations. – Note that the squared deviations are taken around the baseline value, not as would be the case for a true variance around the mean.

– Rule NOM → CR

The table shows that as an inflation target is added into the nominal GDP rule, the average of individual inflation rate variances falls, and the average covariance falls by more, thereby reducing the variability of the aggregate further. This explains the result shown in Table 2 where Euroland inflation variability fell by more than any individual country.

– Rule CR → INFT1

Moving to a pure inflation target the individual country variances rise, and again the covariance structure of the Euroland inflation changes. The rise in the covariance is larger than the rise in the average variance thereby increasing the total variance for Euroland inflation by more than the simple average would imply. Again we saw this in Table 2 where Euroland inflation variability rose by more than in any individual country.

– Rule INFT1 → INFT1.5

The average variance falls very slightly as the coefficient on inflation is increased to 1.5 but again the fall in the average covariance is larger so that Euroland inflation variability falls further than individual countries.

It is clearly possible that the average variance could rise whilst the covariance falls by more, hence inducing a conflict between the Governing Council and the Executive Board. The former would be concerned with minimising the variability of individual inflation variances and the latter would be concerned with minimising the variance of Euroland inflation as a whole. Thus regional conditions could influence policy and evidence in the United States shows that local conditions can influence the votes of regional bank governors (see Havrilesky, Gildea 1992, 1995; McGregor 1996). However while it is quite possible for this to be the case for the European Monetary Union, we find that the different policy rules we consider in this paper would not result in such a conflict. The two principal decision making bodies of the ECB would both choose the combined rule as both Euroland inflation variability and individual country inflation variabilities are minimised under this rule.

7. Conclusions

In this paper we have used stochastic simulation techniques on the National Institutes Global Econometric Model, NiGEM to investigate the stabilisation properties of different monetary policy regimes. We repeatedly applied historical shocks to the model, and then calculated the subsequent variances of economic variables. This then allows a comparison to be made between the different rules and judgements to be made as to their performance in terms of economic stability. A rule is judged to be superior if it reduces the variability of certain economic variables.

We find that a combined nominal GDP and inflation targeting rule is superior to both a nominal GDP targeting rule and a pure inflation targeting rule in terms of stabilising Euroland output and inflation and so is the ECB's preferred rule. The results also clearly point to this rule being the preferred rule for individual member countries. We also show the variance of Euroland inflation is not the same as the average of individual country variances and so there could be a situation when the ECB and the individual member countries prefer different rules. The covariance structure of Euroland inflation would influence this possibility. We decompose Euroland inflation into its components – the weighted sum of individual inflation variabilities and the weighted sum of the covariances, and find that while the covariance structure changes over the rules, there is no immediate conflict within the decision making bodies of the ECB.

References

Ball, L. (1997), Efficient Rules for Monetary Policy. *International Finance* 2 (1): 63–93.

Barrell, R., K. Dury and N. Pain (1998), *Working under Different Rules: An Analysis of Different Monetary Policy Feedback Rules.* Paper presented at Money Macro Finance Conference, September 1998.

Barrell, R., K. Dury and I. Hurst (1999), An Encompassing Framework for Evaluating Simple Monetary Policy Rules. NIESR Discussion paper 156. National Institute of Economic and Social Research, London.

Barrell, R., K. Dury and I. Hurst (2000), International Monetary Policy Coordination: An Evaluation of Cooperative Strategies using a large Econometric Model. NIESR Discussion paper 160. National Institute of Economic and Social Research, London.

Barrell, R., K. Dury and N. Pain (2001a), *Decomposing Forecast Uncertainty.* National Institute of Economic and Social Research, London, mimeo.

Barrell, R., K. Dury, I. Hurst and N. Pain (2001b), *Modelling the World Economy: The National Institute Global Econometric Model, NiGEM.* National Institute of Economic and Social Research, London, mimeo.

Barrell, R. and J. Sefton (1997), Fiscal Policy and the Maastricht Solvency Criteria. *Manchester School of Economic Studies* 65 (3): 259–279.

Batini, N. and A. Haldane (1999), Forward-Looking Rules for Monetary Policy. Bank of England Working Paper 91. Bank of England, London.

Benhabib, J,. S. Schmitt-Grohé and M. Uribe (1998), The Perils of Taylor Rules. Working Paper RR9837. CV Starr Centre of Applied Economics at New York University, New York.

Blake, A. (1996), Forecast Error Bounds by Stochastic Simulations. *National Institute Economic Review* 156: 72–79.

Blake, A. (2000), Optimality and Taylor Rules. *National Institute Economic Review* 2000 (4): 80–91.

Bryant, R.C, P. Hooper and C.L. Mann (1993), *Evaluating Policy Regimes: New Research in Empirical Macroeconomics.* Washington, DC: Brookings.

Christiano, L. and C. Gust (1999), Taylor Rules in a Limited Participation Model. *De Economist* 147 (4): 437–460.

Clarida, R., J. Gali and M. Gertler (2000), Monetary Policy Rules and Macroeconomic Stability: Evidence and Some Theory. *Quarterly Journal of Economics* 115: 147–180.

Clements, M.P. and D.F. Hendry (1999), *Forecasting Non-Stationary Economic Time Series.* Cambridge, MA: Cambridge University Press.

Duisenberg, W. (1998), *A Stability Oriented Monetary Policy for the ESCB.* European Central Bank, Franfurt.

Fair, R (1998), Estimated Stabilisation Costs of the EMU. *National Institute Economic Review* 1998 (2): 90–99.

Havrilesky, T. and J. Gildea (1992), Reliable and Unreliable Partisan Appointees to the Board of Governors. *Public Choice* 73 (4): 397–417.

Havrilesky, T. and J. Gildea (1995), The Biases of Federal Reserve Bank Presidents. *Economic Inquiry* 33 (2): 274–284.

McGregor, R.R. (1996), FOMC Voting Behaviour and Electoral Cycles: Partisan Ideology and Partisan Loyalty. *Economics and Politics* 8 (1): 17–32.

National Bureau of Economic Research (ed.) (1999), *Monetary Policy Rules.* Chicago: University of Chicago Press.

NIESR (ed.) (2001), *World Model Manuals.* National Institute of Economic and Social Research, London, mimeo.

Orpanides, A. (1998), Monetary Policy Rules Based on Real Time Data. Finance and Economic Discussion Series 1998-3. Board of Governors of the Federal Reserve System, Washington, DC.

Rudebusch, G.D. and L. Svensson (1999), Policy Rules for Inflation Targeting. In National Bureau of Economic Research (ed.) (1999), 203–262.

Svensson, L. (1997), Inflation Forecast Targeting: Implementing and Monitoring Inflation Targets. *European Economic Review* 41 (6): 1111–1146.

Svensson, L. (1999), Price Level Targeting versus Inflation Targeting: A free Lunch? *Journal of Money, Credit and Banking* 31 (3): 277–295.

Svensson, L. (2000), Open-Economy Inflation Targeting. *Journal of International Economics* 50 (1): 155–183.

Taylor, J.B. (1985), International Co–ordination in the design of Macro-economic Policy Rules. *European Economic Review* 28: 53–81.

Taylor, J.B. (1993), Discretion Versus Policy Rules in Practice. *Carnegie-Rochester Conference Series on Public Policy* 39: 195–214.

Taylor, J.B. (1999a), An Historical Analysis of Monetary Policy Rules. In National Bureau of Economic Research (ed.) (1999), 319–348.

Taylor, J. B. (1999b), The Robustness and Efficiency of Monetary Policy Rules as Guidelines for Interest Rate Setting at the European Central Bank. In National Bureau of Economic Research (ed.) (1999), 263–318.

Vestin, D. (1999), Price Level Targeting versus Inflation Targeting in a Forward- Looking Model. Sveriges Riksbank Working Paper 106. Sveriges Riksbank, Stockholm.

Christian Schumacher and Christian Dreger

Money Demand in Europe:
Evidence from Panel Cointegration Tests[1]

1. Introduction

Money demand in Europe, especially in the Euro area, is a widely discussed topic in applied research and economic policy, especially monetary policy. The Eurosystem has given money a prominent role in its monetary policy strategy (European Central Bank 2000, 2003). For that purpose, the existence of stable money demand behaviour is an important prerequisite. Before the implementation of the common currency in the Euro area, a lot of econometric exercises have been undertaken to show that a stable money demand function for the Euro area exists (see Lütkepohl, Wolters 1999 and the survey of Browne et al. 1997).

Money demand studies are usually based on two estimation strategies. First, money demand functions for member countries are estimated. The results can show heterogeneity across EMU member countries; but if for all countries stable relationships are found, one can conclude that there should be a stable money demand on the aggregate level, too. Secondly, after applying an appropriate aggregation method, Euro area wide money demand functions are estimated (see Coenen, Vega (1999). In short, the results of these studies can be summarized as follows. Single country studies often find stable money demand functions after imposing corrections for outliers and structural breaks. Area wide money demand functions generally tend to perform better than the single country equations. For a pool of fourteen European countries, Fagan/ Henry (1998) find that some of the single country demand equations show no cointegration whereas the aggregated European money demand function has clearly better statistical properties. In addition, it is shown that aggregate money demand functions are more stable because of statistical averaging effects between member country demand functions.

---

[1] This paper represents the authors' personal opinions and does not necessarily reflect the views of the Deutsche Bundesbank.

One critique of these econometric approaches is that they don't use the full information contained in the data. To use the full time series and cross section information set available, the money demand behaviour in Europe is investigated with panel cointegration methods in this paper. In detail, the recently proposed methods of Pedroni (1999) are applied. Time series tests often suffer from low power when applied to short time series. The idea of pooling data across panel members avoids these problems by making available more information to check the cointegration properties. The panel cointegration techniques allow the econometrician to selectively pool information regarding common long-run relationships from across the panel while allowing the short-run dynamics and fixed effects to be heterogeneous across the panel members. The null is that for each member of the panel the variables are not cointegrated. Due to higher efficiency, the panel tests could shed more light on the cointegration properties of money demand in the Euro area and whether the good statistical properties of the aggregated money demand functions are the result of an averaging effect.[2]

The paper proceeds as follows: The panel cointegration methods are explained in chapter 2. In chapter 3, a money demand in Europe is investigated with these methods. Chapter 4 discusses the methodology and chapter 5 concludes.

2. Econometric methodology

In this paper, a widely used specification of money demand equations is chosen (Ericsson 1999; Goldfeld, Sichel 1990). The money aggregate depends on a scale variable, here output, opportunity costs of holding money including inflation:

$$M^d / P = f(Y, R, \pi), \qquad (1)$$

where M^d is nominal money, P is the price level, Y is output, R represents the interest rates of various assets, and π is the inflation rate. In this equation price homogeneity is assumed to hold in the long-run.[3] The effect of the scale variable is expected to be positive. Own yields have a positive effect on money demand, while the interest rates of alternative assets have a negative impact. Moreover, inflation enters money demand negatively. This can be interpreted as the opportunity costs of holding money in spite of holding real assets (Wolters, Lütkepohl 1997).

---

[2] Moreover, different statistical properties than the single country equations could be due to the aggregation schemes that are used to convert the countries' data into a common currency. Although there is no consensus which scheme is the appropriate one, some authors show that the effect of using different aggregation methods results is rather small; see Coenen, Vega 1999. On the problems of aggregation, see Wesche 1998.

[3] The empirical reason for this is that money and the price level may be I(2) variables and are cointegrated to form the I(1) variable real balances.

Different combinations of explanatory variables are tested. R will be represented by two interest rates representing money's own rate and opportunity costs or only the long term rate.[4] Due to data considerations and for the sake of comparability to other recent money demand studies the inclusion of other variables is avoided.

2.1 Pedroni (1999) cointegration tests

The panel cointegration methods by Pedroni (1999) that are employed here can be understood as natural extensions of the residual based Engle/Granger (1987) cointegration technique. Calculations are performed in a two stage process. First, the cointegration equation is estimated for each cross section unit in the usual time series fashion. In a second step, the time series properties of deviations from the cointegration relationships are analysed by means of unit root tests. If the null hypothesis is true, the variables considered are not cointegrated. Under the alternative, they are, but the cointegrating vector might not be the same for each unit. The tests control for different fixed effects and short run dynamics, and also for different long run relationships across the panel members. Hence, heterogeneity is allowed between the various cross section units.

The cointegration regression for a cross section member i is formulated as follows:

$$y_{it} = \alpha_i + \delta_i t + \beta_i X_{it} + e_{it}. \tag{2}$$

X_{it} denotes the matrix of explanatory variables. In addition to the slope vectors β_i, the fixed effect α_i and trend parameters δ_i of this equation are allowed to vary across different pool members.

The second step of the procedure can be carried out in different ways. All test statistics are functions of simple OLS estimators. The main distinction is between the panel statistics on the one hand and group statistics on the other. In the former, pooling of the residuals is along the within dimension, while in the latter pooling is along to the between dimension of the panel. To be more specific, the within dimension computation requires to sum both the numerator and denominator of the test statistics over the cross section dimension separately. After summing up, the division is performed. In contrast, the between statistics arise by first dividing the numerator by the denominator, and then summing over the cross section. The panel statistics effectively pool the autoregressive coefficients of the residuals across the panel units. Equivalently, it is assumed that the autoregressive coefficient is the same for all cross section members. Instead, the group statistics rely on the average of individual test

---

[4] For alternative specifications see Browne et al. 1997 or Lütkepohl, Wolters 1999.

statistics. Obviously, in the group statistics, the autoregressive coefficients may vary among the individuals. Hence, group statistics allow an additional source of potential heterogeneity across the panel members.

Notice that in the panel statistics framework, the null of an autoregressive coefficient of unity is tested against the alternative, that this coefficient is smaller than one and equal across all individuals. In the group statistics, the alternative has changed markedly. If the null is false, the autoregressive coefficient is smaller than one and may be different across the panel members.

Within the panel and group statistics, the unit root tests for cointegration rely on well known time series procedures. In the case of the panel statistics, two unit root tests tests make use of non parametric corrections following Phillips/Perron (1988) according to their ρ- and t-statistic. Another statistic is a modification of the parametric ADF-test. In the group statistics framework, two tests are simply averages of the Phillips/Perron tests applied to each cross section unit and one test is again based on the ADF principle.

In the following, we first explain the group statistics, since they can be directly derived from the time series case.

2.1.1 Group statistics

The group ρ-statistic and the group t-statistic in non-parametric form are

$$\text{Group } \rho\text{-statistic (PP): } \tilde{Z}_{\hat{\rho}NT^{-1}} = \sum_{i=1}^{N} \frac{\sum_{t-1}^{T} \left(\hat{e}_{it-1} \Delta \hat{e}_{it} - \hat{\lambda}_i \right)}{\sum_{t=1}^{T} \hat{e}_{it-1}^2}, \tag{3}$$

$$\text{Group t-statistic (PP): } \tilde{Z}_{tNT} = \sum_{i=1}^{N} \frac{\sum_{t-1}^{T} \left(\hat{e}_{it-1} \Delta \hat{e}_{it} - \hat{\lambda}_i \right)}{\left(\hat{\sigma}_i^2 \sum_{t=1}^{T} \hat{e}_{it-1}^2 \right)^{1/2}}. \tag{4}$$

For each cross section member, the ρ-statistic is nothing but the Phillips/Perron (1988) ρ-statistic. The same is true for the t-statistic. In both statistics, the last element $\hat{\lambda}_i$ is the correction for autocorrelation. To test for unit roots, Phillips/Perron (1988) estimate an AR(1) model without taking into consideration the possible autocorrelation. In our case, this regression is

$$\hat{e}_{it} = \hat{\rho}_i \, \hat{e}_{it-1} + \hat{\mu}_{it}. \tag{5}$$

The residuals $\hat{\mu}_{it}$ are then used to calculate the correction term

$$\hat{\lambda}_i = (1/T) \sum_{s=1}^{k_i} \left(1 - \left(s/(k_i+1)\right)\right) \sum_{t=s+1}^{T} \hat{\mu}_{it} \hat{\mu}_{it-s}, \tag{6}$$

which leads to the individual cross section member long-run variance through

$$\hat{\sigma}_i^2 = (1/T) \sum_{t=1}^{T} \hat{\mu}_{it}^2 + 2\hat{\lambda}_i. \tag{7}$$

Given this variance, the coefficient ρ_i can be transformed into the Phillips/Perron (1998) t-statistic above.

The last group statistic is closely related to the widely used ADF test. To test for unit roots in contrast to the Phillips/Perron test, here the AR(1) regressions are augmented by lags of first differences of the cointegration residuals:

$$\hat{e}_{it} = \hat{\rho}_i \hat{e}_{it-1} + \sum_{k=1}^{k_i} \hat{\gamma}_{ik} \Delta \hat{e}_{it-k} + \hat{\mu}_{it}^*. \tag{8}$$

$\hat{\gamma}_{ik}$ are the autoregressive coefficients and $\hat{\mu}_{it}^*$ are the residuals of this equation. The parametric t-statistic based on this regression is

$$\text{Group t-statistic (ADF): } \tilde{Z}_{t_{NT}}^* = \sum_{i=1}^{N} \frac{\sum_{t-1}^{T} \hat{e}_{it-1} \Delta \hat{e}_{it}}{\left(\hat{s}_i^{*2} \sum_{t=1}^{T} \hat{e}_{it-1}^2\right)^{1/2}}. \tag{9}$$

Here, $\hat{s}_i^{*2}$ is the variance of the residuals of equation (8):

$$\hat{s}_i^{*2} = (1/T) \sum_{t=1}^{T} \hat{\mu}_{it}^{*2}, \tag{10}$$

that gives the t–statistic. The statistic is simply the sum of the individual ADF t-statistics and therefore closely analogous to the IPS-test, where an average of t-statistics are used to detect panel unit roots.

2.1.2 Panel statistics

The panel statistics include three different tests. The first statistics are the panel ρ-statistic and t-statistic, again analogous to the pure time series Phillips/Perron unit root tests:

Panel ρ-statistic (PP):

$$Z_{\rho NT^{-1}} = \left(\sum_{i=1}^{N} \sum_{t=1}^{T} \hat{L}_{11i}^{-2} \cdot \hat{e}_{it-1}^2 \right)^{-1} \sum_{i=1}^{N} \sum_{t=1}^{T} \hat{L}_{11i}^{-2} \left(\hat{e}_{it-1}^2 \Delta \hat{e}_{it} - \hat{\lambda}_i \right), \tag{11}$$

Panel t-statistic (PP):

$$Z_{t_{NT}} = \left(\tilde{\sigma}_{NT}^2 \sum_{i=1}^{N} \sum_{t=1}^{T} \hat{L}_{it-1}^{-2} \cdot \hat{e}_{it-1}^2 \right)^{-1/2} \sum_{i=1}^{N} \sum_{t=1}^{T} \hat{L}_{11i}^{-2} \left(\hat{e}_{it-1}^2 \Delta \hat{e}_{it} - \hat{\lambda}_i \right). \quad (12)$$

The cross section unit long-run variance for the residuals $\hat{L}_{11i}^2$ is used to obtain appropriate distributions. This nuisance parameter $\hat{L}_{11i}^2$ can be understood as a cross section unit long-run variance for the residuals. It is defined as

$$\hat{L}_{11i}^2 = (1/T) \sum_{t=1}^{T} \hat{\eta}_{it}^2 + (2/T) \sum_{s=1}^{K_i} \left(1 - \left(s/(k_i + 1) \right) \right) \sum_{t=s+1}^{T} \hat{\eta}_{it} \hat{\eta}_{it-s} \quad (13)$$

and can be recovered as the long run variance of the residuals $\hat{\eta}_{it}$ resulting from an additional regression between the differenced variables in the cointegrating relationships

$$\Delta y_{it} = \sum_{m=1}^{M_i} \hat{b}_{mi} \Delta X_{mit} + \hat{\eta}_{it}. \quad (14)$$

To transform the autoregressive parameter ρ into the t-statistic, the panel long-run variance $\tilde{\sigma}_{NT}^2$ is needed. It is defined as

$$\tilde{\sigma}_{NT}^2 = (1/N) \sum_{i=1}^{N} \hat{L}_{11i}^{-2} \hat{\sigma}_i^2, \quad (15)$$

with $\hat{\sigma}_i^2 = \hat{s}_i^2 + 2\hat{\lambda}_i$, the long-run variance of the residuals $\hat{\mu}_{it}$ from the AR(1) regression $\hat{e}_{it} = \hat{\rho}_i \hat{e}_{it-1} + \hat{\mu}_{it}$.

The next statistic is the panel parametric t-statistic. This is closely related to the single time series ADF-test. The statistic is

Panel t-statistic (ADF):

$$Z_{t_{NT}}^* = \left(\tilde{s}_{NT}^{*2} \sum_{i=1}^{N} \sum_{t=1}^{T} \hat{L}_{11i}^{-2} \cdot \hat{e}_{it-1}^2 \right)^{-1/2} \sum_{i=1}^{N} \sum_{t=1}^{T} \hat{L}_{11i}^{-2} \hat{e}_{it-1} \Delta \hat{e}_{it}, \quad (16)$$

where $\tilde{s}_{NT}^{*2}$ is the contemporaneous panel variance estimator

$$\tilde{s}_{NT}^{*2} = (1/N) \sum_{i=1}^{N} \hat{s}_i^{*2}, \quad (17)$$

with $\tilde{s}_i^{*2} = (1/T) \sum_{t=1}^{T} \hat{\mu}_{it}^{*2}$, the estimated individual contemporaneous variance, and $\hat{\mu}_{it}^*$ are the residuals from the augmented unit root regression (8). This panel statistic effectively pools the autoregressive coefficients of the residuals across the panel units and, hence, is the same for all cross section members.

When both the cross section and the time series dimension become large and after normalizing using the underlying Brownian motion functionals, Pedroni reaches statistics that are standard normal distributed:

$$\frac{\tilde{Z}-\mu\sqrt{N}}{\sqrt{v}}, \tag{18}$$

where $\tilde{Z}$ are the test statistics explained above, appropriately standardized for the time series and cross section dimensions. μ and v are functions of the moments of the underlying Brownian motion functionals and are tabulated in Pedroni (1999, table 2). They depend on the deterministic specification of the model, that is, whether individual constants or time trends or both are included in the cointegration equation, and the number of regressors.

One sided tests can be applied for each statistic. The null of no cointegration is rejected when test values are large and negative as in the pure time series case.

2.2 Fully modified OLS estimators of the cointegration vector

To investigate the shape of the cointegration relation, several methods can be applied. Here, we use the fully modified OLS estimator of Phillips/Hansen (1990), extended to the panel case by Pedroni (1996) and Kao/Chiang (1995). In contrast to the usual OLS estimator, the modifications correct serial correlation in the residuals and endogeneity of the regressors in the above equation. The model is

$$y_{it} = \alpha_i + \delta_i t + \beta_i x_{it} + e_{it}, \tag{19}$$

$$x_{it} = x_{it-1} + \tau_{it}. \tag{20}$$

The residuals $\omega_{it} = (e_{it}, \tau_{it}^{'})'$ have the covariance matrix $\Omega_i = \Omega_i^0 + \Gamma_i + \Gamma_i^{'}$, where Ω_i^0 is the contemporaneous covariance and $\Gamma_i = \sum_{j=1}^{\infty} E(\omega_{it} \omega_{it}^{'})$, measured as a weighted sum of autocovariances. The aim of the FMOLS estimator is to consider the correlation between e_{it} and τ_{it} as well as the autocorrelation in the system. The covariance matrix is partitioned into

$$\Omega_i = \begin{pmatrix} \Omega_{ie} & \Omega_{ie\tau} \\ \Omega_{i\tau e} & \Omega_{i\tau} \end{pmatrix}, \tag{21}$$

where the off diagonal blocks are not necessarily equal to zero. The estimated slope vector is

$$\hat{\beta}_{FM} = N^{-1} \sum_{i=1}^{N} \frac{\sum_{t=1}^{T} (x_{it} - \bar{x}_i) y_{it}^* - T\gamma_i^*}{\sum_{t=1}^{T} (x_{it} - \bar{x}_i)^2}, \tag{22}$$

with the t-statistic

$$t_{\hat{\beta}_{FM}} = N^{-1/2} \sum_{i=1}^{N} \frac{\sum_{t=1}^{T} (x_{it} - \bar{x}_i) y_{it}^* - T\gamma_i^*}{\left(\hat{\Omega}_{e.\tau} \sum_{t=1}^{T} (x_{it} - \bar{x}_i) \right)^{1/2}}, \tag{23}$$

where $y_{it}^* = y_{it} - \bar{y}_i - \hat{\Omega}_{ie\tau} \hat{\Omega}_{i\tau}^{-1} \Delta x_{it}$ is the transformation of the endogeneous variable that corrects for endogeneity. The modified regression (19) has residuals e_{it}^* that are uncorrelated with the τ_{it} by construction (see Phillips, Hansen (1990: 112). The variance of residuals of the modified regression is $\Omega_{ie.\tau} = \Omega_{ie} - \Omega_{ie\tau} \Omega_{i\tau}^{-1} \Omega_{i\tau e}$, which is needed to transform the coefficient estimators into the t-statistics. The term $\gamma_i^* = (\hat{\Omega}_{ie\tau}^0 + \hat{\Gamma}_{ie\tau}) - (\hat{\Omega}_{i\tau}^0 + \hat{\Gamma}_{i\tau}) \hat{\Omega}_{i\tau}^{-1} \hat{\Omega}_{i\tau e}$ corrects for serial correlation (see Kao/Chiang 1995: 8). The panel coefficients and the corresponding t-statistic are simply averages of the individual member coefficients and t-statistic. Pedroni (1996) shows that the t-statistic is standard normal for both the time series and the cross section dimension goes to infinity.

3. An empirical application to money demand in Europe

In this section the tests described before are applied to money variables in Europe. A panel of fourteen countries including Austria, Belgium, Denmark, Finland, France, Germany, Great Britain, Greece, Ireland, Italy, Netherlands, Portugal and Spain is investigated. The money concept is M3H, which is the "old" concept of harmonized M3 developed in the context of the BIS. Hence, the statistics are not fully consistent with the new concept of Euro area wide M3 now used by the ECB. The scale variable is real GDP and the price index is the GDP deflator. The interest rates are short-term money market-rates and long-term bond yields. The sample period is from the first quarter of 1981 to the fourth quarter of 1995. More information about the quarterly data set, such as data sources and integration properties, is given in the appendix.

To test the cointegration properties and get an impression about the stability of the results, we choose different specifications. We test cointegration relations including only the long term rate or additionally the short term interest rate. In line with the theoretical suggestions optionally the inflation rate is included. The general specification is

Table 1

Panel cointegration tests for EU-14

	Money demand specification:			
	ltr_{it}	ltr_{it}	ltr_{it}, str_{it}	ltr_{it}, str_{it}
	No π_{it}	π_{it}	No π_{it}	π_{it}
	Statistics:			
Panel ρ	0.64	0.73	1.94	1.56
Panel t	–0.46	–0.36	0.52	0.46
Panel ADF	–0.35	–0.76	0.72	–0.46
Group ρ	1.39	2.44	2.91	2.63
Group t	0.26	1.45	1.28	1.35
Group ADF	0.42	1.24	1.22	0.34

Authors' calculations. – *: 95 % significance level; in each case the left hand side variable is real money, right hand side variables are output plus interest rates and inflation as indicated in the table; variables: *str*: short term rate, *ltr*: long term rate, π: annualized quarterly change in the GDP deflator; cross sections = 14.

$$m3r_{it} = \alpha_i + \beta_{i1} y_{it} + \beta_{i2} ltr_{it} + \beta_{i3} str_{it} + \beta_{i4} \pi_{it}, \qquad (24)$$

where $m3r_{it}$ denotes the real money stock in natural logarithms, y_{it} is real output in natural logarithms, str_{it} the short term rate, ltr_{it} the long term rate and π_{it} is annualized quarterly change in the GDP deflator. The results of the Pedroni cointegration tests for the alternative specifications are displayed in Table 1.

All specifications show no sign of cointegration. The additional inclusion of a short-term rate as well as inflation doesn't improve the results. We also investigated the inclusion of deterministic time trends in the cointegration relationships. But again, the null of no cointegration could not be rejected.

In the next step, the number of cross section units was reduced and the same cointegration tests were carried out with different country groups. Unfortunately, for the countries of the Euro area, the results were not different.

Only for a subgroup of Germany, France, Austria, the Netherlands and Belgium the results show cointegration in some of the specifications (Table 2).

Concerning the different specifications the implications from this exercise are twofold. Firstly, after the additional inclusion of the short term interest rate, cointegration is mostly found with high significance. This implies that the short-term and long-term interest rates together seem to be a more accurate representation of the opportunity costs of holding money, since only the long term interest rate doesn't reflect the own yield of the broad money chosen here. Secondly, the inflation rate doesn't improve the cointegration properties. In each specification the null of no cointegration is not rejected. Although there are theoretical justifications for the inflation rate to enter the money

Table 2

Panel cointegration tests for EU-5:
Germany, France, Austria, the Netherlands and Belgium

	Money demand specification:			
	ltr_{it}	ltr_{it}	ltr_{it}, str_{it}	ltr_{it}, str_{it}
	No π_{it}	π_{it}	No π_{it}	π_{it}
	Statistics:			
Panel ρ	−1.29	−0.25	−1.24	−0.32
Panel t	−1.73*	−0.83	−2.22*	−1.35
Panel ADF	−1.81*	−0.58	−1.83*	−0.70
Group ρ	−0.48	0.33	−0.57	0.36
Group t	−1.56	−0.61	−2.22*	−1.24
Group ADF	−1.97*	−0.67	−2.16*	−0.26

Authors' calculations. – *: 95 % significance level; in each case the left hand side variable is real money, right hand side variables are output plus interest rates and inflation as indicated in the table; variables: *str*: short term rate, *ltr*: long term rate, π: annualized quarterly change in the GDP deflator; cross sections = 5.

demand equation, there is no concensus about the empirical importance of this variable.[5] The results are supported by both the group and panel statistics. The allowance of more heterogeneity doesn't have an impact on the cointegration results.

The shape of the money demand equation is now investigated using FMOLS estimators of the cointegration equations. Although the cointegration tests before showed no sign of cointegration when the inflation rate was included, the corresponding cointegration vectors are calculated to get an impression about the robustness of the other estimates.

The specification only with the long term rate shows the expected signs at the panel level. At the individual level, the semi elasticity of the long term interest rate rate has the wrong sign and is insignificant. The output elasitcity is significantly above one except for Austria. After the additional inclusion of the short term rate, the shape of the money demand function is quite similiar. The short rate is significant only at the 10 % level.

The above results show cointegration properties that are in favour of an economically meaningful money demand function for the EU-5. In contrast to the results obtained with a broader data set, the countries where monetary policy was tightly linked with the German Bundesbank seem to have a similiar money demand behaviour.

---

[5] We tried also deterministic trends, but as was the case with the EU-14 data set, no improvements arised. Economically, deterministic trends can absorb long-run developments in the velocity of money due to possible structural changes in the money demand behaviour. But a lot of single country studies find plausible cointegration equations without time trends. In only a few studies time trends are needed. See Juselius 1998.

Table 3

FMOLS estimators of the money demand functions for EU-5

Sample: 1981-1 to 1995-4

		Variables:			
		y	ltr	str	π
Individual	Germany	1.08 (21.60*)	−2.60 (4.10*)		
	France	1.60 (7.35*)	0.47 (0.89)		
	Austria	0.90 (11.79*)	−2.43 (−2.90*)		
	Netherlands	2.26 (21.23*)	−2.42 (−2.82*)		
	Belgium	2.01 (9.33*)	−0.94 (−1.30)		
Panel	EU–5	1.57 (14.26*)	−1.58 (−2.04*)		
Individual	Germany	1.10 (24.52*)	−2.23 (−3.84*)		−0.49 (−2.16*)
	France	1.60 (7.09*)	0.56 (0.90)		−0.09 (−0.23)
	Austria	0.89 (11.76*)	−2.23 (−2.66*)		−0.15 (−1.00)
	Netherlands	2.26 (21.35*)	−2.40 (−2.72*)		−0.03 (−0.34)
	Belgium	1.99 (9.27*)	−0.92 (−1.25)		−0.11 (−0.34)
Panel	EU–5	1.57 (14.80*)	−1.44 (−1.91*)		−0.17 (−0.77)
Individual	Germany	1.09 (23.39*)	−1.19 (−1.19)	−0.61 (−1.48)	
	France	1.47 (11.07*)	−2.09 (−3.65*)	2.60 (5.28*)	
	Austria	0.91 (11.27*)	−2.43 (−1.72*)	0.17 (0.25)	
	Netherlands	2.19 (20.79*)	−4.87 (−3.39*)	1.94 (2.00*)	
	Belgium	2.08 (10.05*)	−2.46 (−2.09*)	1.41 (1.66*)	
Panel	EU–5	1.55 (15.31*)	−2.61 (−2.41*)	1.10 (1.54)	
Individual	Germany	1.11 (25.08*)	−1.43 (−1.52)	−0.38 (−0.94)	−0.38 (−1.61)
	France	1.43 (10.63*)	−1.91 (−3.35*)	2.68 (5.50*)	−0.28 (−1.23)
	Austria	0.90 (11.26*)	−2.36 (−1.69*)	0.22 (0.33)	−0.14 (−0.94)
	Netherlands	2.19 (20.92*)	−4.83 (−3.36*)	1.93 (2.00*)	−0.02 (−0.12)
	Belgium	2.07 (10.10*)	−2.43 (−2.09*)	1.43 (1.69*)	−0.16 (−0.53)
Panel	EU–5	1.54 (15.60*)	−2.59 (−2.40*)	1.18 (1.72*)	−0.20 (−0.88)

Authors' calculations. – *: 95 % significance level; variables: y: real output in natural logarithms, str: short term rate, ltr: long term rate, π: annualized quarterly change in the GDP deflator; t–values are in parentheses.

4. Discussion of methods and results

Although for a subgroup of countries cointegration could be shown, some drawbacks of the used methods must be taken into consideration when the overall usefulness of the methods applied here should be judged.

Most panel methods require independent cross section members for estimation. For an application to money demand equations in a highly integrated economic area, this requirement maybe not fulfilled. A frequently used method for controlling for such common time effects in panels is to demean the data over the cross section dimension. But if the coefficients are allowed to vary between the different cross section members, this is not equivalent to use common time dummies directly in the tests. Hence, very different money demand functions in the EU-14 case may distort the cointegration results presented here. But as it is known from the panel unit root literature (O'Connell 1998), the cross section dependence leads to an overrejection of the null of integration. This can also be expected in the case of cointegration. Therefore, the results obtained in the EU-14 case may be even more in favour of no cointegration if the cross section dependence could be considered more accurately.

In the above cointegration technique, a cointegration rank of one was assumed to hold. Other long-run equilibrium relationships may also hold among the variables. For example, the real interest rate or the interest rate spread can be stationary. Although the empirical relevance of these relations may be given, even in the pure time series case identification problems arise since money demand usually includes all of these variables (Coenen, Vega 1999). A first contribution to test for multiple cointegration vectors for each cross section unit in panels was made by Hall et al. (1999) in a principal components framework. However, asymptotics for their test are not available yet.

Single country studies often need country specific modifications of the money demand equations. Especially in the time series regressions one can control for outliers and structural breaks using dummy variables. It is expected that allowing for further heterogeneity in this sense could help to improve the cointegration properties although this would shift the asymptotic distribution of the tests.

The parameters of the aggregated FMOLS cointegration relation are simple averages of the individual coefficients and rely on the assumption that each panel member has a similiar size. The results concerning the shape of the cointegration vectors presented here can't directly be compared with results obtained from time series methods for the Euro area based on aggregated data.

Finally, one can criticize the two-step procedure of the estimation strategy according to Engle/Granger (1987) in general. The cointegration residuals are recovered from a static regression. Hence, a natural extension of the above method would be the use of dynamic set ups such as the Stock (1987) approach where the test of cointegration applies to a model with short-run dynamics.

5. Conclusions

The results of the analysis concerning the cointegration properties are somewhat mixed. Whereas there is no sign of cointegration in the whole EU-14 panel, for a subgroup of Germany, France, Austria, the Netherlands and Belgium cointegration can be found. This is an indication of averaging out effects when aggregated time series data are used to estimate cointegration models. Other studies before reached similiar conclusions, for example on the grounds of higher t-statistics of aggregated time series regressions in contrast to the national single cross section equations. This implies that the statistical properties of aggregated money demand functions for Europe could indeed be the result of an statistical averaging effect that overestimates the quality of the empirical measures.

Although these results seem to be quite interesting at first sight, one should be cautious when interpreting the panel methods employed here. Some drawbacks of the panel cointegration tests were discussed. The pure time series methods to analyze models of money demand are in general far more developed. Hence, it can be questioned whether the advantage of higher efficiency due to the inclusion of the cross section dimension overcompensates these drawbacks. But with further extensions, panel cointegration methods may become more powerful econometric tools in the future.

Data appendix

The data set used here is the same as in Fagan/Henry (1998). The time series are quarterly and seasonally adjusted. The sample period is from first quarter 1981 to fourth quarter 1995. The money stock is M3H from the EMI database. The transaction variables are represented by real GDP and prices are GDP deflators. Source is the BIS database. Interest rates are short-term money market rates and long-term bond yields, again taken from BIS database and, in addition, from IMF and OECD and national data. All series have been adjusted by Fagan/Henry (1998) and are not to be considered as official BIS, ECB or EMI time series.

To justify the cointegration analysis, the integration properties of the data set have to be analyzed. For this purpose, the now common panel unit root test of Im et al. (1997) is applied. In contrast to the usual time series unit root tests the statistic employed here also includes the cross section dimension. For each cross section, a time series ADF statistic is calculated separately:

$$\Delta y_{it} = \alpha_i + \rho_i \, y_{it-1} + \sum_{j=1}^{p_i} \beta_{ij} \Delta y_{it-j} + e_{it}. \tag{A1}$$

The heterogeneity of the panel members is considered with this test, because the autoregressive parameters can diverge between the different cross section units. Moreover, deterministic terms and short-run dynamics can be different. The IPS-statistic is based on the mean of the individual t-statistics for the individual autoregressive parameters:

$$IPS = \sqrt{N} \cdot \frac{\bar{t} - E(\bar{t})}{\sqrt{V(\bar{t})}}, \tag{A2}$$

with $\bar{t} = (1/N) \sum_{i=1}^{N} t_i$. Here, $E(\bar{t})$ und $V(\bar{t})$ are approximations to the moments of the individual t-statistics. The moments are simulated and reported in Im/Pesaran/Shin (1997). The standardized mean of the t-values is distributed standard normal for large N and T. In addition, N/T has to converge to a constant that is not required to be zero.

The results of the IPS-test for the time series in the money demand equation are shown in Table 4. The IPS-tests indicate that all variables are nonstationary. The test is standard normal distributed and rejects the null for large negative values. No test statistic reaches the 95% critical value. The null of nonstationarity for the short run interest rate and the inflation rate is not rejected clearly in the IPS-test. Therefore, also the autocorrelations and single series unit root tests were analyzed. The autocorrelations of both series decline very slowly with increasing lag order.

Table 4

IPS Panel unit root test results

	m3r	y	str	ltr	π
IPS–statistic	2.43	0.97	−1.54	−1.26	−1.43

Notes: * = 95 % significance level; the estimates are standard normal distributed and explained in detail in the text; Variables: $m3r$ = real money stock in natural logarithms, y = real output in natural logarithms, str = short term rate, ltr = long term rate, π = annualized quarterly change of the logged GDP deflator; Time trends and constants were included in the regressions.

References

Browne, F., G. Fagan and J. Henry (1997), Money Demand in EU Countries: A Survey. EMI Staff Paper 7. European Monetary Institute, Frankfurt a.M.

Coenen, G., J.-L. Vega (1999), The Demand for M3 in the Euro Area. ECB Working Paper 6. ECB, Frankfurt.

Engle, R. and C. Granger (1987), Co-Integration and Error Correction: Representation, Estimation and Testing. *Econometrica* 55: 251–276.

Ericsson, N.R. (1999), Empirical Modelling of Money Demand. In H. Lütkepohl and J. Wolters (eds.) (1999), 29–49.

European Central Bank (2000), The Two Pillars of the ECB's Monetary Policy Strategy. *ECB Monthly Bulletin* 2000 (11): 37–48.

European Central Bank (2003), The outcome of the ECB's evaluation of its monetary policy strategy. *ECB Monthly Bulletin* 2003 (6): 79–92.

Fagan, G. and J. Henry (1998), Long-run Money Demand in the EU: Evidence for Area-wide Aggregates. *Empirical Economics* 23: 483–506.

Goldfeld, S. and D. Sichel (1990), The Demand for Money. In B.M. Friedman and F.H. Hahn (eds.), *Handbook of Monetary Economics*. Amsterdam: North Holland, vol. 1, 299–356.

Hall, S., S. Lazarova and G. Urga (1999), A Principal Components Analysis of Common Stochastic Trends in Heterogeneous Panel Data: Some Monte Carlo Evidence. *Oxford Bulletin of Economics and Statistics* 61 (Special Issue 1999): 749–767.

Im, K., H. Pesaran and Y. Shin (1997), Testing for Unit Roots in Heterogeneous Panels. Department of Applied Economics Working Paper 9526, Revised December 1997. Cambridge.

Juselius, K. (1999), Changing Monetary Transmission Mechanisms within the EU. In H. Lütkepohl and J. Wolters (eds.) (1999), 189–215.

Lütkepohl, H. und J. Wolters (eds.) (1999), Money Demand in Europe. Studies in Empirical Economics. Heidelberg et al.: Physica.

O'Connell, P. (1998), The Overvaluation of Purchasing Power Parity. *Journal of International Economics* 44: 1–19.

Pedroni, P. (1995), Panel Cointegration. Asymptotic and Finite Sample Properties of Pooled Time Series Tests with an Application to the PPP Hypothesis. Working Paper Series 95-013. Indiana University, Bloomington, IN.

Pedroni, P. (1996), Fully Modified OLS for Heterogeneous Cointegrated Panels and the Case of Purchasing Power Parity. Working Paper Series 96-020. Indiana University, Bloomington, IN.

Pedroni, P. (1999), Critical Values for Cointegration Tests in Heterogeneous Panels with Multiple Regressors. *Oxford Bulletin of Economics and Statistics* 61 (Special Issue 1999): 653–670.

Phillips, P. and B. Hansen (1990), Statistical Inference in Instrumental Variables Regression with I(1) Processes. *Review of Economic Studies* 57: 99–125.

Phillips, P. and P. Perron (1988), Testing for a Unit Root in Time Series Regression. *Biometrika* 75: 335–346.

Zentrum für Europäische Integrationsforschung (ed.) (1998), EMU Monitor: Press Statement, July 9, 1998. Bonn.

Wesche, K. (1998), Die Geldnachfrage in Europa: Aggregationsprobleme und Empirie. Wirtschaftswissenschaftliche Beiträge 154. Heidelberg et al.: Physica.

Wolters, J. und H. Lütkepohl (1997), Die Geldnachfrage für M3: Neue Ergebnisse für das vereinigte Deutschland. *Ifo-Studien* 43 (1): 35–54.

List of Authors

György Barabas, Rheinisch-Westfälisches Institut für Wirtschaftsforschung, Essen

Ray Barrell, National Institute of Economic and Social Research, London

Michael Beeby, Research Officer at the Centre for International Macroeconomics, University of Oxford

Jean Louis Brillet, Unit for Technical Cooperation, National Institute for Statistics and Economic Studies, France

Karen Dury, National Institute of Economic and Social Research, London

Gabriel Fagan, Directorate General Research, European Central Bank, Frankfurt a.M.

Christian Dreger, IWH Institute for Economic Research, Halle/Saale

Stephen G. Hall, Professor of Economics at Imperial College Management School, London, and a visitor to the Oxford Centre

Ullrich Heilemann, Rheinisch-Westfälisches Institut für Wirtschaftsforschung, Essen

Jérôme Henry, Directorate General Research, European Central Bank, Frankfurt a.M.

S.G. Brian Henry, Director of the Centre for International Macroeconomics, University of Oxford

Ian Hurst, National Institute of Economic and Social Research, London

Mika Kortelainen, Bank of Finland

Lawrence R. Klein, Benjamin Franklin Professor of Economics (emeritus), Department of Economics, University of Pennsylvania, Philadelphia

David G. Mayes, Adviser to the Board, Bank of Finland

Ricardo Mestre, Directorate General Research, European Central Bank, Frankfurt a.M.

Hiltrud Nehls, Rheinisch-Westfälisches Institut für Wirtschaftsforschung, Essen

David Rae, Economics Department, OECD, Paris

Maria Dos Santos, DEA (Specialized Studies Diploma) student, Paris XIII University, France

Christian Schumacher, Deutsche Bundesbank, Frankfurt a.M.

David Turner, Economics Department, OECD, Paris